# Enhancing Business Continuity and IT Capability

# Enhancing Business Continuity and IT Capability

## System Administration and Server Operating Platforms

Nijaz Bajgorić

Lejla Turulja

Semir Ibrahimović and

Amra Alagić

CRC Press

Taylor & Francis Group

Boca Raton  London  New York

CRC Press is an imprint of the
Taylor & Francis Group, an **informa** business

AN AUERBACH BOOK

First Edition published 2021
by CRC Press
6000 Broken Sound Parkway NW, Suite 300
Boca Raton, FL 33487-2742

and by CRC Press
2 Park Square, Milton Park, Abingdon, Oxon OX14 4RN

© 2021 Taylor & Francis Group, LLC

CRC Press is an imprint of Taylor & Francis Group, LLC

ISBN 13: 978-0-367-65261-6 (pbk)
ISBN 13: 978-0-367-61698-4 (hbk)
ISBN 13: 978-1-003-10609-8 (ebk)

# Contents

# Foreword

Most businesses today depend on the availability of their information systems; therefore, enterprise servers and server operating systems are becoming more important given that applications' availability is determined by these so-called server operating platforms. Not only e-businesses but other businesses as well simply go "out of business" if some sort of downtime occurs.

Modern businesses implement information technologies in several forms of enterprise information systems that are expected to be "up and running" on a continuous or "always-on" basis. This applies not only to businesses, but also to most non-business organizations such as governmental, infrastructure, and so on.

Enterprise servers, server operating systems, and system administration play an important role in "keeping business in business" as their crashes are the main causes of "going out of business". Other causes include human error, hackers' activities, natural disasters, and the like. Therefore, modern information technology management addresses these problems and tries to offer solutions that may help in reducing downtime and achieving higher levels of uptime.

The book entitled *Enhancing Business Continuity and IT Capability: System Administration and Server Operating Platforms*, by Bajgorić, Turulja, Ibrahimović, and Alagić (published by Taylor and Francis Group) addresses several aspects of how modern server operation environments and system administration can help reduce downtime and ensure higher levels of applications availability. The book is structured in such a way that it first introduces the concepts of system downtime, business continuity, business continuity management, disaster recovery, disaster recovery management, and IT capability, and then presents the main high-availability features of modern servers and server operating environments and establishes some connections between these concepts and technologies on one side and IT capability and a firm's performance on the other side.

*Ajay Vinze*
Dean and Professor
Robert J. Trulaske, Sr., College of Business
University of Missouri, Columbia, USA

# Acronyms and Abbreviations

| | |
|---|---|
| **AIA** | application impact analysis |
| **ASP** | application service provider |
| **AWS** | Amazon Web Services |
| **BBN** | Bayesian belief networks |
| **BC** | business continuity |
| **BCI** | Business Continuity Institute |
| **BCM** | business continuity management |
| **BCMM** | business continuity maturity model |
| **BCMS** | business continuity management system |
| **BCP** | business continuity plan |
| **BCP** | business continuity planning |
| **BI** | business intelligence |
| **BIA** | business impact analysis |
| **BS** | British Standard |
| **BSI** | British Standards Institute |
| **CDP** | continuous data protection |
| **CI** | configuration item |
| **CIO** | chief information officer |
| **CIP** | critical infrastructure protection plan |
| **CISA** | certified information system auditor |
| **CISO** | chief information security officer |
| **CMM** | capability maturity model |
| **CMMI** | capability maturity model integration |
| **COBIT** | control objectives for information and related technology |
| **COOP** | continuity of operations plan |
| **COSO** | Committee Of Sponsoring Organizations |
| **CP** | contingency planning |
| **CPT** | conditional probability table |
| **CPU** | central processing unit |
| **CR** | control risk |

| | |
|---|---|
| **CRM** | customer relationship management |
| **DAG** | directed acyclic graph |
| **DAR** | desired audit risk |
| **DAS** | direct attached storage |
| **DHCP** | dynamic host configuration protocol |
| **DNS** | domain name service/domain name system |
| **DR** | detection risk |
| **DR** | disaster recovery |
| **DRaaS** | Disaster Recovery as a Service |
| **DRBD** | distributed replicated block device |
| **DRD** | dynamic root disk |
| **DRM** | disaster recovery management |
| **DRP** | disaster recovery plan |
| **ECC** | error correcting code |
| **EIS** | enterprise information system |
| **ERM** | enterprise risk management |
| **ERP** | enterprise resource planning |
| **ESG** | Enterprise Strategy Group |
| **ESX** | Elastic Sky X (server virtualization platform from VMware) |
| **FaaS** | Function as a Service |
| **FC** | fiber channel |
| **HA** | high availability |
| **HBA** | host bus adapter |
| **HCI** | hyperconverged infrastructure |
| **IaaS** | Infrastructure as a Service |
| **ICT** | information communication technology |
| **IDC** | International Data Corporation |
| **IDP** | intrusion detection prevention |
| **IEC** | International Electrotechnical Commission |
| **IP** | internet protocol |
| **IR** | inherent risk |
| **IS** | information system |
| **IS AUDITOR** | information systems auditor |
| **ISACA** | Information Systems Audit and Control Association |
| **ISCP** | information system contingency plan |
| **ISCSI** | internet small computer systems interface |
| **ISO** | International Organization for Standardization |
| **ISO 27001** | International Organization for Standardization 27001 |
| **ISO/IEC** | International Organization for Standardization/International Electrotechnical Commission |
| **ISP** | internet service provider |
| **IT AUDIT** | information technology audit |
| **IT** | information technology |

| | |
|---|---|
| **IT-CMF** | IT capability maturity framework |
| **ITIL** | Information Technology Infrastructure Library |
| **IVI** | Innovation Value Institute Ireland |
| **JFS** | journalized file system |
| **KPI** | key performance indicator |
| **LAN** | local area network |
| **LDAP** | lightweight directory access protocol |
| **LVM** | logical volume manager |
| **MAN** | metropolitan area networks |
| **MAO** | maximum acceptable outage |
| **MOF** | operations service management function |
| **MQ** | message queueing |
| **MTD** | maximal tolerable downtime |
| **MTTR** | mean time to recovery |
| **NAS** | network attached storage |
| **NFPA** | national fire protection |
| **NIC** | network interface card |
| **NIST** | National Institute of Standards and Technology |
| **NVM** | non-volatile memory |
| **OEP** | occupant emergency plan |
| **OS** | operating system |
| **PaaS** | Platform as a Service |
| **PCI DSS** | payment card industry data security standard |
| **PDCA** | plan, do, check, act |
| **PRISMA** | preferred reporting items for systematic reviews and meta-analyses |
| **RA** | risk assessment |
| **RACI** | responsible, accountable, consulted, informed |
| **RADIUS** | remote authentication dial |
| **RAID** | redundant array of independent disks |
| **RAID** | redundant array of inexpensive disks |
| **RAIM** | redundant array of independent memory |
| **RAM** | random access memory |
| **REST** | representational state transfer |
| **RPO** | recovery point objective |
| **RTO** | recovery time objective |
| **SaaS** | Software as a Service |
| **SAMBA** | server message block |
| **SAN** | storage area network |
| **SCM** | supply chain management |
| **SDO** | service delivery objective |
| **SIC** | standard industrial classification |
| **SLA** | service level agreement |

| | |
|---|---|
| **SLM** | service level management |
| **SMB** | server message block |
| **SOE** | server operating environment |
| **SOS** | server operating system |
| **SSHA** | single system high availability |
| **SWOT** | strengths-weaknesses-opportunities-threats |
| **TCO** | total costs of ownership |
| **TCP/IP** | transmission control protocol/internet protocol |
| **UPS** | uninterruptable power supply |
| **VLDB** | very large database |
| **VLM** | very large memory |
| **VM** | virtual machine |
| **WAN** | wide area network |
| **WOS** | Web of Science |
| **WRT** | work recovery time |
| **ZB** | zetabyte |

# Preface

Enterprise servers play a mission-critical role in modern computing environments, especially from a business continuity perspective. Servers and server operating systems are expected to provide an operating environment that must meet much more rigorous requirements than a standard PC and desktop operating system. Such platforms are of special interest for businesses in the digital age that require "zero downtime" and an "always-on" computing environment. With regard to availability, reliability and scalability, servers and server operating systems are crucial for modern business as they run platforms for business-critical applications, such as Enterprise Resource Planning, Customer Relationship Management, Supply Chain Management, and Electronic Commerce. Modern server operating systems include a set of additional features to support higher levels of availability, reliability, and scalability. Therefore, system administration should be seen as critical managerial activities on server operating platforms with regard to reducing both system downtime and data recovery time.

Information technologies in general are implemented today within information centers based on several types of information architectures (e.g., client-server, on-premises, cloud based). They form different types of information infrastructures and are operated/managed by information centers. Information technology (IT) infrastructure and IT operations are considered critical components of a firm's IT capability. Several models of IT capability have been introduced over the last two decades. This book aims at proposing a new model of IT capability.

Chapter 1 contains some introductory information on the topics addressed in the book.

The objective of Chapter 2 is twofold: first, it provides some introductory insights on system downtime and the economics of downtime by providing information from some recent reports on how modern business suffers from downtime. Several reports are cited and summarized with the main aim of demonstrating the costs of being "out of business" due to downtime. The second objective is to present the main framework for the book; in other words, to establish the relationship between downtime on one side and business continuity and IT capability on the other side, and how system administration and modern server operating platforms can help in improving business continuity (BC) and IT capability.

Chapter 3 aims at defining the main concepts addressed in the book: business continuity and IT capability and their importance in modern business. A short overview of business continuity planning (BCP) is given, followed by a description of BCP strategies and a brief statement of methodologies for business continuity planning. Then, a short introduction to disaster recovery planning (DRP) and contingency planning (CP) is provided, as well as some of the existing business continuity management (BCM) maturity models. The concept of IT capability is presented along with the relationship between BCM and organizational IT capability.

Chapter 4 addresses several aspects of so-called server operating environments (SOEs) and how modern SOEs can contribute to minimizing downtime, achieving higher levels of uptime, continuous computing, business continuity, and IT capability. Several technologies are presented that are used in establishing such SOEs in order to have an operating environment that can support continuous computing and always-on business.

Chapter 5 explores the role of system administration in ensuring higher levels of system availability, system scalability, and business continuity. Several high-availability–oriented features of most widely used server operating systems are presented (commercial UNIX, Linux, Windows Server). The business perspective of server operating systems is presented as well as the main framework for a course related to system administration for business continuity.

In Chapter 6, some methods, techniques, and tools for enhancing availability and business continuity are presented. The frameworks for business impact analysis, assessing the downtime impact, and designing an optimal BC solution are presented in Chapter 6.

Chapter 7 discusses some aspects and relations between IT auditing and business continuity, that is, how IT auditing can help in ensuring business continuity, the role of system administration in IT auditing, and how IT auditing is performed with regard to BC and disaster recovery (DR). This chapter covers IT auditing as a process of gathering data and evidence to evaluate whether the company's information system is efficient and effective and whether it meets business goals. Some mechanisms associated with the audit process, such as audit risks, audit methods, audit objectives, and so on, are also explained.

Chapters 8 and 9 suggest some frameworks and guidelines on how to measure/assess IT capability and how IT capability affects a firm's performance, with some notions on the so-called IT paradox. These chapters aim at presenting a conceptual framework for organizational IT capability, methods of measuring and evaluating this capability, as well as its relationship with organizational business performance. The concept and measurement of IT capability are mapped.

Chapter 10 contains some excerpts from cases and white papers that describe real world stories related to the topics addressed in the book.

We would like to thank Professor Ajay Vinze for his Foreword.

A further special note of thanks goes the managerial, acquisition, editorial, publishing, and marketing teams at Taylor & Francis Group.

# Chapter 1

# Introduction: Downtime and Modern Business

## Background

Advances in and the proliferation of modern portable computing devices and the wide availability of mobile and LAN/WAN/Internet connections have created an environment in which people connect to their favorable applications and/or websites on a continuous basis. They want to be "always on" in accessing business data, getting up-to-date information, responding to busines and private e-mails, posting files on social networks, and so on. However, in spite of powerful servers, the wide availability of the Internet, Wi-Fi and mobile connections, and high data transfer rates, end users still experience messages such as "server is down", "site is temporary unavailable", "your request can't be completed now, try later", "DNS failure", "service unavailable", "down for maintenance", "sorry, something went wrong", "network is unreachable", "we'll be back soon, thank you for your patience", and so on. If users get these messages when they connect to Facebook, Instagram, and other social network sites, just from sharing messages/files, such messages do not result in negative financial effects for them. However, these and similar messages will in most cases result in, for instance, customers' decisions to switch to another site/vendor/provider when trying to connect to an e-business/e-commerce site and consequently yield some negative financial effects to the company/vendor/provider. Not only "out of use" messages but also delays in application servers' response time may cause customers to immediately switch to competitors and hence the loss of customers and money.

From a technology point of view, such messages can be the result of several types of hardware and software origins, such as server hardware glitches, server operating system crashes, application bugs, failures in data communication devices and lines, network disconnections, and bad IT operations. However, application servers may also go down and/or become unreachable for several hours/days due to electricity cuts, power outages, natural disasters, and pandemic diseases as well.

Technical issues related to IT infrastructure devices may occur within all types of information architecture models that are in use today such as the client-server on-premises model and client-cloud model. In many cases, these problems may cause the unavailability of application servers or of whole networks, which simply means the unavailability of information. If an application server goes down or a network is unreachable for some time, this situation is known as "system downtime", and can be caused by a server hardware glitch, a server operating system crash, network component failure, and similar issues. These so-called downtime points in both on-premises client-server architecture and client-cloud architecture are considered mission critical for continuous computing and business continuity in the modern e-business world. According to the *IT Disaster Recovery Preparedness Council Report* (2015), one hour of downtime can cost small companies as much as $8,000, midsize companies up to $74,000, and large enterprises up to $700,000. Ponemon Institute (2016) reported that the average cost of a data center outage has steadily increased from $505,502 in 2010 to $740,357 today (or a 38% net change). An Information Technology Intelligence Consulting (ITIC) report (ITIC Report, 2016) found that 98% of organizations say a single hour of downtime costs over $100,000; 81% of respondents indicated an amount of over $300,000. And a record one-third, or 33%, of enterprises report that one hour of downtime costs their firms $1 million to over $5 million.

Emerson Network Power and the Ponemon Institute (2016) revealed that the average cost of data center downtime across industries was approximately $7,900 per minute. Raphael (2013) reported that a 49-minute failure of Amazon's services on January 31, 2013, resulted in close to $5 million in missed revenue. Similar outages happened in January/February/March 2013 to Dropbox, Facebook, Microsoft, Google Drive, and Twitter. According to *Aberdeen Report* (2014), the average cost of an hour of downtime for large companies is $686,250; $215,638 for medium companies; and $8,581 for small companies. Gartner (2014) noted that "Based on industry surveys, the number we typically cite is $5,600 p/minute, which extrapolates to well over $300K p/hour". With regard to network downtime, "the cost of improving availability remains high and downtime is less acceptable, making rightsizing network availability the key goal for enterprise network designers". (Gartner, 2014). *Emerson Report* (2014) found that the most frequently cited total expense of unplanned outages includes: IT equipment failure; cyber-crime; UPS system failure; water, heat, or CRAC failure; generator failure; weather incursion; accidental/human error. International Data Corporation (IDC) (2014) noted that IT applications and services have become a critical element in how companies interact with their customers, deliver new products and services, and improve the productivity of their own workforce. The biggest cloud outages in 2014 include those of Amazon Web Services, Verizon Wireless, Dropbox, Adobe, Samsung,

Microsoft Lync, and Microsoft Exchange Online (Raphael, 2013). An Avaya report (2014) revealed that 80% of companies lose revenues when the network goes down, with the average company losing $140,003 per incident. *Quorum Report* (2013) found that hardware failures are the most common type within small and mid-sized businesses with the percentage of 55%, while in 22% of disasters, the reason was human error (system and network administrators' mistakes).

According to the 2017 *Veeam Availability Report* (2017), 82% of enterprises face a gap between what users expect and what IT can deliver. This "availability gap" is significant – unplanned downtime costs enterprises an average of $21.8 million each per year. The Uptime Institute's report (2018) revealed that the number of respondents that experienced an IT downtime incident or severe service degradation in the past year (31%) increased over last year's survey (about 25%). And in the past three years, almost half of 2018 survey respondents had an outage. This is a higher-than-expected number. The *Veeam Data Availability Report* (2017) revealed that, on average, each downtime incident lasts about 90 minutes, costs on average $150k per outage, and represents $21.8M per year in losses. Gartner reported that the average cost of an IT outage is $5,600 per minute, and because there are so many differences in how businesses operate, downtime, at the low end, can be as much as $140,000 per hour, $300,000 per hour on average, and as much as $540,000 per hour at the higher end (Opiah, 2019). Veeam (2016) reported that

> company executives, including CIOs and CFOs, have zero tolerance for downtime and data loss. These companies have established high availability requirements for the applications and critical data the organization uses on a daily basis. Sadly, most companies have not found a way to match these expectations with the harsh realities of maintaining the demands of the Always-On Enterprise™. In fact, 82% of CIOs admit to not being able to meet the demand for 24.7.365 Availability of IT services.

Recent Uptime Institute research (Uptime Institute report, 2019) found that major failures are not only still common, but that the consequences are high, and possibly higher than in the past – a result of our high reliance on IT systems in all aspects of life. In 2018, there were major outages of financial systems, daylong outages of 911 emergency service call numbers, aircraft losing services from ground-based IT landing systems, and healthcare systems lost during critical hours. The number of respondents that experienced an IT downtime incident or severe service degradation in the past year (31%) increased over last year's survey (about 25%). And in the past three years, almost half of our 2018 survey respondents had an outage. This is a higher-than-expected number. The Business Continuity Institute (BCI Report, 2018) reported that the uptake of business continuity arrangements has experienced an upward trend. An increasing number of organizations embed business continuity to protect their supply chains, which also has a positive impact on other areas such as insurance and top management commitment.

Application defects, hardware failures, and operating system crashes may take different forms, such as bugs in programs, badly integrated applications, and process/file corruptions. Network problems, in addition to hardware glitches on data communication devices, include problems such as those related to Domain Name System (DNS) servers, network configuration files, network protocols. Human error may also cause data unavailability, which includes accidental or intentional removal of files, fault operations, and hazardous activities including sabotage, strikes, and vandalism. Accidental or intentional removal of system files performed by a system administrator can shut down the whole server and make applications/data unreachable. Another example is the loss of key IT personnel or the leaving of expert staff due to several reasons, for example, bad managerial decisions on IT staffing policy.

Adeshiyan et al. (2010) stated that traditional high-availability and disaster recovery solutions require proprietary hardware, complex configurations, application specific logic, highly skilled personnel, and a rigorous and lengthy testing process. Jarvelainen (2013) proposed a framework for business continuity management to the context of business information systems. Zambon et al. (2011) stated that having a reliable information system is crucial to safeguard enterprise revenues. Martin (2011) cited the results of a study by Emerson Network Power and the Ponemom Institute that revealed that the average data center downtime event costs $505,500, with the average incident lasting 90 minutes. *ITIC Report* (2009) revealed that "server hardware and server operating system reliability has improved vastly since the 1980s, 1990s and even in just the last two to three years". This report underscores that common human error poses a bigger threat to server hardware and server operating system reliability than technical glitches. Venkatraman (2013) noted that more than a third of respondents viewed human error as the most likely cause of downtime. Clancy (2013) stated that it takes an average of 30 hours to recover from failures, which can be devastating for a business of any size. Sun et al. (2014) proposed a Markov-based model for evaluating system availability and estimating the availability index. Bhatt et al. (2010) considered IT infrastructure as the "enabler of organizational responsiveness and competitive advantage". Versteeg and Bouwman (2006) defined the main elements of a business architecture as business domains within the new paradigm of relations between business strategy and information technologies. Yoo (2011) stated that the shift to cloud computing also means that applications providers will place less emphasis on the operating system running on individual desktops and greater focus on the operating system running on the relevant servers. Duffy et al. (2010) stated that "although the operating system is an integral component of a computer-based information system, for many MIS majors the study of operating systems falls into this 'dry' category" Lawler et al. (2008) explored the risks of IT application downtime and the increasing dependence on critical IT infrastructures and discussed several disaster tolerance techniques. Brende and Markov (2013) considered the most important risks inherent to cloud computing and focused on the risks that are relevant to the IT function being migrated to the cloud. Sandvig (2007) noted that four server-side technologies are needed to support e-business: a web server, server side programming technology, a database application, and a server operating system. *ITIC Report* (2009) indicated that "server hardware and server operating system reliability has improved vastly since the 1980s, 1990s". According to this report, common human error poses a bigger threat to server hardware and server operating system reliability than technical glitches. In summary, it is more than evident that continuous computing features of modern server operating systems in terms of their availability, scalability, and reliability affect a business in such a way that more or less downtime simply means more or fewer financial losses. CIO (2013) reported that "Web-based services can crash and burn just like any other type of technology". Marshall (2013) related a story about the cloud service provider Nirvana that "has told its customers they have two weeks to find another home for their terabytes of data because the company was closing its doors and shutting down its services". Clancy (2013) stated that "Hardware failure is the biggest culprit, representing about 55 percent of all downtime events at SMBs, while human error accounts for about 22 percent of them". According to *Information Today Report* (2012), network outages (50%) were the leading cause of unplanned downtime within the last year. Human error (45%), server failures (45%) and storage failures (42%) followed closely behind. An example of human error is an accidental or intentional operation of removing files by the system administrator on any server. For instance, just by using a very simple command on the root level (# **rm** –R \*.\*) on a UNIX or Linux server, the system administrator can remove all the files. The same will happen if the system administrator executes a very simple "drag and drop" GUI-based operation of the main MyDocuments folder or root directory on any application server. Csaplar (2012) quoted the Aberdeen Group's report that found that between June 2010 and February 2012, the cost per hour of downtime increased on average by 65%. Forrester (2013) noted that there is less and less tolerance for any kind of downtime across all industries and predicted that the global cloud computing market will grow from $40.7 billion in 2011 to more than $241 billion in 2020 (Dignan, 2011). Leitch (2016) argued that downtime has reached an estimated cost of $700 billion per year to US businesses in 2016. The Ponemon Institute and Emerson Network Power (Ponemon Institute Report, 2016) reported that the average cost of a data center outage has steadily increased from $505,502 in 2010 to $740,357 today (or a 38% net change). However, as IDC stated (IDC, 2014), "Business cannot tolerate the same levels of planned and unplanned downtime that they could before they started on their digital transformation journey".

## Framework for the Book

Today, as many organizations are operating on a "24x7x365" basis, most of their applications simply become "business-critical" or "mission-critical". As these applications are installed and implemented on application servers, depending on the servers' availability, reliability and scalability, the whole business operates with more or less downtime. More downtime simply means higher negative financial effects, disgruntled customers, and a bad reputation. From an IT perspective, the issues mentioned above are considered IT issues that cause system/application downtime. They occur on several so-called "downtime points" within the information system infrastructure, both hardware and software, such as server hardware, server operating system, server application, network devices, and network infrastructure. The downtime points, in turn are considered mission critical in creating a "continuous computing platform", which is a must for continuous business given that even a few minutes of system downtime may result in thousands or even millions of dollars in lost revenues, bad decisions, disgruntled customers, or the broken image of the company.

Information technologies are implemented via several forms of enterprise information systems with the main objective of achieving "always-on" computing or, in more realistic terms, reducing downtime/increasing availability ratios. These systems (applications) rely mainly on the stability of server operating systems that run servers. Most e-businesses today depend on the availability of their IT infrastructures; therefore, the roles of enterprise servers and server operating systems are becoming more important given that applications availability is determined by these so-called server operating platforms. Not only e-businesses but also most businesses generally simply go "out of business" if some sort of downtime occurs, be it on the application server, the Data Base Management System (DBMS) server, network infrastructure, or storage infrastructure. Therefore, most businesses today are expected to be "up and running" on a continuous or always-on basis. And this applies not only for businesses but also for most non-business organizations such as governmental, interorganizational, and infrastructure.

Business continuity management (BCM) is a relatively new discipline established in the field of IT management with the primary goal of providing the right technical, organizational, and managerial solutions to ensure continuous computing and business continuity. In its extended form, BCM implies other factors as well, such as: pandemic diseases, floods, earthquakes, strikes, acts of terrorism, not only IT-based factors and not only those factors that have an impact on an organization's IT platform. BCM is a strategic issue for the organization because it helps the organization retain value derived from competitive advantage. A particular technical aspect of BCM is related to the availability, reliability, and scalability of the computer servers on which modern business computing and efficient management of information resources, which are of particular importance for modern business.

Business continuity planning (BCP) is a BCM process that defines the strategies that an organization must implement to ensure its survival when an event/crisis that causes a business interruption occurs and that mitigates the impact on the organization.

Organizational IT capability represents the way an organization uses IT to manage information resources successfully. IT capability includes the possession of information technologies as well as their adequate use to meet the information needs of an organization. BCM is considered an integral part of the organization's IT capabilities. To evaluate their IT capabilities, it is essential that organizations evaluate their BCM as well. Most IT maturity models also address BCM. When it comes to more technical research, they treat the technical/infrastructure side of IT capability and BCM as an integral part of it. Chapter 3 briefly introduces the concept of BCM, followed by an overview of BCP, a description of BCP strategies, and a brief statement of methodologies for business continuity planning. Then, clarification of DRP is provided, as essential parts of BCP, as well as some of the existing BCM maturity models. The second part of the chapter introduces the concept of organizational IT capability. Finally, in the third part, the relationship between BCM and organizational IT capability is introduced. This chapter mainly deals with the conceptualization of BCM and related terms, while the technical aspects are explained in the chapters after that.

Servers and server operating systems play a crucial role in "keeping business in business" as their crashes and outages are the main causes of "going out of business". Other causes of going out of business include server hardware glitches, server applications' defects, human error, hackers' activities, natural disasters, and the like. Human errors are mainly related to faulty operations performed by system administrators. Server operating environments include core and advanced built-in features related to continuous computing such as: automatic failover, system recovery, fault-tolerance, reloadable kernel, online upgrade, 64-bit computing, crash-handling techniques, memory mirroring, workload management, high-availability clustering, TCP/IP failover, and storage scalability. Modern server configurations include technologies that are critical for reducing downtime and improving uptime: fault tolerant RAM technologies such error correcting code (ECC), built-in redundant technologies for overcoming single points of failure, and hot-swappable components − the hardware components that can be swapped without shutting down the servers. No matter which model of IT architecture is implemented, traditional client-server, cloud-based, or newly introduced modifications called converged, hyperconverged, or composable models, it is evident that in all these models enterprise servers still play a critical role. The server is a central component of the so-called server operating environment and this applies to both on-premises and cloud-based implementations. Servers run applications that are accessed by the client side, which is either PC/thin or thick client or mobile devices based. Server operating systems should be considered from a business perspective due to their role in minimizing downtime and hence enhancing the availability ratios of business applications. They represent a core component of a "server operating environment", which includes several server applications and extensions for fault tolerance, disaster tolerance/recovery, and high availability/reliability/scalability.

System administration skills are very important in reducing system downtime and improving the process of system recovery. The system administrator has a critical role in keeping the server and server operating system up and running, and providing troubleshooting solutions when the system goes down. A skilled and experienced system administrator can resolve quickly most of the problems that occur on the server or the server operating system level when the server shuts down or the server operating system crashes, and hence reduce significantly the time required for system recovery in terms of Recovery Time Objective (RTO) and Recovery Point Objective (RPO). However, the system administrator's privileges (data access rights) should be kept "under control" and implemented by following the compliance regulations such as FDCC, Sarbanes–Oxley, PCI, HIPAA, GLBA, including solutions such as: Fine-Grained privileges and Role-based Access Control. According to IDC's White Paper (2009), by adopting industry best practices compliance regulations (e.g., ITIL, CobiT), companies can lower annual downtime by up to 85%, greatly reducing interruptions to daily data processing and access, supporting business continuity, and containing operational costs. System administration is considered a critical activity on servers and server operating systems with regard to their role in modern business. System and network administrators, if properly educated and skilled, can significantly reduce recovery time after the downtime occurs for any reason. Several other specialists exist as well, such as network administrators, database administrators, security managers, business continuity managers, business continuity analysts, business continuity specialists, business continuity administrators, business resilience architects, disaster recovery specialists, and the like.

With the introduction of several agile methodologies in the field of software development such as XP, Scrum, Lean software development, and Kanban during the last decade, many organizations have started adopting the so-called DevOps software development method that has appeared as an upgrade to agile methodologies. The impact of modern software architectures and the DevOps framework on business continuity and system administration (sysadmin 4.0) has been addressed as well. In addition, an approach to optimize investments in BC by using the Bayesian belief network model for availability analysis is presented in order to identify the factors affecting Information System (IS) availability.

The processes of controlling and auditing information systems are important in today's competitive business world. Control and audit are global concerns, especially in areas like electronic payment systems, electronic funds transfer, and wireless technology. Digital transformation, cybercrime, and protection of personal data have a tremendous impact on the audit, control, and security of IT in business and our lives. Therefore, the whole audit process consisting of preparation and planning, performance of audit procedures, preparation of an audit report, and post-audit activities should be addressed as well. Various types of tools, techniques, and methods available for the auditor to use are described as well as their advantages and disadvantages. As new information technologies are integrated and become commercially profitable, so too must the skills of IT auditors be at the level to meet the challenge and comply with professional practice standards. Some best practices for an effective audit of Business Continuity and Disaster Recovery, VMware virtualization administration, application containers, and cloud administration can be identified. Although the process of performing the audit will change little, the tools to do it with and the quality of reporting with follow-up of management actions will change to be profitable, competitive, and efficient.

Chapter 8 aims to present a concept of organizational IT capability, methods of measuring and assessing IT capability, as well as its relationship with organizational business performance. A citation and co-citation bibliometric analysis of "IT capability" research has been conducted. The conceptualization and measurements of IT capability are mapped. The results indicate that there are two approaches to assess organizational IT capability: one is present in scientific studies, mainly in the field of management, and the other is present in the practice and international standards and good practices addressing BCM. In this regard, this chapter critically reviews the available methods for assessing organizational IT capability.

The framework presented in the book (Figure 1.1) includes the following core concepts:

a) Always-On Business
b) Downtime Costs
c) Server Operating Environment
d) System Administration
e) Continuous Computing Technologies
f) Business Continuity Management
g) Auditing and Compliance Regulations
h) IT Capability
i) Firm's Performances

This book aims to offer scholars and IT practitioners an overview of the BCM concept and its relation to the IT capability presented in the scientific and professional literature. There are two basic goals that this book aims to fulfill. First, the presentation of BCM so that the reader understands the essence of the concept itself as well as the basic methods, technologies, and system administration. Second, a critical evaluation of organizational IT capability. Both these topics are a matter of interest in management as well as in IT.

In this regard, the book consists of three related sections:

In **the first part**, the concept of downtime is presented after the introductory section, followed by the introduction of BCM, and its connection to the IT capability of a contemporary organization. This type of structure is rational because downtime as a potential threat to the business of contemporary organizations is the reason for establishing BCM. In other words, after understanding downtime and its potential effect on business implications, the need for BCM and BCP becomes clear, so understanding the concept itself is

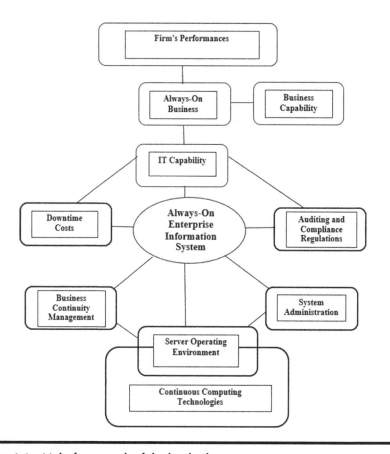

**Figure 1.1  Main framework of the book: the core concepts.**

required. These three chapters can be considered as the first part of this book, which aims to help the reader understand downtime and the concept of BCM.

In **the second part**, the server operating platforms for BCM are presented, as well as system administration for BCM, followed by methods, techniques, and technologies to enhance business continuity. This may be considered as the second part of the book, in which the reader is introduced to BCM's technical solutions. Moreover, the basics of IT auditing and its relationship to business continuity are presented.

**The third part** deals with the comprehensive addressing of the concept of an organization's IT capability. In this regard, Chapter 8 offers a systematic literature review of the concept of IT capability to answer the following questions: 1) What is organizational IT capability? 2) How can organizational IT capability be measured? and 3) What is the relationship between

BCM and organizational IT capability? Based on the literature review, the adequacy of the available IT capability measures is discussed, especially considering the importance of BCM. Finally, Chapter 9 critically reviews the conceptualizations offered, proposing a reconsideration of the IT capability concept in order to include BCM and IT audit.

Through these three sections of the book, the reader is able to understand the need for BCM, the concept of BCM itself, as well as the methods, techniques, and technology of BCM. Finally, the reader is offered the conceptualization of organizational IT capability, which raises the question of critical consideration of the scientific approach and the methods present in standards.

The book is devoted to IT professionals, business people, and students of both IT and business programs in different ways:

a) System administrators and other IT professionals will benefit from an additional perspective of system administration enhanced with a BC perspective.
b) IT managers/CIOs will get some insights into why stable, available, reliable, and scalable IT infrastructure is important for modern business.
c) IT managers/CIOs will benefit from a new perspective on the role of system administrators in modern business, meaning that hiring and/or firing system administrators is much more than a technical issue.
d) Students of IT-related programs (computer science, computer engineering, information technology, and so on) will benefit from such an approach as it brings an additional perspective – a business perspective of server configurations, server operation systems, data communications, computer networks, and system administration.
e) Students of business/business administration programs will gain at least some introductory information on the importance of modern server configurations, and information infrastructures for modern business.

## Conclusions

Disruption of business in today's competitive market can lead to a decline in the organization's credibility or a loss of reputation. Business continuity management is based on a holistic operating model that allows companies to operate more effectively and efficiently in their daily operations. IT is now an integral part of almost any business process. However, possessing adequate technology does not imply value generation. Therefore, understanding the IT capability, which includes owning IT as well as its adequate use in business activities, is necessary. Consequently, it is of great importance to understand what IT capability is, how to measure it, and how IT capability interacts with other organizational factors.

## Discussion Questions

1. Explain the main terms of continuous computing: availability, reliability, and scalability.
2. Define the concepts of "continuous computing" and "continuous computing technologies".
3. Discuss the factors that affect system availability.
4. Define the concept of business continuity drivers.
5. Identify the main server hardware – based continuous computing technologies.
6. List some redundant devices that are used in assuring higher levels of availability.
7. List some advanced server technologies for business continuity.
8. How do the networking and security affect business continuity?
9. Explain briefly why server configurations are important for modern business.
10. List some frequently used applications or frequently used websites that have experienced downtime issues recently.

## References

Aberdeen Report. (2014). Preventing Virtual Application Downtime. Retrieved from https://statuscast.com/preventing-virtual-application-downtime-2/

Adeshiyan, T. et al. (2010). Using virtualization for high availability and disaster recovery, *IBM Journal of Research and Development*, 53(4), 587–597.

Avaya Report. (2014). Network Downtime Results in Job, Revenue Loss, March 2014. Retrieved from www.avaya.com/usa/about-avaya/newsroom/news-releases/2014/pr-140305/

Bajgoric, N. (Ed.). (2010b). Always-On Enterprise Information Systems for Business Continuance: Technologies for Reliable and Scalable Operations, IGI-Global, XVI-XX.

Bajgoric, N. (2014). Continuous Computing Technologies for Enhancing Business Continuity, IGI-Global, 2008.

BCI Report. (2018). BCI Supply Chain Resilience Report 2018. Retrieved from www.thebci.org/uploads/assets/uploaded/c50072bf-df5c-4c98-a5e1876aafb15bd0.pdf

Bhatt, G., Emdad, A., Roberts, N., Grover, V. (2010). Building and leveraging information in dynamic environments: The role of IT infrastructure flexibility as enabler of organizational responsiveness and competitive advantage, *Information & Management*, 47(7–8), 341–349.

Brende, N., Markov, I. (2013). Risk perception and risk management in cloud computing: Results from a case study of Swiss companies, *International Journal of Information Management*, 33, 726–733.

CIO Report. (2013), The Worst Cloud Outages of 2013 (So Far), InfoWorld, July 1, 2013. Retrieved from www.cio.com/slideshow/detail/108561/The-Worst-Cloud-Outages-of-2013–So-Far-?source=CIONLE_nlt_cloud_computing_2013-07-08

Clancy, H. (2013). Most Common Cause of SMB Downtime? The Answer May Surprise You, ZDNET. Retrieved from www.zdnet.com/most-common-cause-of-smb-downtime-the-answer-may-surprise-you-7000011137

Csaplar, D. (2012). The Cost of Downtime Is Rising. Retrieved from http://blogs.aberdeen. com/it-infrastructure/the-cost-of-downtime-is-rising/

Dignan, L. (2011). Cloud Computing Market: $241 Billion in 2020. Retrieved from www. zdnet.com/blog/btl/cloud-computing-market-241-billion-in-2020/47702

Duffy, K.P., Davis, M.H. Jr., Sethi, V. (2010). Demonstrating operating system principles via computer forensics exercises, *Journal of Information Systems Education, 21*(2), 195–201.

Emerson Report. (2014). The Lowdown on Data Center Downtime: Frequency, Root Causes and Costs, Retrieved from www.emersonnetworkpower.com/en-US/Solutions/ByApplication/DataCenterNetworking/Data-Center-Insights/Pages/Causes_of_Downtime_Study.aspx

Forrester Report. (2013). How Organizations Are Improving Business Resiliency with Continuous IT Availability, February 2013. Retrieved from www.emc.com/collateral/analyst-report/forrester-improve-bus-resiliency-continuous-it-avail-ar.pdf

Gartner. (2014). The Costs of Downtime, July 2014. Retrieved from http://blogs.gartner. com/andrew-lerner/2014/07/16/the-cost-of-downtime    www.thebci.org/uploads/assets/uploaded/c50072bf-df5c-4c98-a5e1876aafb15bd0.pdf

IDC White Paper. (2009). Reducing Downtime and Business Loss: Addressing Business Risk with Effective Technology, IDC, August 2009

IDC White Paper. (2014). DevOps and the Cost of Downtime: Fortune 1000 Best Practice Metrics Quantified. Retrieved from www.idc.com/getdoc.jsp?containerId=253155

Information Today Report. (2012). Enterprise Data and the Cost of Downtime: 2012 IOUG Database Availability Survey. Retrieved from www.oracle.com/us/products/database/2012-ioug-db-survey-1695554.pdf

IT Disaster Recovery Preparedness Council Report. (2015). Retrieved from www. techadvisory.org/2016/01/the-importance-of-disaster-recovery/

ITIC Report. (2009). ITIC 2009 Global Server Hardware and Server OS Reliability Survey, Information Technology Intelligence Corp. (ITIC), July 2009.

ITIC Report. (2016). Retrieved from https://itic-corp.com/blog/2016/08/cost-of-hourly-downtime-soars-81-of-enterprises-say-it-exceeds-300k-on-average/

Jarvelainen, J. (2013). IT incidents and business impacts: Validating a framework for continuity management in information systems, *International Journal of Information Management, 33*, 583–590.

Lawler, C.M., Harper, M., Szygenda, S., Thornton, M., (2008), Components of disaster-tolerant computing: Analysis of disaster recovery, IT application downtime and executive visibility, *International Journal of Business Information Systems, 33*, 3(3):317–331.

Leitch, G. (2016). The True Cost of Downtime in 2016. Retrieved from www.soscanhelp. com/blog/start-investing-in-uptime-instead-of-losing-money-to-downtime

Marshall, D. (2013). Cloud Storage Provider Nirvanix Is Closing Its Doors. InfoWorld. Retrieved from www.infoworld.com/d/virtualization/cloud-storage-provider-nirvanix-closing-its-doors-227289

Martin, N. (2011). The True Costs of Data Center Downtime. Retrieved from http://itknowledgeexchange.techtarget.com/data-center/the-true-costs-of-data-center-downtime/

Opiah, A. (2019). Outages. Downtime. System Failures. 2019's IT Meltdowns. Retrieved from https://data-economy.com/outages-downtime-system-failures-2019s-it-meltdowns/

Ponemon Institute Report. (2016). Cost of Data Center Outages. Retrieved from www. emersonnetworkpower.com/en-US/Resources/Market/Data-Center/Latest-Thinking/Ponemon/Documents/2016-Cost-of-Data-Center-Outages-FINAL-2.pdf

Quorum Report. (2013). *Quorum Disaster Recovery Report*, Q1 2013. Retrieved from www.quorum.net/news-events/press-releases/quorum-disaster-recovery-report-exposes-top-causes-of-downtime

Raphael, J.R. (2013). The Worst Cloud Outages of 2013 (So Far), InfoWorld, July 1, 2013. Retrieved from www.cio.com/slideshow/detail/108561/The-Worst-Cloud-Outages-of-2013–So-Far-?source=CIONLE_nlt_cloud_computing_2013-07-08

Sandvig, J.C. (2007). Selection of server-side technologies for an E-business curriculum, *Journal of Information Systems Education, 18*(2), 215–226.

Sun, J., Dong, X., Zhang, X., Gong, W., Wang, Y. (2014). High availability analysis and evaluation of heterogeneous dual computer fault-tolerant system, *5th IEEE International Conference on Software Engineering and Service Science (ICSESS)*, 2014, 460–464.

Uptime Institute. (2018). Uptime Institute's Eighth Annual Data Center Industry Survey Report. Retrieved from https://uptimeinstitute.com/2018-data-center-industry-survey-results

Uptime Institute. (2019) Publicly Reported Outages 2018-10. Retrieved from https://uptimeinstitute.com/publicly-reported-outages-2018–19

Veeam Availability Report. (2017). Retrieved from www.veeam.com/wp-availability-report-2017-brief.html

Veeam Report. (2014). The Veeam Data Center Availability Report 2014. Retrieved from www.veeam.com/wp-availability-report-2014.html

Veeam White Paper. (2016). 5 Fundamentals for Modern Data Center Availability. Retrieved from www.veeam.com/wp-backup-davis-five-fundamentals-of-modern-data-protection.html

Venkatraman, A. (2013). Human Error Most Likely Cause of Datacentre Downtime, Finds Study, Computerweekly. Retrieved from www.computerweekly.com/news/2240179651/Human-error-most-likely-cause-of-datacentre-downtime-finds-study

Versteeg, G., Bouwman, H. (2006). Business architecture: A new paradigm to relate business strategy to ICT, *Information Systems Frontiers, 8*, 91–102.

Yoo, C.S. (2011), Cloud computing: Architectural and policy implications, *Review of Industrial Organization, 38*, 405–421.

Zambon, E., Etalle, S., Wieringa, R.J., Hartel, P. (2011). Model-based qualitative risk assessment for availability of IT infrastructures, *Software and Systems Modeling, 10*, 553–580.

# Chapter 2

# Economics of Downtime

## Background

Hardware glitches on processors, RAM, and network adapters; server operating system crashes; Internet disconnections; application bugs, and system administrators' mistakes are examples of some critical points in the information system infrastructure on which a downtime may occur (Figure 2.1).

In addition, natural disasters such as fires, floods, hurricanes, tropical storms, extreme heat, earthquakes, and pandemic diseases may also result in application servers' unavailability, which may bring financial losses in today's dominant e-business environment (Figure 2.2).

Downtime may occur not only in an on-premises model of IT infrastructure but in the cloud computing model as well as cloud providers hosting applications on the servers, and these servers can also go down and become unreachable. Each time the cloud provider's application server is down, for any reason, the customer faces a problem with data accessibility. Similarly, all kinds of network-related disconnections and related problems may occur in the cloud model as well. Therefore, the role of system/network administration remains important no matter which model of IT-architecture or infrastructure is used.

What follows is a list of some stories that demonstrate downtime issues.

Reuters (2017) reported that a technological failure which stranded tens of thousands of British Airways (BA) passengers in May 2017 cost the company around 80 million pounds ($102.19 million). BA suffered a disruption at London's Heathrow and Gatwick airports when a power surge knocked out its IT system, forcing it to cancel almost two-thirds of all flights on May 27, 2017, which fell on a busy bank holiday weekend. Sverdik (2016) noted that the Delta Airlines data center outage in 2016 cost the company $150,000,000. Even small companies lost an average of over $8,000 per hour. *Forbes* (2018) reported, for example, in

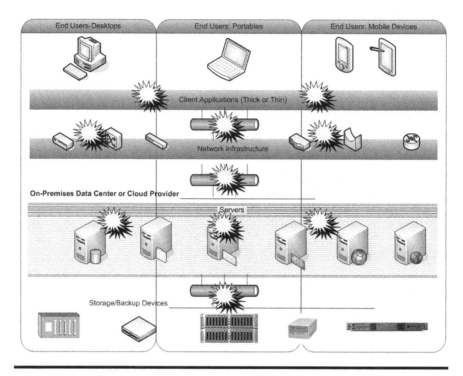

**Figure 2.1    Major downtime points in a client-server architecture. Bajgoric, (2010a).**

2017, organizations were losing an average $100,000 for every hour of downtime on their site. A *Business Insider* story (2018) reported that the website glitches and downtime that Amazon experienced during its annual Prime Day sale may have cost it more than just some unhappy customers – the company is believed to have missed out on tens of millions of dollars in sales. The downtime is estimated to have cost Amazon $72 million to $99 million in lost sales. Cloud Pro reported (2019) that in January 2019, the Microsoft Office 365 platform went down across Europe. Customers were unable to use their Office 365 e-mail accounts for more than nine hours.

Miller (2019) asked the questions, "Is cloud computing reliable? Can I trust Internet services with my mission-critical business workloads?" And he answered, "for some cloud prospects, last week's cluster of outages for major Internet brands may raise fresh questions about the reliability of online service delivery. Several of the Internet's most widely used platforms suffered prolonged outages, including Google Cloud, Apple Pay and iCloud, Facebook, Instagram, WhatsApp, and the CloudFlare content delivery service, which impacted thousands of customer websites. Similar outages happened in September 2018 when users across the world were unable to

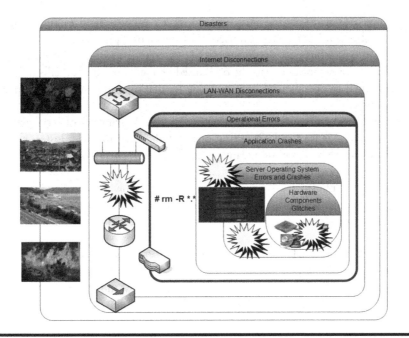

**Figure 2.2  Downtime issues including natural disasters.**

access critical Microsoft services, including Office 365 and Azure, for more than 24 hours after a "severe weather event" knocked one of its data centers offline".

Forrester (2015) stated:

> Nearly every application is considered critical. With the increased focus on serving both internal and external customers, critical applications are driving the demand for the always-on enterprise. On average, survey respondents reported that 39% of their organization's applications were business-critical, and another 36% were mission-critical.

Forty-five percent of IT and business managers and executives surveyed cited the loss of customer confidence as the most significant business impact of downtime. The IT and business managers and executives surveyed cited loss of customer confidence (45%), lost revenue (44%), loss of employee productivity (40%), and damaged corporate reputation (39%) as the top implications of poor availability.

Uptime Institute (Bednarz, 2019) defined a scale (a rating system) that has five tiers:

1) Level 1 is a negligible outage. The outage is recordable, but there's little or no obvious impact on services and no service disruptions.

2) Level 2 is characterized as a minimal service outage. Services are disrupted, but there's minimal effect on users, customers, or reputation.

3) Level 3 is a business-significant service outage. It involves customer or user service interruptions, mostly of limited scope, duration, or effect. There's minimal to no financial impact. Some reputational or compliance impact is incurred.

4) Level 4 is a serious business or service outage. Disruption of service and/or operations is involved. Ramifications include some financial losses, compliance breaches, reputation damage, and possibly safety concerns. Customer losses are possible.

5) Level 5 is a business- or mission-critical outage involving major and damaging disruption of services and/or operations. There are possible large financial losses, safety issues, compliance breaches, customer losses, and reputational damage.

A key finding from this Uptime Institute research is that power is less implicated in overall failures, while the network and IT systems are more implicated.

What follows is a list of common causes, according to this report:

On the network front, common causes of outages include:

a) Fiber cuts outside the data center, with insufficient routing alternatives.
b) Intermittent failure of major switches, with secondary routers not deployed.
c) Major switch failure without backup.
d) Incorrect configuration of traffic during maintenance.
e) Incorrectly configured routers and software-defined networks.
f) Loss of power to non-backed-up single components, such as switches and routers.

When IT is the culprit, some of the causes cited include:

a) A poorly managed upgrade with insufficient testing at the software level.
b) The failure and subsequent data corruption of large disk drives or storage area networks. This is likely caused by hardware failure, exacerbated by configuration or programming errors.
c) Failure of synchronization or programming errors across load balancing or the traffic management system.
d) Incorrectly programmed failure/synchronization or disaster-recovery systems.
e) Loss of power to non-backed-up single components, such as servers or large disk drives.

When power is the culprit, some of the leading causes of outages include:

a) Lightning strikes, leading to surges and lost power. Backup software/configuration failed.

b) Intermittent failures with transfer switches, leading to failure to start generators, or transfers to a second data center.

c) Uninterruptible Power Supply (UPS) failures and failure to transfer to a secondary system.

d) Operator errors, turning off or misconfiguring power.

e) Utility power loss and subsequent failure of generator or UPS.

f) Damage to IT equipment caused by power surges.

g) IT gear not equipped with dual power suppliers to switch to secondary feed.

Table 2.1 summarizes some reports that demonstrate the downtime costs.

## Business Computing in the Digital Age: Always-On Information System and Always-On Business

As more and more businesses tend to have their operations on a "follow the sun" basis, they try to find a solution to "keep business in business" even if some sort of disaster occurs. Most organizations in the digital age seek such an information system that supports "continuous computing" (Bajgoric, 2006, 2008b), which is called an "always-on information system" (Bajgoric, 2006, 2010b). Theoretically, such an information system, if implemented and managed properly, can provide "%100" uptime, or "zero downtime".

**Always-On Business** is at the same time the main requirement for a business system and the main objective of **an always-on enterprise information system**. All business functions, divisions and departments, employees, customers, and suppliers expect such a kind of information infrastructure (information system) that will be available on continuous basis and with zero downtime, in other words – "always-on". Messages such as: "system is down, please try later", "something went wrong", "DNS error occurred" are not an option from an end-user perspective, be it an employee, CEO, CIO, customer, or supplier.

**Downtime/Uptime** is a measure of performance of an always-on enterprise information system. The goal is to reach a "100%" uptime or "zero downtime". However, given that it is not easy to achieve such an availability, the uptime objective is usually expressed by so-called high-availability ratios and in terms of "number of nines" (e.g., four nines – 99,99%, five nines – 99,999%, etc.), or in number of minutes/hours of downtime per year (e.g., "five minutes per year", "five hours per year").

By using a literature review approach on several aspects on downtime costs and their impact on modern business, and several approaches in designing new business models, and by applying a systems approach, we came up with a framework for creating a concept of an "always-on information system" or a "business continuity-oriented information system" (Figures 2.3 and 2.4).

**Table 2.1   Reports on Downtime Costs**

| Report | Findings |
|---|---|
| Butler (2013) | A 49-minute failure of Amazon's services on January 31, 2013, resulted in close to $5 million in missed revenue. |
| Aberdeen Report (2014) | The average cost of downtime for large companies is $686,250 per hour, $215,638/hour for medium companies, and $8,581/hour for small companies. |
| Gartner (2014) | Based on industry surveys, average downtime is $5,600 p/minute. |
| Avaya Report (2014) | 80% of companies lose revenue when the network goes down. |
| IDC (2014) | For the Fortune 1000, the average total cost of unplanned application downtime per year is $1.25 billion to $2.5 billion. |
| Veeam Data Availability Report (2014) | Sixty-eight percent of those organizations modernizing their data centers are doing so in order to enable 24/7, always-on business operations. |
| IDC Report (2015) | For a large firm, the mean cost of downtime per hour is nearly $1.7 million, with some specific industries approaching $10 million lost per hour of downtime. |
| IT Disaster Recovery Preparedness Council Report (2015) | One hour of downtime can cost small companies as much as $8,000, midsize companies up to $74,000, and large enterprises up to $700,000, according to a 2015 report from the IT Disaster Recovery Preparedness (DRP) Council. |
| Report (2015) | Disaster recovery service provider Zetta showed that more than half of companies surveyed (54%) had experienced a downtime event that lasted more than eight hours over the past five years. Two-thirds of those surveyed said their businesses would lose more than $20,000 for every day of downtime. |
| Ponemon Institute Report (2016) | The average cost of a data center outage has steadily increased from $505,502 in 2010 to $740,357 today (or a 38% net change). |
| ITIC (2016) | ITIC's latest survey data finds that 98% of organizations say a single hour of downtime costs over $100,000; 81% of respondents indicated that 60 minutes of downtime costs their business over $300,000. And a record one-third, or 33%, of enterprises report that one hour of downtime costs their firms $1 million to over $5 million. |

*(Continued)*

**Table 2.1 (Continued)    Reports on Downtime Costs**

| Report | Findings |
|---|---|
| Aberdeen Report (2016) | Recent research has shown that the average cost of an hour of downtime is about half a million dollars,1 and this will only increase with the continued digitization of industries. |
| Veeam Data Availability Report (2017) | Eighty-two percent of enterprises face a gap between what users expect and what IT can deliver. This "availability gap" is significant – unplanned downtime costs enterprises an average of $21.8 million each per year. |
| Uptime Institute (2015) | Costs to businesses can include lost work time, downtime, OSHA investigations, fines, medical costs, litigation, lost business, equipment damage, and most tragically, loss of life. |
| Uptime Institute (2018) | The number of respondents that experienced an IT downtime incident or severe service degradation in the past year (31%) increased over last year's survey (about 25%). And in the past three years, almost half of our 2018 survey respondents had an outage. |
| Veeam Data Availability Report (2018) | On average, each downtime incident: Lasts about 90 Minutes, Costs on average $150k per outage, Represents $21.8M per year in losses |
| Uptime Institute (2019) | The three main findings in this report are:<br>a) Major and damaging outages continue to trouble the IT industry, despite improvements in technology and management. There is clear evidence that availability does not match marketing claims (service-level promises).<br>b) Major publicly recorded outages are now more likely to be caused by IT and network problems than a year or two years ago, when power problems were a bigger cause.<br>c) Public cloud-based services account for a significant number of reported service outages, with causes ranging from power to wide-area synchronization issues. Although the reliability/availability of their services is generally good, their scale and complexity mean that their outages are likely to have a highly visible, clear and well-recorded impact. |

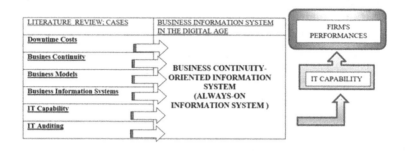

**Figure 2.3   BC-oriented information system – always-on information system: Conceptual model of the book.**

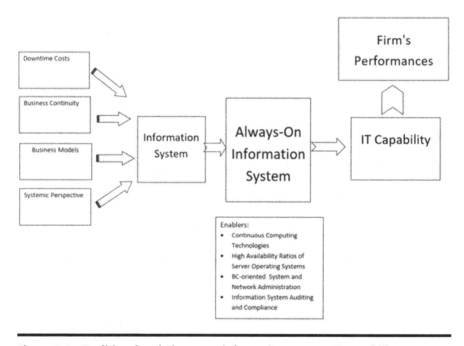

**Figure 2.4   Traditional and always-on information system; IT capability.**

Narman et al. (2014) pointed out that the availability of enterprise information systems is a key concern for many organizations. Butler and Gray (2006) underscored the question of how system reliability translates into reliable organizational performance. Lump et al. (2008) provided an overview of state-of-the-art architectures for continuous availability concepts such as high-availability (HA) clustering platforms. Niemimaa (2017) stated that organizations' value creation is dependent on the reliable and continuous operations of their inherently unreliable information systems (IS). Year after year, industry and academic surveys show that IS-related incidents persist as a top concern on IS managers' agenda. He argued that leading IS journals provide little contribution on this perspective and identified the IS-BC relationship as "a timely question" (Niemimaa, 2015). Niemimaa, Jarvelainen, and Heikkila (2019) argued that the innovative business models enabled by technological development provide significant opportunities for the companies that have innovated them but pose significant BC threats for other established companies and their business models. By focusing on the continuity of resources that implement the current business model, the business model itself is left out of consideration despite the strategic threat it poses to BC. They argued that existing business continuity approaches have eclipsed issues related to business models.

Turban et al. (2010) identified a set of "business pressures" related to the modern business environment: market pressures, technology pressures, and societal pressures. They argued that businesses employ information technologies in order to provide responses to business pressures and business risks. However, the modern e-business environment has created a set of additional pressures that are related to business continuity. This is shown in Figure 2.5.

Business continuity, in other terms, "always-on business", relies on such a kind of business (enterprise) information system that provides "continuous computing" or an "always-on information system", which is, in short, an infrastructure that is expected to be "always-on", and with "zero downtime". However, achieving "zero downtime" is not an easy task and requires numerous resources; therefore, most

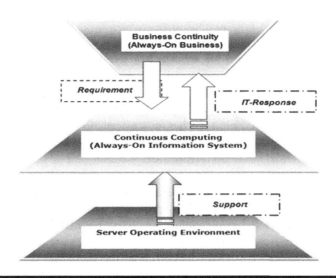

**Figure 2.5   Business continuity (always-on business): an Internet era's requirement and business pressure.**

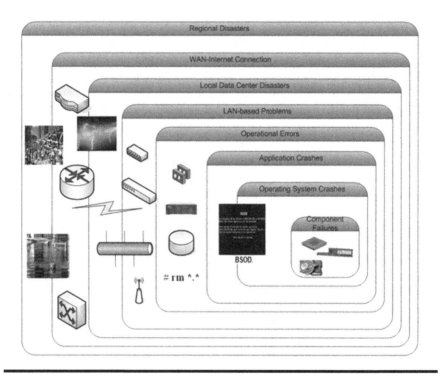

**Figure 2.6    Major threats that cause downtime. Bajgoric (2008).**

organizations tend to reach more realistic, but still acceptable, so-called high-availability ratios. These ratios are measured in terms of "number of nines", for example, 99.99% availability.

Today's enterprises are exposed to several types of business risks, either from outside or from inside the system. In addition, modern business can suffer from IT-related issues such as technical glitches on server platforms, physical damage on IT infrastructure, server operating system crashes, application defects, operational mistakes, human error, and so on (Figure 2.6).

Physical threats result from any kind of physical damage that may occur on IT centers, servers, hardware components, or communication devices. Natural catastrophic events such as fires, lightning, floods, earthquakes, and hurricanes can damage IT centers and cause applications/data unavailability for some time. Logical threats may have different forms, such as deleted system files, corrupted files, broken processes or programs, a corrupted file system, or a crashed operating system. Technical glitches relate to hardware component failures that may occur on computer components/devices within the IT infrastructure (memory chips, fans, mainboards, hard disks, disk controllers, tapes or tape drivers, network cards, switches, routers, communication lines, power supply units). System crashes are situations that make all applications and data stored on enterprise server which underwent the crash unavailable for end users, for example, "BSOD" on Windows Servers.

In today's e-business age, system downtime equals financial losses and simply means going "out of business". Particularly, this is something that applies to enterprise servers running business-critical applications. Therefore, running business applications effectively and keeping enterprise servers up and running on a continuous or always-on basis is a crucial task for IT managers. No matter how these applications are implemented, be it "in-house/home-grown" or "off-the-shelf" running within an on-premises platform, or cloud computing based, these applications are expected to run on a continuous basis, with zero or near-zero downtime.

Messages such as "the server is down", "down for maintenance", "sorry, something went wrong" "site is temporary unavailable", "DNS failure", "service unavailable", "network is unreachable", "we'll be back soon, thank you for your patience" all mean that due to some technical problems on the server or IT infrastructure, a particular application or application server cannot be reached. A second type of problems that are common when accessing any server (website, portal, server-based application) are those related to response time – if the application server is not capable of responding or is not scalable enough to resolve all clients' requests in a short or reasonable period of time. Such situations as well may bring financial losses, for instance, if a prospective customer decides immediately to switch to another site/vendor after waiting for some time to access data or open the site. Therefore, most businesses try to identify so-called downtime points and resolve them by implementing continuous computing technologies in order to avoid or minimize downtime/increase uptime.

Katoa and Charfoentrab (2018) underscored that there is a need for "business[es] [...] to integrate disaster risk management, including business continuity, into [their] business models and practices through disaster-risk-informed investments, especially in micro, small, medium-sized enterprises". Folkers (2017) argues that while the future in the form of potentially disruptive events certainly matters in BCM, continuity managers rely less on future scenarios than on the analysis of systemic features of an organization. This perspective indicates another dimension of temporality associated with the temporal order of business processes and the adequate sequence of emergency management procedures. Thus, BCM shifts the key focus from futurity to continuity, from the time of anticipation to the now time of operations. Soufi, Torabi, and Sahebjamnia (2019) stated that BCM can be implemented as a managerial system according to the international standard ISO 22301 (2012). However, the lack of effective methods and frameworks to develop suitable BCPs has led to the loss of resources happening after a disruption. In other words, the current qualitative approaches are not able to fully satisfy managerial obligations through BCM programs. To fill this gap, they proposed a quantitative model for selecting the most effective and efficient BCPs by taking into account the interrelationships between the main requirements of BCMs. Schattera et al. (2019) pointed out that BCM forms part of supply chain risk management and is an important competitive factor for companies by ensuring the smooth functioning of critical business processes in the case of failures. If business operations are severely disrupted, a company's decision maker is confronted with a situation that is characterized by a high degree of uncertainty, complexity, and time pressure. In such a context, decision support can be of significant value. They presented a decision support methodology that leads to an improved and more robust BCM for severe disruptions caused by disasters.

According to Faertesa (2018), BCM continues to evolve strongly in response to the volatility of the business environment, increased global competition, and the effect of customer choice. These forces are driving companies in every sector to reinvent themselves and compete on the basis of flexibility, speed, and customer responsiveness. The pervasive influence of technology and concepts of lean management have further revolutionized how companies conduct their business. Though the value of BCM in business planning is widely understood, managers still hold the view that it is a specialist function that deals with day-to-day operational activities in relation to its strategic possibilities. Faertesa (2018) outlined the challenges of establishing business continuity as a critical success factor that supports business performance and proposed an incremental three-stage approach to introduce discipline into different levels of corporate activities. The intent is to establish business continuity as a key driving force in your company that contributes to successful strategy development and management excellence.

## The Role of the Server Operating Environment and System Administration

Modern businesses operating in the e-business environment are in most cases run by different forms of business-critical applications. These applications are hosted by application servers and accessed by end users over the network based dominantly on the client-server architecture (c/s). Such an architecture consists of one or more servers hosting applications and a number of clients accessing them. Depending on the server infrastructure's availability, reliability, and scalability, the whole business operates with more or less downtime, which, in turn, has more or less impact on its financial performance. Information technologies are implemented within information systems that are characterized by different levels of availability,

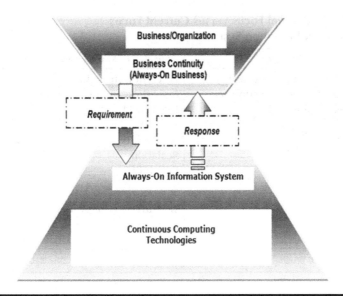

**Figure 2.7    Always-On business: A digital age's requirement and business pressure.**

scalability, and reliability, with the main objective of achieving "always-on" computing (Bajgoric, 2006).

In addition to availability, both scalability and reliability of e-business application platforms are business critical, as well as modern e-businesses are expected to be "always-on", with zero or "near-zero" downtime. Such businesses aim at providing products and services on a continuous basis as each hour, even each minute, of downtime can be easily expressed as financial losses. As shown in Figure 2.7, "always-on" business relies on continuous computing technologies that should be implemented in a specific form of an "always-on" information system or a "highly available" information system as system having "near-zero-downtime". In other words, this can be translated into available data, an always-on application platform, and consequently an always-on information system.

The role of servers and the server operating environment remains almost the same in cloud computing-based architectures as - applications are run now and again by server computers, with the only difference being that servers reside within the boundaries of the cloud computing provider but not in the business's computer center.

Table 2.2 demonstrates the changes in the main features of information systems.

Figure 2.8 indicates the transition from the traditional information system to the "always-on" information system by showing main drivers and enablers.

**Table 2.2 Traditional Focus versus Current Focus
on Enterprise Information Systems**

| *Traditional IS – focus on:* | *Always-On IS: focus on:* |
|---|---|
| Efficient transaction processing<br>Reporting and decision support<br>Integrated systems<br><br>**Technology framework:**<br>**Information Technology** | Efficient transaction processing<br>Reporting and decision support<br>Integrated systems<br>+<br>Availability<br>Scalability<br>Reliability<br>IT Capability<br><br>**Technology framework:**<br>**Business technology**<br>... |

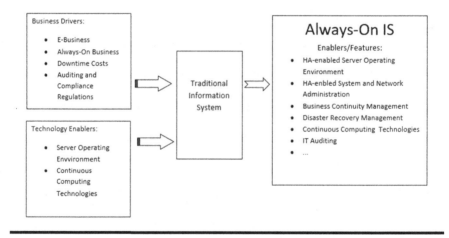

**Figure 2.8    From traditional IS toward always-on IS.**

# Conclusions

In modern business computing, that of the e-business era, system downtime is not a merely technical issue. It simply translates into financial losses. The more critical a business application, the more financially negative effects a business will suffer from the downtime that occurs on such application server. Therefore, modern IT management seeks such solutions: technical, software, organizational, operational, that will mitigate the negative effects of system downtime. Several approaches, methods, techniques, and technologies are developed in order to enhance the availability of application servers and reduce downtime costs. This book proposes a framework for discussing the roles of server operating environments, system administration, and IT auditing in enhancing business continuity.

## Discussion Questions

1. Define the concepts: downtime and uptime.
2. What is the meaning of high availability?
3. Explain the concept of the "economics of downtime".
4. Does every business need a high available IT system?
5. Explain the principal IT risks of downtime for your company.
6. Explain the concept of "mission-critical" applications. What are these in your business?
7. Which term is the most appropriate one in explaining the role of IT in modern business: "business resilience", "always-on business", "continuous business"?
8. Explain the term "keeping business in business".
9. Identify at least ten IT-related problems that might cause a situation in which a business might suffer.
10. Explain the main differences among these terms: availability, reliability, and scalability

## References

Aberdeen Report. (2014). Preventing Virtual Application Downtime. Retrieved from https://statuscast.com/preventing-virtual-application-downtime-2/

Aberdeen Report. (2016). Maintaining Virtual System Uptime in Today's Transforming IT Infrastructure, The Aberdeen Group, 2016. Retrieved from https://247uptime.co.uk/maintaining-virtual-system-uptime-in-todays-transforming-it-infrastructure/

Arcserve Report. (2015). Retrieved from www.arcserve.com/data-protection-resources/gruver-secured-business-continuity-and-reduced-downtime/

Avaya Report. (2014). Network Downtime Results in Job, Revenue Loss, March 2014. Retrieved from www.avaya.com/usa/about-avaya/newsroom/news-releases/2014/pr-140305/

Bajgoric, N. (2006). Information systems for e-business continuance: A systems approach, *Kybernetes: The International Journal of Systems and Cybernetics, 35*(5), 632–652.

Bajgoric, N. (2008a). Toward Always-On Enterprise Information Systems, in: Gunasekaran, A. (ed.), *Modeling and Analysis of Enterprise Information Systems – Advances in Enterprise Information Systems*, IGI Global, 250–284.

Bajgoric, N. (2008b). *Continuous Computing Technologies for Enhancing Business Continuity*, IGI-Global.

Bajgoric, N. (2010a). Server operating environment for business continuance: Framework for selection, *International Journal of Business Continuity and Risk Management, 1*(4), 317–338.

Bajgoric, N. (ed.). (2010b). *Always-On Enterprise Information Systems for Business Continuance: Technologies for Reliable and Scalable Operations*, IGI-Global, xvi–xx.

Bednarz, A. (2019). Network Issues Are Causing More Data-Center Outages, Network World, March 20, 2019, Retrieved from www.networkworld.com/article/3373646/network-problems-responsible-for-more-data-center-outages.html?utm_source=Adestra&utm_medium=email&utm_content=Title%3A%20Network%20issues%20are%20causing%20more%20data-center%20outages&utm_campaign=Networkworld%20Data%20Center%20Alert&utm_term=Editorial%20-%20Data%20Center%20Alert&utm_date=20190327054907

Business Insider. (2018). Amazon's One Hour of Downtime on Prime Day May Have Cost It up to $100 Million in Lost Sales. Retrieved from www.businessinsider.com/amazon-prime-day-website-issues-cost-it-millions-in-lost-sales-2018-7

Butler, B. (2013). Amazon.com Suffers Outage: Nearly $5M Down the Drain?, Network World, January 31. Retrieved from www.networkworld.com/article/2163191/cloud-computing/update–amazon-com-suffers-outage–nearly–5m-down-the-drain-.html

Butler, B.S, Gray, P.H. (2006). Reliability, mindfulness, and information systems, *MIS Quarterly, 30*(2), 211–224.

Cloud Pro Report. (2019). Microsoft Office 365 Goes Down across Europe. Retrieved from www.cloudpro.co.uk/saas/7905/microsoft-office-365-goes-down-across-europe

Faertesa, D. (2018). Reliability of supply chains and business continuity management, *Procedia Computer Science, 55*, 1400–1409.

Folkers, A. (2017). Continuity and catastrophe: Business continuity management and the security of financial operations, *Economy and Society, 46*(1), 103–127.

Forbes Report. (2018). Why CTOs and CIOs Should Care More about the Cost of Downtime. Retrieved from www.forbes.com/sites/forbestechcouncil/2018/04/26/why-ctos-and-cios-should-care-more-about-the-cost-of-downtime/#5dcc201a131c

Forrester Report. (2015). The Ongoing IT Struggle: Delivering Availability 24x7x365. Retrieved from http://cstor.com/wp-content/uploads/2016/03/Forrester_Ongoing-IT-Struggle-Delivering-Availability_White-Paper.pdf

Gartner. (2014, July). Network Downtime. Retrieved from http://blogs.gartner.com/andrew-lerner/2014/07/11/network-downtime/, accessed: November 19, 2014

IDC Report. (2014). High-Value Business Applications on x86: The Need for True Fault-Tolerant Systems, May. Retrieved from: www8.hp.com/h20195/v2/GetPDF.aspx/4AA5-8631ENW.pdf

IDC White paper. (2014). DevOps and the Cost of Downtime: Fortune 1000 Best Practice Metrics Quantified. Retrieved from www.idc.com/getdoc.jsp?containerId=253155

IT Disaster Recovery Preparednedd Council report (2015). The Importance of Disaster Recovery, Retrieved from http://www.techadvisory.org/2016/01/the-importance-of-disaster-recovery/

ITIC Report (2009), ITIC 2009 Global Server Hardware and Server OS Reliability Survey, Information Technology Intelligence Corp. (ITIC), July 2009

Katoa, M., Charoentrab, T. (2018). Business continuity management of small and medium sized enterprises: Evidence from Thailand, *International Journal of Disaster Risk Reduction, 27*, 577–587.

Lump, T., Schneider, J.M., Holtz, J., Muller, M., Lenz, N., Biazzeti, A., Peterson, D. (2008). From high availability and disaster recovery to business continuity solutions, *IBM Systems Journal, 47*(4), 605–619.

Miller, R. (2019). The Cloud's Worst Week: Will Outages Slow Enterprise Momentum? Retrieved from https://datacenterfrontier.com/the-clouds-worst-week-will-outages-slow-enterprise momentum/?mkt_tok=eyJpIjoiWVRRMFpEVTRNbU0wTkROaCIsInQiO iIrRkpJdVA3SDNjOXdNbWVlUVZlNkhmaFpVaU9zOFFyS0V4eXBBIdmR5YVROb HRuemcxRlVrVDdGRUNRTE1WcEFFHYjR6ZVk2c29PYm9cL0UyVFNHeStyOTlc L2NtaVAzSlRFVTNvRkFyNFFNcLzJuMG95cFQ4TXZQMzFnRTFwYXpidjFFUVSJ9

Närman, P., Buschle, M., & Ekstedt, M. (2014). An enterprise architecture framework for multi-attribute information systems analysis. *Software and Systems Modeling, 13*(3), 1085–1116.

Niemimaa, M. (2015). Interdisciplinary review of business continuity from an information systems perspective: Toward an integrative framework, *Communications of the Association for Information Systems, 37*, 69–102.

Niemimaa, M. (2017). Information systems continuity process: Conceptual foundations for the study of the "social", *Computers and Security, 65*, 1–13.

Niemimaa, M., Jarvelainen, J., Heikkila, M., Heikkila, J. (2019). Business continuity of business models: Evaluating the resilience of business models for contingencies, *International Journal of Information Management, 49*, 208–216.

Ponemon Institute Report (2016), Cost of Data Center Outages, available on: http://www.emersonnetworkpower.com/en-US/Resources/Market/Data-Center/Latest-Thinking/Ponemon/Documents/2016-Cost-of-Data-Center-Outages-FINAL-2.pdf, accessed on July 21, 2016

Reuters. (2017). British Airways CEO Puts Cost of Recent IT Outage at 80 Million Pounds, June. Retrieved from www.reuters.com/article/us-iag-ceo/british-airways-ceo-puts-cost-of-recent-it outage-at-80-million-pounds-idUSKBN1961H2

Schattera, F., Hansenb, O., Wiensa, M., Schultmanna, F. (2019). A decision support methodology for a disaster-caused business continuity management, *Decision Support Systems, 118*, 10–20.

Soufi, H.R., Torabi, A.A., Sahebjamnia, N. (2019). Developing a novel quantitative framework for business continuity planning, *International Journal of Production Research, 57*(3), 779–800.

Sverdik, Y. (2016). Delta: Data Center Outage Cost Us $150. Retrieved from www.datacenterknowledge.com/archives/2016/09/08/delta-data-center-outage-cost-us-150m

Turban, E., Volonino, L. (2010). *Information Technology for Management – Transforming Organizations in the Digital Economy*, 7th ed. Wiley.

Uptime Institute (2015). Arc Flash Mitigation in the Data Center, retrieved from https://journal.uptimeinstitute.com/arc-flash/

Uptime Institute. (2018). Uptime Institute's Eighth Annual Data Center Industry Survey Report. Retrieved from https://uptimeinstitute.com/2018-data-center-industry-survey-results

Uptime Institute. (2019). How Planning Reduces the Impact of Outages. Retrieved from https://uptimeinstitute.com/resources/research-and-reports/how-planning-reduces-the-impact-of-outages

Veeam Availability Report. (2017). Retrieved from www.veeam.com/wp-availability-report-2017-brief.html

Veeam Data Availability Report. (2018). Retrieved from: www.verustechnology.com/files/2018/11/veeam_availability_suite_9_5_datasheet_en.pdf

Veeam Report. (2014). The Veeam Data Center Availability Report 2014. Retrieved from www.veeam.com/wp-availability-report-2014.html

# Chapter 3

# Business Continuity and IT Capability

*"He who fails to plan
is planning to fail".*

**Winston Churchill**

*"To [...] not prepare is the greatest of crimes;
to be prepared beforehand to any contingency
is the greatest of virtues".*

**Sun Tzu**

## Business Continuity Management

Business globalization is increasingly contributing to market dynamics that drive competition, creating a business environment that requires higher levels of service quality and efficiency, and better responds to customer demands. In such a market economy, customer expectations 24-7 completely exclude the possibility of business interruption. Even a minor disaster or business interruption can cause irreparable damage to the organization and its image. In other words, business disruptions have significant negative effects on customer loyalty and organizational reputation in general (Järveläinen, 2012).

For this reason, organizations are increasingly concerned about the risks that threaten the continuity of their operations. There is also increased pressure on organizations to take action to ensure service availability and business continuity. Furthermore, the need for business continuity has also risen due to increasing threats, ranging from natural causes to businesses' increasing dependence on complex information systems (Herbane, 2010). The declaration of COVID-19 as a pandemic highlights the importance of business continuity planning (BCP). As the expansion of COVID-19 and measures to combat it bring about drastic changes in the workplace, companies have to find a way to continue to provide their services while ensuring the health and safety of employees and customers. Business continuity refers precisely to the provision of services for the operation of the company and the generation of income. In the literature, the management segment, whose primary objective is to meet these requirements, is known as business continuity management.

Business continuity management (BCM) is a discipline established in the field of information technology (IT) management with the primary goal of providing the right technical, organizational, and managerial solutions to ensure continuous computing and business continuity (Sagita, Supriadi, & Pheng, 2018). BCM is often considered part of information security. Specifically, information security breaches are one of many possible threats to business continuity, and achieving data availability is a primary goal of business continuity from an information systems perspective (Järveläinen, 2012). However, it should be emphasized that the wider context of BCM also implies the influence of other factors on business (pandemic diseases, floods, earthquakes, strikes, acts of terrorism, etc.), not only IT-based and not only those factors that have an impact on an organization's IT platform. In this regard, the old BCM approach was a more IT-oriented approach, while the new approach involves incorporating all factors that impair business continuity. In other words, the old BCM approach was only about disaster recovery or crisis response. However, today, BCM is a set of business processes that brings together a wide range of management disciplines. The review presented in Figure 3.1 shows that BCM has evolved into a more holistic approach that represents a broader strategic organizational mindset that focuses on its business values (Sagita et al., 2018).

| Considerations for Business Continuity Management | |
| --- | --- |
| STANDARD PRACTICE | BETTER PRACTICE |
| OLD | NEW |
| DISASTER RECOVERY | BCM |
| IT focus | Value chain focus |
| IT staff | Multi-disciplinary team |
| Existing structure | New structure |
| Protect core operations | Protect entire organization |
| Sustain current position | Create sustainable advantage |
| Parochial view | Open system view |
| Recovery emphasis | Prevention emphasis |

**Figure 3.1  Old and new BCM approach. Sagita et al., 2018.**

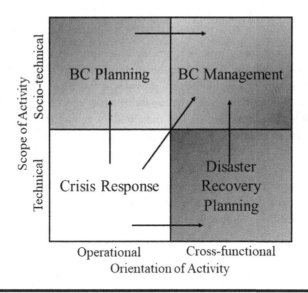

**Figure 3.2 Typology of continuity approaches. Herbane et al., 2004.**

BCM is a strategic issue for the organization because it helps the organization retain value derived from competitive advantage. However, organizations vary depending on the level of awareness of BCM importance and implement it differently. Figure 3.2 distinguishes between different approaches to crisis management and BCP, depending on whether the scope of the activity is designed to address a technical or socio-technical crisis and whether the activity is potentially strategic. Strategic orientation is defined as a business-based approach in reference to a combination of planning and management (Herbane, Elliott, & Swartz, 2004).

A specific technical aspect of BCM relates to the availability, reliability, and scalability of computer servers on which modern business computing and effective information resources management are centered, which are of particular importance to modern business. The reasons are numerous and, as already mentioned, the most important can be cited as follows:

■ Modern business globalization requiring the development of "24x7x365" applications,
■ A focus on customers' requirements – a customer-oriented business.

BCM encourages business flexibility to respond to operational challenges and threats, ensuring maximum operational efficiency for critical business processes. Organizational culture must encourage employees to be aware of constant danger and ensure that every employee is responsible for mitigating risk.

Hence, BCM can be defined as a

> holistic management process that identifies potential threats to an organization and the impacts to business operations those threats, if realized, might cause, and which provides a framework for building organizational resilience with the capability of an effective response that safeguards the interests of its key stakeholders, reputation, brand, and value-creating activities.
>
> (The British Standards Institution, 2012)

BCM seeks to recognize, reduce, or plan potential risks so that business processes and services proceed without interruption (Järveläinen, 2012). BCM should ensure that the organization is responsive to major disruptions that threaten its survival. This concept refers to the management of processes, resources, and systems in the event of a disaster. In addition, it deals with the integration, planning, and control of various elements of business practice in a unique way before, during, and after a crisis or disaster (Sadgrove, 2016). BCM is an umbrella discipline and covers all the response, resumption, recovery, and restoration plans for specific threats. Figure 3.3 shows the BCM umbrella, emphasizing BCM as a core concept that encompasses potential disaster planning, response, and recovery. BCM also includes planning processes (methodology) and also the results (plans).

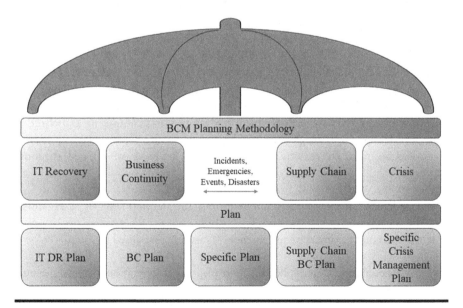

**Figure 3.3   BCM Institute – Business Continuity Management Umbrella. Elliott et al., 2010.**

## *Brief Business Continuity History*

Business continuity has become one of the essential elements of strategic planning for organizations. BCM is based on a holistic operating model that enables businesses to function more efficiently and effectively in their day-to-day operations. Understanding the basics of BCM is imperative to understanding its history.

The following years are important for BCM's evolution:

- 1950: Organizations begin to back up their critical records.
- 1960: The reliance on data increases. The frequency of backups increases from weekly to daily.
- 1970: Organizations start contracting alternative sites with vendors.
- 1983: The United States Office of the Comptroller of the Currency (OCC) requires financial institutions to develop documented recovery plans.
- 1989: The United States Federal Financial Institutions Examinations Council (FFIEC) requires the documentation, maintenance, and testing of recovery plans.
- 1990: The revolution in distributed computing enables organizations to recognize the need for operational recovery. The term "business continuity" is becoming increasingly used.

Traditional BCM arose from concerns about the failure of the computer and information systems. Therefore, the roots of the BCM discipline lie in protecting information systems. The development of BCM has gone from its original emphasis on technology to broader strategic requirements. The evolution of BCM can be viewed through the evolution of the organizational mindset in three stages (Elliott, Swartz, & Herbane, 2010) (see Figure 3.4):

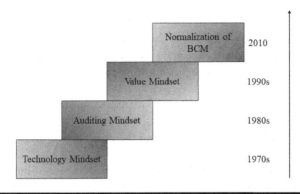

**Figure 3.4   Evolution of BCM concept and practice. Elliott et al., 2010.**

1. **Technology mindset** of the 1970s: the focus was on protecting computer systems, primarily corporate mainframe systems, from external physical threats such as bombs, floods, or fires.
2. **Auditing mindset** in the 1980s: technological changes have moved the IT element from the mainframe system to the end user. At this stage, the focus is still on technology, but factors other than technological are also taken into account.
3. **Value mindset** of the 1990s: During this phase, BCM becomes a factor aligned with the strategic planning of the organization and other aspects such as maintaining competitive advantage, including customers and suppliers, as well as the social, economic, and human factors of the entire organization.

## *BCM Implementation*

The four main components that must be considered when implementing BCM in an organization (Sagita et al., 2018) are the following:

- **Policies**: Senior management must identify policies for the implementation of BCM by staff. Policies should set the priorities, values, and strategy of the organization, which will determine what has to be done and act as a framework and support for all BCM areas.
- **Processes**: A collection of activities identifying objectives, performance, and evaluation criteria for achieving the BCM policy goals. They include formal controls and a documentation process.
- **People**: Participation of different business units should be identified in the organization. The roles and responsibilities of staff involved in the organization's BCM activities should be clearly defined.
- **Infrastructure**: The organization should allocate resources to support critical business functions against potential risk events. This requires a good understanding and application of available technology and equipment and physical capacities to respond to the occurrence of a risk.

The BCM planning methodology is the planning process for implementing any business continuity plan. According to guidelines of the Business Continuity Management Institute, it includes the following phases:

- Project management – planning and managing resources and tasks to achieve defined objectives.
- Risk analysis and review – identifying the existing risks and threats to which the organization is exposed.
- Business impact analysis (BIA) – analyzing the impact of business interruption on business functions.
- Business continuity strategy – a review of the prevention, crisis response, and recovery measures to be carried out between the occurrence of a disaster and the resumption of normal operations.

- Plan development – identify strategies for informing responsible people and assessing organizational efficiency, and establish steps to minimize the risk of disruption and resume normal operations following the disruption. The result of this phase is the BC Plan or DR Plan.
- Testing and exercising – testing of a developed recovery plan to ensure its functioning.
- Program management – updates and maintenance of the plan in line with changes in business, plan revision, managing the entire BCM program.

Today, BCM is used in different types of organizations. Due to different business environments, firms have developed different procedures to overcome different types of crises. Some of them have also focused not only on business continuity but also on continuity of service to their clients. The simplest way to implement BCM in an organization is by following the recommendations of one of the standards or best practices. Multiple standards address the issue of BCM in organizations. Some standards are intended to primarily address this issue, while most other standards dealing with information security in general, at least in one part, address the BCM.

In the UK, the Business Continuity Institute (BCI) has developed a business continuity certification standard. In addition, BCI has also published the BCM Standard (BS25999: 1-2006) as a Business Continuity Management Code of Practice and can be considered an implementation guide for those who intend to understand BCM principles and practice more comprehensively. Both the US Business Continuity Institute (BCI) and BSI America have joined forces to help organizations better prepare for disasters by encouraging the adoption of BS 25999. This standard is also aligned with the US National Business Continuity Standard (NFPA 1600: 2007 – National fire protection 2007) (Sagita et al., 2018).

ISO officially launched ISO 22301: Societal Security – Business Management System – Requirements, an international standard for business continuity management (BCMS). ISO 22301 was developed in 2012 to help organizations minimize the risk of business disruption. This standard is similar to previous BCM standards but has some enhancements to BCM implementation, such as:

- greater emphasis on goal setting, performance monitoring, and metrics;
- clearer expectations from the management; and
- ,ore careful planning and preparation of the resources needed to ensure business continuity.

ISO 22313: Social Security – Business Continuity Management Systems – The Guideline complements ISO 22301 by clarifying the concepts introduced in ISO 22301 and providing explanations and examples to assist organizations during implementation.

Watters (2014) provides a summary of standards addressing BCM, which are presented in Table 3.1.

**Table 3.1  Summary of BCM Standards**

| Standard | Description |
|---|---|
| AS/NZ HB 221 | HB 221 identifies the minimum level of acceptable performance and what infrastructure and resources are required to sustain it. |
| AS HB 292 | HB 292 summarizes best practices from Australia, the United States, and the United Kingdom. |
| BCI: Good Practice Guidelines | The Business Continuity Institute (BCI) guidelines outline best practices for building or improving a business continuity program. |
| BS ISO/IEC 17799:2005 | ISO/IEC 17799:2005 is a code of practice for information security, which includes business continuity within its scope. |
| BS 25777 (2008) | BS 25777 describes how to implement IT service continuity or IT disaster recovery if you prefer. |
| BS25999 Business Continuity Management BS25999 | BS25999 provides a BCM framework and supporting management system. |
| DRII: Ten Professional Practices (1999) | The Ten Professional Practices established the necessary skills and competencies for individuals focused on business continuity. |
| FFIEC: Business Continuity Planning | The booklet outlines basic standards for BCM within US financial institutions. |
| ISO 22301 | This is the new international standard and is an evolution of BS25999, which it replaced in November 2012. |
| NFPA 1600 | This is the established US standard for business continuity. It covers business continuity, emergency management, and incident management. |
| TR19 | TR19 is a voluntary standard that addresses the question of business continuity management and the recovery of critical processes. |
| SS 540 | SS540 is a Singapore-based certifiable standard (that replaces TR 19 (2004)). SS540 establishes a framework for organizations to analyze and implement strategies, processes, and procedures. |

*Source*: Watters (2014)

The methods, techniques, and technologies of BCM implementation are explained in more detail in Chapter 6.

To summarize, the common phases of the business continuity planning process, their description, and outputs are shown in Table 3.2.

BCM has roots in crisis management and disaster recovery, and continuity issues can arise from many sources, including customers, the supply chain, employers, and facilities (Järveläinen, 2012). In other words, BCM is concerned with identifying potential crisis events and, in a nutshell, business continuity and IT recovery planning. Business continuity planning involves a variety of plans, to be discussed below. However, it is necessary to define the concept of a crisis first.

**Table 3.2  Stages of BCM with Basic Explanations**

| Phase | Key tasks | Outputs |
|---|---|---|
| **Project initiation** | Gaining the support and commitment of management Identifying BCM roles and responsibilities Defining BCM Policy Program and budget development | BCM policy BCM program and budget RACI model of responsibility for BCM |
| **BIA & RA** | Preparation and setup Identifying critical activities Business impact assessment and prioritization | Business Impact Profile – prioritizing business activities Risk registry and matrix Resource requirements for business continuity RTO and RPO |
| **Plan development** | Establishment of crisis management and business continuity teams Developing and documenting contingency and disaster recovery plans | The teams BCM Plan Overview Emergency response plan Crisis management plan Continuity and Recovery Plans |
| **Implementation** | Development and implementation of BCM awareness and training programs Creating an ongoing training and maintenance program | BCM training and maintenance plan |
| **Testing** | Testing | Testing reports |
| **Maintenance** | Update plans as needed | Updated plans |

## Crisis

A crisis represents an interruption of normal business operations or processes, which can range from short-term to longer-term unavailability (BCM Institute Dictionary). A business interruption implies any event when the business does not have access to resources for normal operation. Business interruptions that are at the heart of business continuity management are those events that cause significant interruptions or loss of key business processes, resulting in a very high negative impact and serious consequences for the organization. There are different definitions that use different terminology to define concepts related to a crisis, such as a disaster, emergency, incident, and event. Crises are characterized by an intrinsic sense of urgency of the organization's ability to cope with and resolve them. A crisis is an event that threatens some aspect of the security of an organization and its business, and requires special measures to be taken to resume things to normal functioning.

All crises can be classified into three broad categories (Tucker, 2015):

- **Natural hazards** such as floods, hurricanes, tornadoes, or earthquakes. Preventing natural disasters is very difficult; measures such as good planning can reduce or avoid losses.
- **Technological hazards**. Technological hazards include cases such as failures in infrastructure, technology, and so on.
- **Man-made hazards**. The hazards caused by humans can be intentional or accidental. Intentional hazards include criminal and cyberattacks, as well as terrorist attacks. Accidental hazards are the result of unintentional mistakes of humans (Snedaker & Rima, 2014).

Although BCP is largely structured around how a company acts when a natural disaster, technical disaster, or man-made disaster occurs, the COVID-19 pandemic has raised the question of business continuity in such emergencies. Pandemics are significantly different from the types of disasters that are usually provided for in business continuity plans. It is not often the case that countries, and especially the world, face a pandemic, but natural disasters, man-made disasters, disruptions, and security threats are all realities. Concerning the awareness of importance of business continuity management and planning, COVID-19 will certainly have a positive effect.

The literature most often encounters a crisis through three basic phases: pre-, trans- and post-crisis (Herbane, 2010) (see Figure 3.5). Hence, a typical crisis consists of some or all the following stages:

- Crisis phase – The crisis phase encompasses the first few hours after an unplanned event has begun or a threat has been identified.

**Figure 3.5  The life cycle of a disaster Focus. Watters, 2014.**

- Response phase – The response phase can last from minutes to hours after a disaster. During this phase, the BCP team will evaluate the situation and decide if the business continuity plan will be activated. A crisis phase doesn't need to occur; it is enough to notice a specific threat or the possibility of a crisis occurring to convene a team to analyze a given threat.
- Recovery phase – The recovery phase can last from a few days to several months after a disaster and ends when the organization's operations continue as before the disaster. During the recovery phase, key business functions will be restarted, in a prime or temporary location in recovery format, until normal business conditions are met.
- Restoration phase – During this phase, business conditions return to normal. It begins by assessing the damage, usually immediately after a disaster, and identifying the resources needed to normalize the business.

BCM has roots in crisis management and disaster recovery, and continuity problems may arise from many sources: the supply chain, customers, employers, and facilities (Järveläinen, 2012). Crisis management means the ability of an organization to cope with any disaster that may affect the organization. All organizations must have the capability to respond to unexpected events in a manner that is fully satisfactory in order to sustain their business. Disasters cannot be completely avoided, but they can be managed in such a way that their impact is reduced or eliminated. Every organization today faces the different types of risks outlined above, but their goal is to try to reduce those risks and keep business as normal as possible. In other words, BCM, in addition to BCP, implies adequate crisis management planning. The management of disasters can be split into four different phases: mitigation, preparedness, response, and recovery (Schätter, Hansen, Wiens, & Schultmann, 2019).

It is important to note that the risks of disaster events are not the same for all organizations, so the planning process for avoiding or mitigating them once they happen is not the same for all companies. For the same reason, the complexity of designing and refining plans is not the same. What is common to all types of accidents, however, is a financial risk, a real danger to all companies. Possible financial losses are easily calculated, taking into account only the loss of some business process in the organization, the loss of some raw material or part of the equipment, and assuming some time to reestablish that part of the business. It is then easy to assess how important it is to have a good plan for avoiding or mitigating and reducing such events.

## Business Continuity Planning

BCP is the result of BCM and provides a basis for how an organization responds to and recovers from an incident or disruption (Drewitt, 2013). In other words, the outcome of BCM implementation is to develop a set of procedures or plans that include, primarily, an IT disaster recovery plan, a business continuity plan, and a crisis management plan. Some authors consider all these processes as business continuity planning. Thus, Botha and Von Solms (2004) state that in order to fully understand the BCP, it is necessary to observe two necessary aspects. First, it should be ensured that an organization can continue in business as usual or at an acceptable level during a disaster. Second, IT should be restored to a state similar to the one that preceded the disaster. To better understand these two components of BCP, the concepts of emergency planning (CP) and disaster recovery plan (DRP) need to be considered. Business continuity has its roots in research on disaster recovery plans from 1970 (Niemimaa, Järveläinen, Heikkilä, & Heikkilä, 2019).

The relationships between BCP, CP, and DRP are presented in Figure 3.6. The smaller circles marked A through I represent different business processes. These processes depend on the services and infrastructure found in the IT department, shown in the white circle in the figure center. Some of these processes are also interdependent, as shown by overlapping circles. The outer circle is a combination of DRP IT departments and contingency plans for different business processes.

Hence, business continuity planning is a BCM process that defines the strategies that an organization must implement to ensure its survival when an event/crisis that

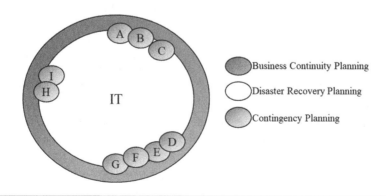

**Figure 3.6   Relationship between BCP, CP, and DRP.** *Botha & Von Solms, 2004.*

causes a business interruption occurs, and that mitigates the impact on the organization. In short, BCP is a set of management tools for identifying and evaluating risk events and their impact on the business, defining and designing measures to avoid the consequences and critical time frames for business recovery, and periodically testing plans to validate them. The BCPs created in this way are periodically tested and revised to increase the organization's resilience to disaster events.

Hence, BCP aims at:

- managing the risks that could lead to disaster events, thereby minimizing the likelihood of these events occurring,
- reducing the time needed to recover when an incident occurs, and
- reducing the risks involved in the recovery process by making critical decisions well in advance rather than in stressful conditions; decisions made during a crisis have a high risk of being wrong, inefficient, and costly.

Business continuity planning can be defined as a

complete process of developing measures and procedures to ensure an organization's disaster preparedness. This includes ensuring that the organization would be able to respond effectively and efficiently to a disaster and that their critical business processes can continue as usual.

(Randeree, Mahal, & Narwani, 2012)

Sagita et al. (2018) state that the following ten issues must be considered before formulating the BCP framework:

1. Policy – creating a policy statement at the managerial level that indicates the company's attitude toward a particular risk and prescribing the goals of such a policy.
2. Methodology – analyzing the assessment processes involved in crisis evaluation and promoting greater commitment to BCP.
3. Accountability – establishing individual responsibility for risk management and ensuring that the nominated person has the appropriate expertise.
4. Management support – determining managerial attitude toward risk assessment and BCM, which is necessary for initiating BCM implementation in the organization.
5. Dependencies – defining the scope of BCP so that each individual is aware of the dependencies involved.
6. Being realistic – management should be prepared to accept certain risks and be willing to spend the necessary resources to mitigate the associated risks.
7. Future actions – determining appropriate business processes to implement or improve, reduce risk to an acceptable level, and assign responsibilities and milestones.

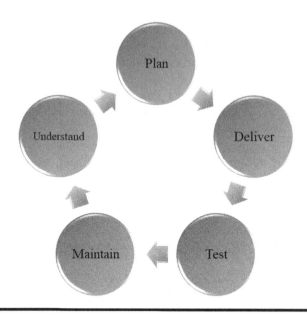

**Figure 3.7    Business continuity life cycle. Watters, 2014.**

8. Performance measures – establishing measurement indicators to enable the assessment and monitoring of the effectiveness of risk management that may be proactive or reactive.
9. Independent expert – appointing an internal or external expert to determine the adequacy of the crisis response.
10. Contingency plan – establishing an alternative contingency plan, not foreseen.

The business continuity process is known as the business continuity lifecycle and describes how any organization should ensure that critical activities are performed no matter what happens (Watters, 2014). The process is first about understanding what constitutes critical processes. Then, support solutions are planned; then, this is tested and then maintained (see Figure 3.7). The cycle is repeated ad infinitum.

In conclusion, **contingency plans**, **disaster recovery plans**, and **business resumption plans** are integrated into the business continuity plan. However, there is no consensus in the literature regarding the plans contained in the BCP. The comprehensive presentation of business continuity plans is shown in Figure 3.8.

## Contingency Planning

Contingency planning is considered an overall process of preparing for unexpected crisis events (Vuong, 2015). Crucial stages for developing contingency plans are BIA and risk analysis (RA). BIA entails identification and analysis of business processes and activities in order to understand the impact of downtime. Risk assessment, on

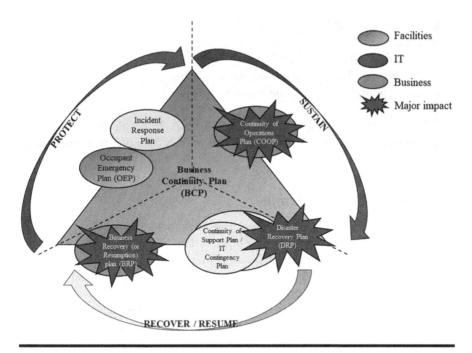

**Figure 3.8   Business continuity types of plan. BCM Dictionary.**

the other hand, involves identifying threats, vulnerabilities, and risks for business. The identified risks become part of the risk register. Developing a contingency plan involves dealing with "what if" questions, and analyzing possible scenarios, which involves constructing possible but equally compelling perspectives on the future.

A contingency plan is a plan that is implemented only when an event occurs, or when certain conditions exist (Kliem & Richie, 2016). That is why it is considered to be actively embracing the crisis. The goal of contingency planning (CP) is to define disaster recovery measures until the recovery phase begins. It can be defined as the process of examining the critical functions of an organization, identifying possible disaster scenarios, and developing procedures to address these issues.

Contingency planning represents:

■ a series of activities of an organization or business unit used in response to a disaster; may include procedures, alternative venues or alternative resources;
■ Emergency planning in anticipation of disasters often based on risk assessment and availability of human and material resources.

Steps in creating a contingency plan are

■ recognizing the need for contingency planning,
■ identifying potential disasters – possible scenarios,

- identifying possible consequences,
- assessing the degree of risk for each scenario,
- identifying strategies for crisis prevention,
- drafting the plan and establishing responsibilities,
- doing disaster simulation and managing plans.

Most of these stages take place during the BIA & RA analyses, which are explained in detail in Chapter 6. The disaster recovery plan is part of the contingency plan (Vuong, 2015).

## *Disaster Recovery Planning*

Disaster recovery as a concept was developed in the mid-1970s when IT department managers began to recognize their organizations' dependency on information systems. During the 1980s and 1990s, awareness of IT disaster recovery and the DR industry itself grew rapidly, driven by the advent of open systems and real-time processing (which increased organizations' dependency on IT systems). Another driving force behind the growth of the industry was regulations mandating business continuity and disaster recovery planning for organizations in various sectors of the economy. With the rapid growth of the Internet in the late 1990s and 2000s, organizations have become increasingly dependent on the continued availability of their IT systems. Many organizations set a target of 99.999% availability of critical systems (Alsultanny, 2013).

The DRP was originally intended for deployment operations to minimize data center downtime. Today, DRP is an active component of BCP and focuses mainly on the recovery of the IT department and all the functions associated with it. Disaster recovery planning is an integral part of a larger business continuity planning process. DRP should include planning for the smooth use of applications, data, hardware, communication devices, and other IT infrastructure. BCP includes planning for non-IT aspects, such as key personnel, facilities, crisis communication, and reputation protection, but also includes a DRP.

A DRP is a comprehensive statement of the activities to be undertaken before, during, and after a disaster. The plan should be documented and tested to ensure business continuity and availability of critical resources if a disaster occurs. The primary objective of a recovery plan is to protect the organization if all or part of its business activities and/or information system are unusable. The key to success is preparedness. The planning process should minimize disruption to business and ensure a certain level of organizational stability and orderly recovery after a disaster.

Disaster recovery planning involves more than off-site storage or backup. Organizations should develop written, comprehensive disaster recovery plans and define all critical operations and business functions. The plan should include documented and tested procedures that will ensure the availability of critical resources and business continuity in the event of a disaster.

Critical processes have been identified in the BIA and RA stages of business continuity planning. These inputs are now being used in further analysis and preparation of the whole disaster recovery planning approach to ensure that normal operations are resumed in the event of any disaster. The recovery process should be based on the business recovery time line, which practically means setting a time line within the overall business continuity process.

Recovery procedures should be:

- Developed based on recovery time line and project management. Gantt charts should include details of the stages of recovery, activities that achieve the goal, tasks that make up each activity, durations, teams, and interdependencies.
- Built on specific standards that define business continuity issues and include methods for maintaining and updating the plan.

Part of the recovery plan is to evaluate how long a business function may be inaccessible, how old the information available to the organization may be, and how acceptable is the time for which all activities can return to normal. That is, the recovery time objective (RTO) and recovery point objective (RPO) should be determined.

- **RTO – Recovery Time Objective** – refers to the time from when an emergency occurs to the time when the business process must be recovered. This is also called a **recovery window**.
- **RPO – Recovery Point Objective** – Describes a point in time to which data must return; outdated information no longer reflects the true state – also called **freshness window**.

The two objectives are not closely linked or completely separate. RTO and RPO should be determined independently, although they will be found to be interconnected due to infrastructure and technological issues. RTO must also include the time needed to decide to implement the plan. The higher the RTO for a particular process, the lower the cost of recovery. However, at the same time, the losses of the inaccessible process are rising.

Moreover, Figure 3.9 shows the maximum tolerable period of disruption (MTPD) is the time it would take before a complete disruption would give rise to unacceptable consequences (Hassel & Cedergren, 2019). These indicators can be estimated based on expert judgments. In addition, integrating Cox's model and Bayesian networks can be used to model business continuity processes (Xing, Zeng, & Zio, 2019).

There is a wide range of DR solutions. These solutions are contingent on business requirements such as RTO and RPO, and constraints such as budget and location. Generally, solutions can be classified into the following categories (Kim & Solomon, 2016; Watters, 2014):

- Hot site
- Warm site

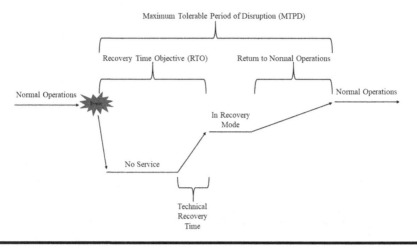

**Figure 3.9    Disaster Recovery Diagram. Watters, 2014.**

- Cold site
- Resilience

A **hot site** involves a duplicate object in another location, with the capacity to absorb additional activities before its termination becomes critical for business survival. The hot site has all the equipment and facilities needed to get the job done. In other words, there is an environment settled in a DR location in a constant state of preparedness. The hardware is adequate in size to support key processes, the operating system is operational, data is updated every second, and applications are ready to download processes.

The hot site applies to architectures where data must be entered in both locations, and records must be validated before the next transaction can be made. This type of DR capability can be divided into greater distances. The cost of this standby is high because it requires a dedicated solution that is maintained as part of the main environment.

A **warm site** provides the environment and basic infrastructure to allow the activity to continue before its termination becomes critical to the survival of the organization. The warm site is similar to the hot site in that the hardware is configured and ready for a startup, and the operating system and applications are kept on standby on the DR device. However, warm recovery systems are generally not online and need to be rebooted, and all applications need to be started from scratch. Generally speaking, data also needs some manual intervention before work begins, which adds to the delay and risk.

A **cold site** is an environment where an operation can be built from the beginning. The cold site does not have any hardware or software prepared or ready to run. The hardware may be previously assigned, but network connectivity and hardware configuration are required to get it up and to run. Operating systems and applications are often installed, and data must be loaded in the event of an unforeseen event. Specialized third-party firms often provide a cold recovery site, and as such, this reduces the cost and need to maintain an additional data center.

Cold, warm and hot sites can be mobile, delivered in trailers with the independent environment, portable, delivered in the form of assembly equipment and independent environment, or static, preinstalled on the premises of a company or supplier (Hiles, 2010).

**Resilience** is not a disaster recovery strategy but a way to avoid the need for DR in a range of scenarios. Resilience is the ability of a system or IT service to continue functioning in the event of a failure or to recover quickly after a failure. In particular, it can avoid the impact of local component failures (e.g., sharing service between two data centers). It is important to note that this solution does not reduce the need for a DR location.

Disaster recovery technologies are explained in Chapter 6.

## *Business Continuity Planning Strategy*

BCP requires more substantial efforts to prioritize business recovery and proactively develop new and innovative recovery strategies (Sagita et al., 2018). The business continuity planning strategy of critical business processes serves as an organization's response to a crisis to maintain an acceptable level of business for each critical business function within a defined period and is used as a business and planning framework to develop a BCP and a DRP. The business processes of organizations are exposed to operational, strategic, and reputational risks, for which the following approaches to their management are available, some of which can be combined as needed (Hiles, 2010):

- **Do nothing** – The "do nothing" option is to wait until a disaster occurs, hoping that everything will be procured and resolved on time. This may be appropriate when the organization's RTO is at a level that it can handle reaction preparatory activities.
- **Bunker** – The bunker or fortress approach will seek to limit the risk to the level at which management will decide that any further recovery planning activities are unnecessary. The bunker can only protect what's inside: operations remain vulnerable.
- **Distributed Processing** – Distributed processing disperses risk across multiple sites.
- **Continuous Processing** – Continuous operation will ensure continuous shadowing or monitoring of production operations from an alternative site with adequate capacity and communication linkage to allow key activities/processes to be transferred to alternative sites with minimal preparation. This can be applied to non-IT departments or IT operations.

Organizations may not take any action; may relocate the process, abolish, or modify the process; and may insure, limit damages, or operate a business continuity system. The choice of a possible strategy is made based on a comparison of the costs of business continuity planning and the possible losses in case of a crisis, that is, the impact of emergencies on business. Moreover, risk and impact analysis, along with resource requirements, help identify and justify an appropriate business continuity strategy (Hiles, 2010).

BCP's strategy includes the following recovery resources:

- Human resources – ensuring the availability of an adequate number of people with the required competencies and knowledge, including external suppliers of goods and services;
- Space – a way of reducing the impact of the unavailability of space;
- Technology – ensuring the availability and sufficiency of the IT infrastructure;
- Data – ensuring the availability, confidentiality, and integrity of business data; and
- Suppliers – reducing the risk of supplier contractual obligations breach.

Instead of addressing all areas of recovery, organizations are suggested to target one or two critical business functions or key processes and develop a recovery plan based on a recovery time line. The advantage of this approach is that it is not necessary to use too many resources for the project, and it is easier to test whether the strategy is feasible or not. It also helps employees understand the full implications of the BCP. Once the purpose, objectives, roles, and responsibilities have been defined, all details should be transferred to the person or persons concerned with the topic. During the development of the plan, the main tasks and interdependencies need to be identified. The staff assigned to the tasks are not the staff who will be responsible for all activities but will be responsible for the implementation of the project in separate departments and for ensuring that all planned activities and testing are carried out. Moreover, the responsibility for maintaining business continuity lies essentially with all employees of the organization.

Hayes and Kotwica (2013) state that business continuity planning is an activity organized daily by an organization that ensures that its critical business functions are accessible to all relevant internal and external stakeholders before, during, and after a crisis. In this regard, they propose a **business continuity program**. This tool places this methodology into a structure that needs to be followed by everyone in the organization to fulfill their business continuity planning needs. The purpose, principles, objectives, and pillars of the program are presented in Table 3.3.

The key principles that support a successful business continuity program are:

- **Commitment to people**: The safety, well-being, and morale of the organization's people, coupled with the organization's commitment, are key priorities of a strong BCP.

- **Overall quality**: Continuous process improvement and identification of the "critical path" of processes, standardization, and management will produce plans that are always current, relevant, fast, and flexible to implement.
- **Growth and innovation**: With innovative, cost-effective planning, the value of an organization can be economically protected and preserved.
- **Customer satisfaction**: BCP strives to maintain organizations' reputation for integrity, reliability, and trustworthiness, to maintain continuity in service and supply of products and services regardless of circumstances or events.

The four BCP pillars are an **assessment** of business needs, **preparedness** for, **response** to, and **recovery** from emergencies (Hayes & Kotwica, 2013). These functions can be performed sequentially or simultaneously, and are not dependent on each other. The diagram can be used as a quick list for security leaders to compare what is currently in their organization and the missing components of the plan (Hayes & Kotwica, 2013). Figure 3.10 shows what is meant by individual pillars. Thus, the establishment of a program involves the identification of goals, scope, budget, roles, responsibilities, and so on. Assessment involves hazard identification, BIA, and vendor resiliency questionnaire. Preparedness includes communication, training, testing, and so on. Response refers to notification levels, locations, emergencies, and so on. Finally, recovery involves checklists, record keeping, and corrective actions.

**Table 3.3   Purpose, Principles, Objectives, and Pillars of BCP**

|  | *Business Continuity Program* |
|---|---|
| **Purpose** | "To enhance the protection of people and assets during a crisis while expediting the resumption of normal operations. The BCP addresses four main elements: assessment, preparedness, response, and recovery". |
| **Principles** | People Commitment<br>Total Quality<br>Growth and Innovation<br>Customer Satisfaction |
| **Objectives** | "To protect and maintain the company's good name and reputation through the effective strategic and tactical management of all major incidents affecting the business, acting at all times to protect the well-being of employees, customers, vendors, and the community at large". |
| **Pillars** | Assessment<br>Preparedness<br>Response<br>Recovery |

*Source*: Hayes & Kotwica (2013)

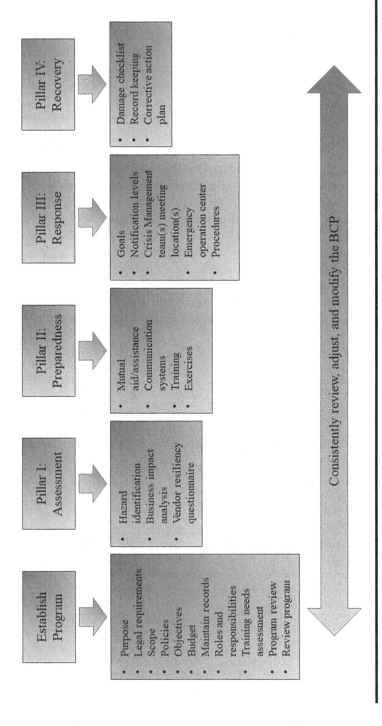

**Figure 3.10** **The four pillars of a successful business continuity program.** *(Source: Hayes & Kotwica, 2013).*

## Methodology for Developing a Business Continuity Plan

The planning process, as well as the methodology itself, can be as useful as a written plan. In order to develop an effective and efficient business continuity plan, all relevant planning items must be considered.

Creating a BCP is a very significant step in an organization's intention to manage its business continuity. The design of the plan itself is a complex process; it is project oriented. In most organizations, adopting some business continuity planning standards or methodologies is essential to ensure that the BCPs developed are consistent and comprehensive. Many methodologies are used today, and they are all different and similar in some ways. In this chapter, we will focus on the characteristics and phases for most of the methodologies analyzed. The project planning phase is necessary to ensure that the business continuity planning project is started properly.

Furthermore, various methodologies tend to view the stages of identifying recovery strategies and their implementation as one stage. Both activities are very important, and it should be emphasized that it is better to view these activities as separate stages. A third notable feature is the lack of testing in some methodologies. Without testing, it is not possible to identify the deficiencies of the business continuity plan prior to its use. In addition, employees would not get the opportunity to exercise their part of the plan in advance. Once developed, the BCP should be maintained regularly.

Based on the study of different existing methodologies and their advantages and disadvantages, it was concluded that a **systematic approach to BCM that includes: identifying key business processes and BIA, defining the BCP strategy, developing BCP and DRP plans, testing plans and establishing procedures for maintaining and improving the BCM process**, is necessary. Hence, the methodology for developing a BCP can be summarized through the following stages:

1. Project Initiation
   - Defining the scope and purpose of business continuity.
   - Establishing a BCP team.
   - Developing a business continuity policy.
2. Business Impact Analysis and Risk Assessment
   - Performing risk analysis and business impact analysis.
   - Considering alternative business continuity strategies.
   - Conducting cost-benefit analysis and strategy selection.
   - Developing a business continuity budget.

BIA is the main technique used to gain a greater understanding of an organization and its process (Garrett, 2012), and it is the backbone of the entire BCM process (Elliott et al., 2010). An organization should evaluate the impact of every identified potential risk on each business activity that supports the delivery of

**Table 3.4   An Example of an Impact Level Scale**

| Level | Name | Definition |
|---|---|---|
| 5 | Catastrophic | Loss of business value that is liable to terminate the organization's existence |
| 4 | Intolerable | Loss of business value exceeding the organization's tolerance, but from which it is likely, eventually, to recover |
| 3 | Major | Major loss of business value |
| 2 | Significant | Significant loss of business value |
| 1 | Minor | Minor loss of business value |

*Source*: Drewitt (2013)

critical products and services, determine the maximum tolerable downtime for each activity, and identify any interdependent activities.

After defining key business functions, risk assessment and business impact analysis should be performed for each of the business functions and then, if necessary, for the infrastructure that supports them. Interdependence analysis should not be neglected either, as a business function that appears as noncritical may support a critical one.

Although the BIA may be useful in calculating maximum impact or loss in the event of a complete disruption of business, its real purpose in BCM terms is to establish priorities for the recovery of various activities or business processes.

In addition to defining key business processes, it is also necessary to identify the possible levels of impact of individual threats. The starting point is to establish an impact level scale, and the most common approach in the context of BCM is the five-point scale. Of course, to use this scale, it is necessary to define each level so that evaluators can assess, as far as possible, how severe the impact is (Drewitt, 2013). Table 3.4 shows an example of a BIA scale of impact level.

After that, a risk assessment should be carried out. Risk assessment involves identifying threats, vulnerabilities, risks, and business impacts of business disruption for each part of the organization. Threats are events that could disrupt a business such as, for example, natural disasters (earthquake, fire, flood), disasters caused by people, acts committed by dissatisfied employees, and mistakes. Vulnerability is the sensitivity to threats (the ability to put an organization at risk). Impacts of these risks on business can be loss of revenue, customer acquisition by competitors, impaired reputation, or employee dissatisfaction (Drewitt, 2013).

The risk assessment should be as comprehensive as possible. Ideally, every risk the organization faces needs to be identified. However, there is no guaranteed way to identify every risk. The identified risks become part of the risk register. A particular threat must be determined by how likely it will occur, the likelihood scale. Any probability scale can be used, and it is ubiquitous to use a risk matrix that uses probability on a scale of 1 to 5 (see Table 3.5).

**Table 3.5   A Typical Likelihood Scale**

| Scale | Name | % | Frequency |
|---|---|---|---|
| 5 | Very high | 25 | More than once a year |
| 4 | High | 5-25 | Every year |
| 3 | Medium | 1-5 | Every 2 to 3 years |
| 2 | Low | 0.2-1 | Every 5 years |
| 1 | Very low | 0.01-0.2 | Every 10 or more years |

*Source*: Drewitt (2013)

**Table 3.6   Assessed Risks**

| Risk | Likelihood | Impact | Risk Score |
|---|---|---|---|
| A | 4 | 2 | 8 |
| B | 4 | 3 | 12 |
| C | 3 | 3 | 9 |
| D | 4 | 2 | 8 |
| E | 4 | 3 | 12 |
| F | 2 | 3 | 6 |
| G | 2 | 5 | 10 |
| H | 5 | 5 | 25 |

*Source*: Drewitt (2013)

Risk consists of two things: the likelihood that an unexpected or unwanted event will occur and the impact that an event will have on a particular process. The generally accepted definition of risk is:

**Risk score = Likelihood (%) × Impact**

Table 3.6 provides a tabular overview of an example in which five different risks were assessed using a standard set of probability and impact criteria, on a scale of 1 to 5.

Assessed risks from Table 3.6 can be presented using the risk matrix, as in Figure 3.11. Once the risk matrix has been created, it is possible to categorize each of the risks. There is no absolute standard for what is low, medium, or high risk. An example of categorization is presented in Figure 3.12.

3. Design and Development
   - Establishing a business recovery team and assigning responsibilities to members.
   - Determining the structure of the plan and its main components.
   - Developing backup and recovery strategies.

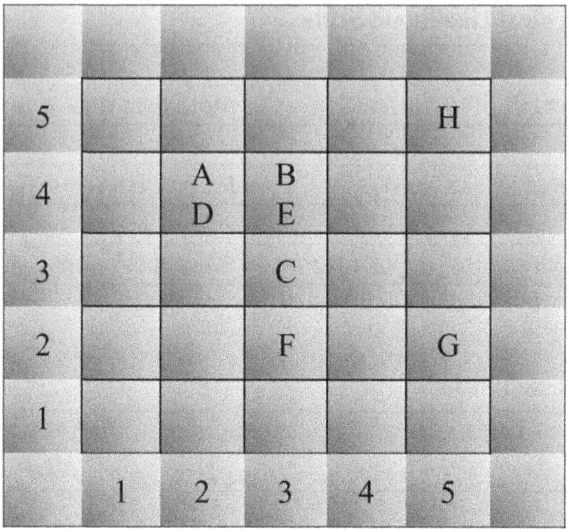

**Figure 3.11    Example of the risk matrix. Drewitt, 2013.**

**Impact Level of Risk**

| | | Insignificant | Minor | Moderate | Major | Catastrophic |
|---|---|---|---|---|---|---|
| | Very High | 3 | 4 | 4 | 5 | 5 |
| | High | 2 | 3 | 4 | 4 | 5 |
| Likelihood Level of Risk | Medium | 2 | 2 | 3 | 4 | 4 |
| | Low | 1 | 2 | 2 | 3 | 4 |
| | Very Low | 1 | 1 | 2 | 2 | 3 |

**Figure 3.12    Example of risk categorization – risk matrix. World Bank, 2016.**

- ◼ Developing plan execution scenarios.
- ◼ Developing criteria for escalation, notification, and plan activation.
- ◼ Developing general policies for plan administration.
- 4. Implementation (Awareness and Training)
    - ◼ Preparing procedures for eliminating hazards.
    - ◼ Preparing command center activation procedures.

- Preparing detailed recovery procedures.
- Preparing contracts with suppliers and procure all resources needed for recovery.
- Ensuring everything is prepared.
- Ensuring that recovery team members know their duties and responsibilities.
5. Testing
- Plan testing based on selected scenarios.
- Develop test reports and evaluation of results.
- Provide training for employees.
6. Maintenance – Updating the Plan
- Periodic review of the plan.
- Update/improve plan.
- Distribution of the plan to members of the recovery and BCP team.

Most phases are scalable in the sense that they may be fully or partially implemented. The various steps of creating a BCP can be categorized into a specific part of the Plan, Do, Check, Act (PDCA) circuit – the cycle of the BS and ISO standards (Figure 3.13).

The "**plan**" process establishes the goals, procedures, and processes for the program to achieve results in accordance with the organization's policies. This includes defining a business continuity management program, setting standards, and appointing a BCP team.

The "**do**" process implements and manages the BCP policies, procedures, and processes. This means that activities related to maintaining business continuity are carried out at this stage. The first step of this phase would be the development of RA and BIA, that is, the impact of a possible disaster on critical business activities and identification of recovery goals. The second step is to identify a disaster recovery strategy. The third is to develop a plan. The final step is to conduct training at the organization level, evaluate strategies and plans through exercises, and launch maintenance programs.

The "**check**" process monitors and analyzes the performance of the identified business continuity management system objectives. The results of the assessment are presented to top-level management through the appointed BCP team. In short, this process ensures that the organization's management is responsible for the program and organization of the entire business continuity system.

The "**act**" process maintains and advances the program on the basis of preventive and corrective action taken, and on the basis of the results of management's evaluation of goals and procedures for the business continuity.

A BCP can be in a variety of formats (Drewitt, 2013) and with a variety of elements. However, Drewitt (2013) states that the business continuity plan should consist of:

- A master plan including:
  - Summary – A clear statement setting out the purpose of the BCP.

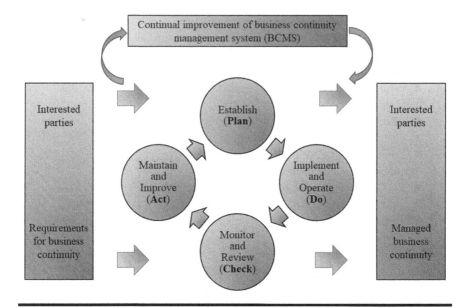

**Figure 3.13  PDCA model applied to business continuity management system (BCMS) processes. The British Standards Institution, 2012.**

- Activation – A statement of who is authorized to activate the BCP.
- Command location – The choice of location.
- Command structure – Detailed lists of duties and responsibilities.
- Priorities and objectives – The recovery objectives established through the BIA.
- Scenario plans (contingency plans).
- Recovery plans – The recovery plans typically set out a short narrative of how and where the activity should be recovered – RTO and RPO.
- Other plan components:
  - Procedures.
  - Incident log.
  - Internal communication.
  - Contact data.

## *BCM Maturity Models*

The concept of process maturity proposes that the process has a life cycle that is evaluated in terms of to what extent it is explicitly defined, managed, measured, and controlled. The concept of process maturity is analogous to the life cycle that takes place in the developmental stages. In other words, the development of the process can be determined by a maturity model, which assumes that progress toward the goal is coming in stages (Randeree et al., 2012). This practically means that when talking about the stages of development of BCM in an organization, the maturity model can be used to evaluate the development stage of BCM. Randeree et al. (2012) state that existing methodologies do not offer a way for assessing where an organization currently stands in terms of BCM maturity, how far they have to go, and what they have to do to get there. Hence, there are several BCM maturity model suggestions in the literature.

Randeree et al. (2012) pointed out the two key BCM maturity models:

■ Complete Public Domain Business Continuity Maturity Model (BCMM) – a tool for objectively measuring a disaster preparedness organization. BCMM distinguishes six different maturity levels. Levels one to three represent organizations that have not yet completed the required program basics needed to launch a sustainable BC program. Levels four through six represent the evolutionary path of the program. Furthermore, the BCMM defines eight corporate competencies that determine the maturity of an organization (Figure 3.14).

■ COBIT maturity model – it is emphasized that this model should not be used to assess the level of adherence to its control objectives but should be used to identify problems and prioritize improvements (Figure 3.15). Organizations can be found at any of the five maturity stages:
  ■ Level 0: Non-existent: No current process in place.
  ■ Level 1: Initial/Ad Hoc: No standardized process in place.
  ■ Level 2: Repeatable but Intuitive: Procedures exist but require highly knowledgeable individuals, and little standardization exists.
  ■ Level 3: Defined Process: Standardized procedures exist but remain unsophisticated.
  ■ Level 4: Managed and Measurable: Standard procedures provide key indicators of success and methods of error detection.
  ■ Level 5: Optimized: Refined, standardized processes exist and maintain strong practice levels that reduce variance.

In addition to the maturity models, organizations can also do benchmarking in accordance with some of the standards outlined in the chapter above.

## Information Technology Capability

Each organization makes significant investments in IT (Rai, Pavlou, Im, & Du, 2012). In this regard, both practitioners and scholars have addressed the issue of return on investment in IT. The most prominent view is that IT investments do not add value to a business without existing and adequate resources available. In this regard, a common way of conceptualizing IT to capture its business value is as **organizational IT capability** (Sambamurthy, Bharadwaj, & Grover, 2003;

| Competency Maturity Level | | Program Basics | | | Program Development | | |
|---|---|---|---|---|---|---|---|
| | | Sr. Mgmt. Commitment | Professional Support | Governance | All Units Participating | Integrated Planning | Cross-Functional |
| Level 1 | Self-Governed | No | No | No | No | No | No |
| Level 2 | Supported Self-Governed | Marginal | Partial | No | No | No | No |
| Level 3 | Centrally Governed | Partial | Yes | Partial | No | No | No |
| Level 4 | Enterprise Awakening | Yes | Yes | Yes | Yes | No | No |
| Level 5 | Planned Growth | Yes | Yes | Yes | Yes | Yes | No |
| Level 6 | Synergistic | Yes | Yes | Yes | Yes | Yes | Yes |

Increasing Business Continuity Competency Maturity

**Figure 3.14 Complete public domain business continuity maturity model (BCMM). Virtual Corporation (2007).**

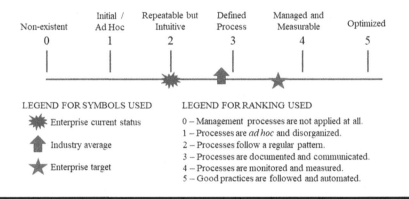

LEGEND FOR SYMBOLS USED

✹ Enterprise current status

⬆ Industry average

★ Enterprise target

LEGEND FOR RANKING USED

0 – Management processes are not applied at all.
1 – Processes are *ad hoc* and disorganized.
2 – Processes follow a regular pattern.
3 – Processes are documented and communicated.
4 – Processes are monitored and measured.
5 – Good practices are followed and automated.

**Figure 3.15 COBIT BCM maturity model. CobiT 4.1.**

Tippins & Sohi, 2003). Organizational IT capability is the way a company uses IT to handle information resources effectively. IT capability includes the possession of information technologies as well as their adequate use to meet the information needs of an organization. In other words, IT capability refers to an organization's ability to employ IT-based resources to gain a completive advantage (Yu, Jacobs, & Chavez, 2016). Consequently, IT capability can be defined as "the implementation and use of IT functionalities with other resources to execute business processes" (Rai et al., 2012). IT is a generic term that refers to computers, software, and telecommunications, while IT capability is a broader term and refers to the use of these technologies to meet the company's information needs (Turulja & Bajgoric, 2016).

In the literature, there are three perspectives on the business value of IT:

- Significance of information for an organization – the importance of IT is explained through the value of information for an organization, and having timely information makes it possible to achieve a competitive advantage (Lai, Zhao, & Wang, 2006). Information technologies serve and facilitate the process of information processing.

- IT investments have a positive impact on long-term organizational performance – IT serves as a catalyst for innovative ideas and is a tool to deliver those ideas (McAfee & Brynjolfsson, 2008). One of the most accepted paradigms for the value of IT is the belief that IT investments can produce long-term benefits for the company if used in transforming business processes (Crawford, Leonard, & Jones, 2011). Within research that has this perspective, IT is viewed as a critical and necessary condition for an organization to succeed in highly competitive environments (Bhatt & Grover, 2005). However, previous research and perspectives emphasize that there is no clear connection and impact of IT on organizational performance, while most contemporary researchers agree that well-positioned IT investments can have a significant impact on long-term business performance (Crawford et al., 2011). In particular, IT in an organization has a dual role; first, IT serves as a catalyst for innovative ideas, and second, IT is the tool that delivers those ideas (McAfee & Brynjolfsson, 2008).

- IT is a dynamic capabilities facilitator – IT supports the creation, modification, and realization of organizational dynamic capabilities. More recent research, instead of focusing on the direct effects of IT investment on organizational performance, address IT supporting the creation, modification, and realization of organizational dynamic capabilities (Crawford et al., 2011; Patrakosol & Lee, 2009; Tippins & Sohi, 2003). The organizational dynamic capability implies the possession of adequate resources, as well as the ability to use them adequately and to improve them continuously.

Organizations' IT capability is considered a significant tool that complements the other organizational capabilities of the company (Pérez-López & Alegre, 2012). IT capability, combined with other organizational capabilities, can generate a positive synergistic effect and increase competitiveness (Liang, You, & Liu, 2010; Pérez-López & Alegre, 2012). The loss of an organization's IT capabilities can have devastating consequences in today's information-intensive business environment (Clitherow, Brookbanks, Clayton, & Spear, 2008). IT has become a strategic tool for all organizations.

Chapter 8 presents in detail the conceptualization of IT capability, as well as measurement models and scales, and the relationship between IT capability and organizational performance using a literature review.

## BCM and IT Capability

After a comprehensive search of IT capability literature and content analysis to identify the conceptualization of the capability and measurement methods, it can be concluded that BCM is hardly considered in the context of IT capability, especially in the scientific literature. A detailed explanation of the definition of IT capability and its measurement available in the relevant literature is presented in Chapter 8. The emphasis here will be on the relationship between BCM and IT capability.

It is clear that organizations are exposed to various risks today. The continuous development of the IT risk landscape requires effective risk management practices for all areas of IT risks, such as but not limited to security, investments, service contracts, data protection and information privacy (Carcary, 2012). Therefore, the ability to effectively manage various information risks should be an integral part of the organizational IT capability. Namely, if the organization does not have the ability to manage IT risks, can it be said that the organization has IT capability? In this regard, Carcary (2012) examines a maturity model developed by the Innovation Value Institute at the National University of Ireland Maynooth (IT Capability Maturity Framework – IT CMF) emphasizing its approach for enhancing the IT capabilities of an organization with particular reference to effective IT risk management (see Figure 3.16).

This model is a systematic framework for understanding the maturity of an organization to generate business value from IT investments. The model represents an IT capability plan and serves as an assessment tool that enables organizations to understand and improve over time their IT capabilities through five levels of maturity – initial, basic, intermediate, advanced, and optimizing.

IT-CMF elements can be presented in three interconnected layers: strategy, macrolayer, and microlayer. The strategic layer underpins the basic elements of IT-CMF that support an approach to strategic thinking that incorporates a business context guided by an organization's vision of its future. The macrolayer consists of both the content and the context of the IT-CMF deployment. Content segments the organization's IT function activities into four macro capabilities: managing IT like a business, managing the IT budget, managing the IT capability, and managing IT for business value. These four integrated IT management strategies underpin the value management of IT (Carcary, 2012). The microlayer contains 33 critical capabilities assigned to individual macro capabilities. They represent the key activities of an IT organization in delivering IT solutions and optimizing the associated generated business value. Applying IT-CMF yields a useful framework to help provide road maps and direction for efforts to improve IT capabilities (Curley, 2008).

It is important to note that this model of an organization's IT capabilities envisages BCM as an integral part of it. It is settled within the "manage IT as a business" macro capability. In other words, risk management focuses on proactively assessing, prioritizing, managing, and monitoring risk to reduce the exposure and

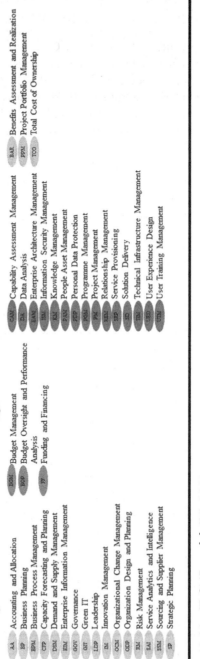

**Figure 3.16  IT CMF model. IVI, 2013.**

potential impact of IT risk. It refers on IT security, data protection, and privacy of information; business continuity and disaster recovery; IT investments; IT program, project, and product life cycles; IT service contracts and suppliers; IT staff; and adherence to regulatory and ethical policies, as well as new risks in these and other categories (Carcary, 2012). Furthermore, Curley (2008) notes that IT capability creates value through two fundamental mechanisms – business continuity and business change. Business continuity ensures that a firm can continue to gain value from its products and services through actions such as process automation, product or service development, service delivery, and so on. Business change brings value when changes to a business model, process, or product/service are made possible by the application of IT.

Weill, Subramani, and Broadbent (2002) identified the IT infrastructure capabilities required for different business activities. An integrated IT infrastructure capability consists of ten service clusters. Ensuring business continuity is part of the cluster "security and risk" (see Figure 3.17).

Further, Peppard and Ward (2004) developed a model of an IS capability that can help organizations deliver value from investments made in IT on an ongoing basis, as shown in Figure 3.18.

This model is based on the IS competencies model (see Peppard, Lambert, & Edwards, 2000). IT capability is defined as "the ability to translate the business strategy into long term information architectures, technology infrastructure and resourcing plans that enable the implementation of the strategy" (Peppard & Ward, 2004). Business continuity and security are micro components of the IS competencies (see 6.6. in Figure 3.19), and it means providing effective recovery, contingency, and security processes to prevent the risk of business failure (Peppard & Ward, 2004).

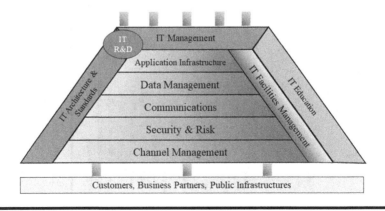

**Figure 3.17   An integrated IT infrastructure with ten capability clusters. Weill et al., 2002.**

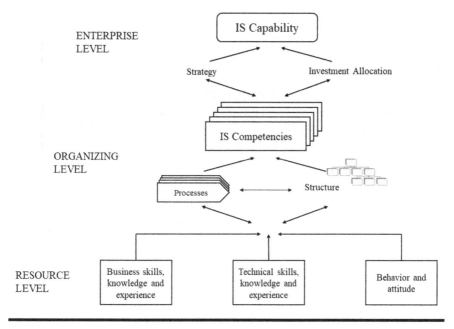

**Figure 3.18   A model of the IS capability. Peppard & Ward, 2004.**

In addition to the technical perspective of IT capability presented in the above-mentioned models, there are several studies in the field of social sciences that do not consider BCM while analyzing an organization's IT capability. For example, Bakar and Udin (2015) analyze IT capability and BCM as separate constructs and investigate the moderating impact of IT capability on the relationship between BCM factors and organizational performance. Analyzing this impact, BCM is viewed through IT objects comprising the BCM infrastructure such as backup system, redundancy in the communication network, data replication strategy, off-site data center, and operation center facilities. On the other hand, the conceptualization of IT capability is adopted from Tippins and Sohi (2003), who consider it a multidimensional construct with dimensions of IT knowledge, IT infrastructure, and IT operations. However, BCM is not an integral part of any dimension.

Based on the discussion, it can be concluded that BCM is an integral part of the organization's IT/IS capabilities. To evaluate their IT capabilities, it is essential that organizations evaluate their BCM as well. Most IT maturity models also address BCM. When it comes to more technical research, they treat the technical/infrastructure side of IT capability and BCM as an integral part of it. However, studies that are more concerned with management and the social sciences employ a narrow conception of IT capability, and BCM is rarely considered part of an organization's IT capability. In other words, IT capability is mostly addressed without BCM.

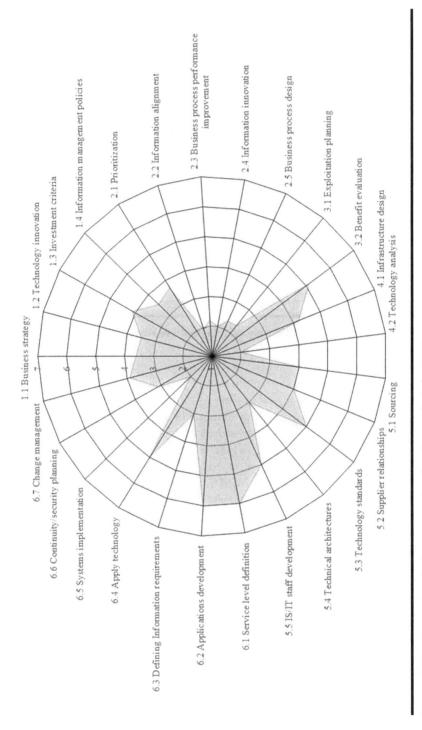

**Figure 3.19 Summary of micro competencies. Peppard et al., 2000.**

# Conclusion

Business process interruptions can cause serious financial losses for an organization. These losses can be immediately visible or measurable, but they may also be negligible or imperceptible at the moment. In the long term, however, these losses can be disastrous for the company's business. Disruption of business, in today's competitive market, can lead to a decline in the organization's credibility or to a loss of the reputation. This leads to long-term financial losses that are not immediately apparent but can ultimately prove decisive. Business continuity planning (BCP) is the process of developing and refining a logistics plan that provides guidance on how to avoid, mitigate, and, in the worst case, recover or restart business after the failure caused by a disaster event. All crises can be classified into three broad categories: natural hazards such as floods, hurricanes, tornadoes, or earthquakes; technological hazards, such as failures in infrastructure, technology, and so on; and human-made hazards. The threats of catastrophe or crisis incidents for all types of organizations are not the same, and plans to avoid or minimize them once they occur are not the same for all companies. For the same reason, the complexity of creating and updating, or changing a plan to keep up with changes in technology and industry, is not the same.

Business continuity has become one of the cornerstones of corporate strategic planning. Business continuity management is based on a holistic operating model that allows companies to operate more effectively and efficiently in their daily operations. Business continuity management, in addition to planning for a response in the event of catastrophic events (e.g., fires, natural disasters, etc.), includes any other events that may cause business interruptions (failure of computer and network systems, interruption of service delivery by suppliers, etc.) that have a direct impact on the business. A systematic approach to BCM includes identification of key business processes and BIA, defining the BCP strategy, development of BCP and DRP plans, testing plans, and establishing procedures for maintaining and improving the BCM process.

The chapter furthermore presents the concepts of BCP and DRP. Business continuity is the strategic and tactical ability of an organization to plan and respond to incidents and disruptions to continue its business activities at a level it has previously defined as acceptable. On the other side, disaster recovery consists of processes, policies, and procedures related to preparing for the recovery or renewal of technological infrastructure critical to the organization following a disaster. Disaster recovery emphasizes technology, while business continuity emphasizes business activity. This is why disaster recovery is part of business continuity, and it can be considered one of the main factors that enable business activities. The BCP implementation methodology is also briefly presented, with basic concepts related to the process itself.

Finally, the second part of the chapter briefly introduces the concept of organizational IT capability and draws a parallel with BCM. Organizational IT capability is how a company uses IT to manage information resources effectively. IT capability includes owning information technologies as well as using them adequately to meet the information needs of the organization.

## Real-World Example

### *Ransomware Hobbles the City of Atlanta*

"There has been no shortage of headline-making ransomware attacks over the last few years. But one that stands out (and whose impact was still reverberating at the time of this writing) was the March 2018 SamSam ransomware attack on the City of Atlanta. The attack devastated the city government's computer systems, disrupting numerous city services, including its police records, courts, utilities, parking services, and other programs. Computer systems were shut down for five days, forcing many departments to complete essential paperwork by hand. Even as services were slowly brought back online over the following later [days], the full recovery took months.

Attackers demanded a $52,000 ransom payment. But when all was said and done, the full impact of the attack was projected to cost more than $17 million. Nearly $3 million alone was spent on contracts for emergency IT consultants and crisis management firms. The Atlanta ransomware attack is a lesson in inadequate business continuity planning. The event revealed that the city's IT was woefully unprepared for the attack. Just two months prior, an audit found 1,500 to 2,000 vulnerabilities in the city's IT systems, which were compounded by "obsolete software and an IT culture driven by 'ad hoc or undocumented' processes", according to StateScoop.

Which vulnerabilities allowed the attack to happen? Weak passwords, most likely. That is a common entry point for SamSam attackers, who use brute-force software to guess thousands of password combinations in a matter of seconds. Frankly, it's an unsophisticated method that could have been prevented with stronger password management protocols.

Despite the business continuity missteps, credit should still be given to the many IT professionals (internal and external) who worked to restore critical city services as quickly as possible. What's clear is that the city did have some disaster recovery procedures in place that allowed it to restore critical services. If it hadn't, the event likely would have been much worse".

The case is adopted from InvenioIT. Available at: https://invenioit.com/continuity/business-continuity-looks-like/ (accessed: February 2020).

## Discussion Questions

1. Discuss the BCM concept.
2. Discuss the relationship between BCM and BCP.
3. Discuss the evolution of BCM.
4. Explain how an organization can implement BCM.
5. What categories of disaster events exist?
6. Discuss the relationship between BCP, CP, and DRP.

7. Explain DRP and how it relates to BCP.
8. Discuss different BCP strategies.
9. Explain the difference between BIA and RA.
10. Explain the concept of organizational IT capability.

# References

Alsultanny, Y. (2013). Fault Tolerance Effect on Computer Networks Availability. *IADIS International Conference Applied Computing* (October 23–25, 2013), 196–200. Fort Worth, TX, USA.

Bakar, Z., Udin, Z. (2015). Business continuity management factors and organizational performance: A study on the moderating role of IT capability, *Journal of Management Info, 7*(1), 12–39.

Bhatt, G.D., Grover, V. (2005). Types of information technology capabilities and their role in competitive advantage: Sn Empirical Study, *Journal of Management Information Systems, 22*(2), 253–277. https://doi.org/ 10.1080/07421222.2005.11045844

Botha, J., Von Solms, R. (2004). A cyclic approach to business continuity planning. *Information Management and Computer Security, 12*(4), 328–337. https://doi.org/ 10.1108/09685220410553541

The British Standards Institution. (2012). ISO 22301: 2012. *Societal security. Business continuity management systems. Requirements.* British Standards Institute, London, 15-19.

Carcary, M. (2012). IT risk management: A capability maturity model perspective. *Electronic Journal Information Systems Evaluation, 16*(3), 3–13.

Clitherow, D., Brookbanks, M., Clayton, N., Spear, G. (2008). Combining high availability and disaster recovery solutions for critical IT environments, *IBM Systems Journal, 47*(4), 563–575. https://doi.org/10.1147/SJ.2008.5386509

Crawford, J., Leonard, L.N.K., Jones, K. (2011). The human resource's influence in shaping IT competence. *Industrial Management & Data Systems, 111*(2), 164–183. https://doi.org/10.1108/02635571111115128

Curley, M. (2008). Introducing an IT capability maturity framework. *Lecture Notes in Business Information Processing, 12*, 63–78. https://doi.org/10.1007/978-3-540-88710-2_6

Drewitt, T. (2013). *A Manager's Guide to ISO22301 – A Practical Guide to Developing and Implementing a Business Continuity Management System.* IT Governance Publishing.

Elliott, D., Swartz, E., Herbane, B. (2010). *Business Continuity Management: A Crisis Management Approach.* Routledge.

Garrett, D.N. (2012). *The Evolution of Business Continuity Management in large Irish enterprises between 2004 and 2009* (Doctoral dissertation, Dublin City University).

Hassel, H., Cedergren, A. (2019). Exploring the conceptual foundation of continuity management in the context of societal safety, *Risk Analysis*, 39(7), 1503–1519. https://doi.org/10.1111/risa.13263

Hayes, B., Kotwica, K. (2013). *Business Continuity Playbook* (D. Correia, Ed.). The Security Executive Council. Elsevier.

Herbane, B. (2010). The evolution of business continuity management: A historical review of practices and drivers. *Business History, 52*(6), 978–1002. https://doi.org/10.1080/00076791.2010.511185

Herbane, B., Elliott, D., Swartz, E.M. (2004). Business Continuity Management: Time for a strategic role? *Long Range Planning, 37*(5), 386–457. https://doi.org/10.1016/j.lrp.2004.07.010

Hiles, A. (2010). *The Definitive Handbook of Business Continuity Management.* John Wiley & Sons.

IVI – Innovation Value Institute (2013). *IT Capability Maturity Framework.* Innovation Value Institute.

Järveläinen, J. (2012). Information security and business continuity management in interorganizational IT relationships. *Information Management & Computer Security, 20*(5), 332–349. https://doi.org/10.1108/09685221211286511

Kim, D., Solomon, M.G. (2016). *Fundamentals of information systems security.* Jones & Bartlett Learning.

Kliem, R.L., Richie, G.D. (2016). *Business Continuity Planning – A Project Management Approach.* CRC Press/Taylor & Francis Group.

Lai, F., Zhao, X., Wang, Q. (2006). The impact of information technology on the competitive advantage of logistics firms in China. *Industrial Management & Data Systems, 106*(9), 1249–1271. https://doi.org/10.1108/02635570610712564

Liang, T., You, J., Liu, C. (2010). A resource-based perspective on information technology and firm performance: A meta analysis. *Industrial Management & Data Systems, 110*(8), 1138–1158. https://doi.org/10.1108/02635571011077807

McAfee, A., Brynjolfsson, E. (2008). Investing in the IT that makes a competitive difference. *Harvard Business Review, 86*, 98–107.

Niemimaa, M., Järveläinen, J., Heikkilä, M., Heikkilä, J. (2019). Business continuity of business models: Evaluating the resilience of business models for contingencies. *International Journal of Information Management, 49*, 208–216. https://doi.org/10.1016/j.ijinfomgt.2019.04.010

Patrakosol, B., Lee, S.M. (2009). IT capabilities, interfirm performance, and the state of economic development. *Industrial Management & Data Systems, 109*(9), 1231–1247. https://doi.org/10.1108/02635570911002298

Peppard, J., Lambert, R., Edwards, C. (2000). Whose job is it anyway?: organizational information competencies for value creation. *Information Systems Journal, 10*(4), 291–322.

Peppard, J., Ward, J. (2004). Beyond strategic information systems: Towards an IS capability. *Journal of Strategic Information Systems, 13*(2), 167–194. https://doi.org/10.1016/j.jsis.2004.02.002

Pérez-López, S., Alegre, J. (2012). Information technology competency, knowledge processes and firm performance. *Industrial Management & Data Systems, 112*(4), 644–662. https://doi.org/10.1108/02635571211225521

Rai, A., Pavlou, P.A., Im, G., Du, S. (2012). Interfirm IT capability profiles and communications for cocreating relational value: Evidence from the logistics industry. *MIS Quarterly, 36*(1), 233–262.

Randeree, K., Mahal, A., Narwani, A. (2012). A business continuity management maturity model for the UAE banking sector. *Business Process Management Journal, 18*(3), 472–492. https://doi.org/10.1108/14637151211232650

Sadgrove, K. (2016). *The complete guide to business risk management.* Routledge.

Sagita, L., Supriadi, R., Pheng, L.S. (2018). *Business Continuity Management in Construction.* Springer Nature Singapore Pte.

Sambamurthy, V., Bharadwaj, A., Grover, V. (2003). Shaping agility through digital options: Reconceptualizing the role of information technology in contemporary firm. *MIS Quarterly, 27*(2), 237–263. https://doi.org/10.1017/CBO9781107415324.004

Schätter, F., Hansen, O., Wiens, M., Schultmann, F. (2019). A decision support methodology for a disaster-caused business continuity management. *Decision Support Systems, 118*, 10–20. https://doi.org/10.1016/j.dss.2018.12.006

Snedaker, S., Rima, C. (2014). *Business Continuity and Disaster Recovery Planning for IT Professionals*. Elsevier.

Tippins, M.J., Sohi, R.S. (2003). IT competency and firm performance: Is organizational learning a missing link? *Strategic Management Journal, 24*(8), 745–761. https://doi.org/10.1002/smj.337

Tucker, E. (2015). *Business continuity from preparedness to recovery: A standards-based approach.* Butterworth-Heinemann (Elsevier Inc.)..

Turulja, L., Bajgoric, N. (2016). Innovation and information technology capability as antecedents of firms' success. *Interdisciplinary Description of Complex Systems, 14*(2), 148–156. https://doi.org/10.7906/indecs.14.2.4

Virtual Corporation, Inc. (2007). *Business Continuity Maturity Model.* Virtual Corporation.

Vuong, J. (2015). Disaster recovery planning. *Information Security Curriculum Development Conference 2015* (October), 1–3. https://doi.org/10.1109/MP.2004.1301248

Watters, J. (2014). *Disaster Recovery, Crisis Response, & Business Continuity – a Management Desk Reference.* Apress.

Weill, P., Subramani, M.R., Broadbent, M. (2002). Building IT Infrastructure for Strategic Agility. Center for Information Systems Research CISR, Massachusetts Institute of Technology.

World Bank. (2016). *The World Bank Risk Assessment Methodology.* World Bank. Retrieved from www.fatf-gafi.org/media/fatf/documents/reports/risk_assessment_world_bank.pdf

Xing, J., Zeng, Z., Zio, E. (2019). Dynamic business continuity assessment using condition monitoring data. *International Journal of Disaster Risk Reduction, 41*, 101334. https://doi.org/10.1016/j.ijdrr.2019.101334

Yu, W., Jacobs, M.A., Chavez, R. (2016). The impacts of IT capability and marketing capability on supply chain integration: A resource-based perspective. *International Journal of Production Research, 55*(14), 4196–4211.

# Chapter 4

# Server Operating Environments for Business Continuity

## Background: Enterprise Information Systems and Information Technology Architectures

Turban et al. (2005) defined "information technology architecture" as "a high-level map or plan of the information assets in an organization, which guides current operations and is a blueprint for future directions".

Jonkers at al. (2006) defined architecture as "structure with a vision" that provides an integrated view of the system being designed and studied. They build their definition on top of a commonly used definition by the IEEE Standard 1471–2000. Kim et al. (2002) proposed new architectural metrics that consist of six dimensions: internal stability, external security, information gathering, order processing, system interface, and communication interface. The six measures were found to be relevant to important technical and managerial aspects of Internet business. Versteeg and Bouwman (2006) define the main elements of a business architecture as business domains within the new paradigm of relations between business strategy and information technologies. Goethals et al. (2006) argue that enterprises are living things; they constantly need to be (rearchitected in order to achieve the necessary agility, alignment, and integration. Balabko and Wegmann (2006) applied the concepts of system inquiry (systems philosophy, systems theory, systems methodology, and systems application) in the context of an enterprise architecture. Alsultanny (2014) considered the weak points in the e-government infrastructure with regard to computer network security.

Information technologies are used in modern business within the concept of enterprise information systems. Enterprise information systems (EIS), or simply enterprise systems (ES), are designed and implemented by using several methods or methodologies of IS analysis and design. They contain servers, desktops, portable computers/devices, data communication/networking technologies, systems and application software, and employ several IT specialists.

EIS are implemented in several forms, such as: (Figure 4.1):

- Enterprise resource planning systems (ERP)
- Messaging/Collaboration systems
- Document management systems (DCM)
- Customer relationships management systems (CRM)
- Supply chain management systems (SCM)
- Business intelligence systems (BI)
- Legacy systems
- …

Most businesses today implemented their information systems based on one of the following models of information architectures:

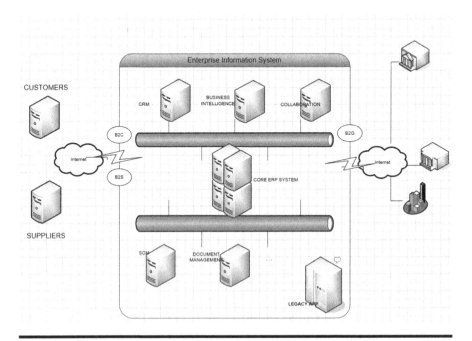

**Figure 4.1   Enterprise information system: typical components.**

a) client-server model implemented "on-premises", with servers installed and implemented "on-premises" – within the boundaries of the company
b) cloud computing-based client-server model, sometime called client-cloud model – the model that uses servers of the cloud provider

Both approaches have advantages and disadvantages. Some businesses still use a mainframe environment, which can be seen as a version of the client-server model with a mainframe computer on the server side. Mainframe plays the role of server in both "on-premises" and cloud-based architectures. In all cases, the client side consists of several client devices such as desktop computers, notebooks, and other portable computer devices. Standard client-server and cloud-client information architectures divide data processing into two major classes of computers: clients and servers.

A client is a computer such as a PC, workstation, portable, or mobile computing device attached to local area network, wide area network, or the Internet. The client side may consist of several dozens (hundreds, thousands, hundreds of thousands) of clients, while the server side contains one or more servers.

The server side of such architecture is called an "enterprise server", which is a core component of a server operating environment. It consists of server hardware, a server operating system, and server-based continuous computing technologies that are used to enhance key server platform features such as reliability, availability, and scalability.

The server provides clients with services. Examples of servers are database servers and e-mail servers. These application servers are accessed by end users that use client software installed on client devices or simply a Web browser (see Figure 4.2).

**A hybrid architecture** is used as well: a combination of a mainframe (legacy) platform with newly implemented "thick" and "thin" client-server applications installed on enterprise servers (Figure 4.3).

The requirements expected from a server operating environment (SOE) depend on the organizational size, complexity, and type of business; however, the following requirements are most common:

a) SOE is expected to be available, scalable, and reliable.
b) SOE is expected to provide storage and backup-recovery capabilities.
c) SOE is expected to exist in a reliable networking environment.

Within the evolution of the client-server architecture, the following models have been identified over the last three decades:

a) File-oriented
b) Shared databases
c) Traditional client-server
d) Advanced client-server; multi-tiered c/s architecture
e) Web-enabled client-server architecture

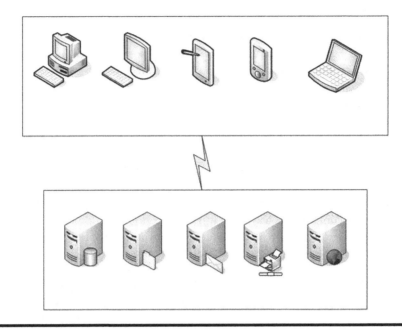

**Figure 4.2   Traditional client-server architecture.**

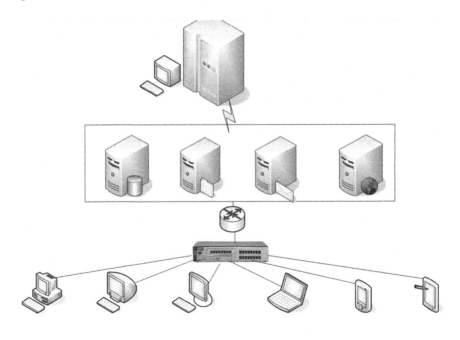

**Figure 4.3   A hybrid architecture (mainframe and client-server); legacy systems and new client-server applications.**

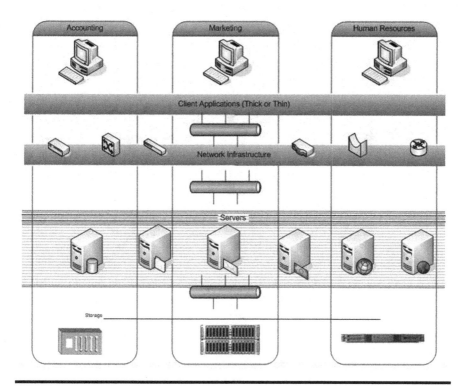

**Figure 4.4   Client-server infrastructure layers and components.**

f) Cloud-computing based (Cloud-client) architecture
g) Converged and Hyper-converged infrastructure
h) Composable infrastructure

Most commonly implemented layers of the client-server architecture can be identified as follows (see Figure 4.4):

a) **Client layer** – consisting of client computing devices that are used to access server applications.
b) **Networking layer** – a set of data communication devices, data communication media, and networking software.
c) **Server operating system layer** – cores OS and additional set of server-based applications.
d) **Storage layer** – storage devices and media used for primary data storage, backup, and recovery.

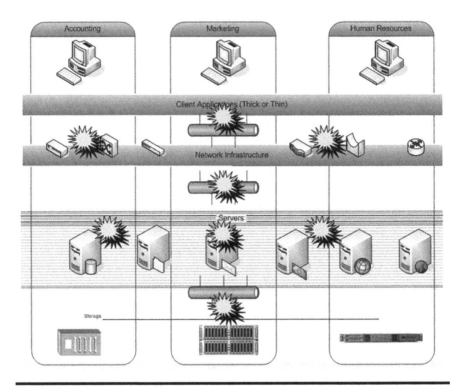

**Figure 4.5   Client-server infrastructure components and possible downtime points. Bajgoric, 2010.**

Within such a kind of information infrastructure, a number of critical points can be identified with regard to possible downtime problems (Figure 4.5):

a) Hardware/Software/Networking issues on client computing devices
b) LAN/WAN/Internet – disconnections
c) Server operating platform – related issues
d) Data storage – related issues
e) Operational mistakes

These downtime points are considered critical in the information system infrastructure that determines the business continuity. Previous figures show traditional implementations of the c/s model with separate application servers, network components, and storage components.

Over the last couple of years, new models of IT infrastructures have emerged such as converged infrastructure, hyperconverged infrastructure, and composable infrastructure. Some authors call them "infrastructures" (Bednarz, 2019a), but some name them "data center architectures" (Scott, 2018).

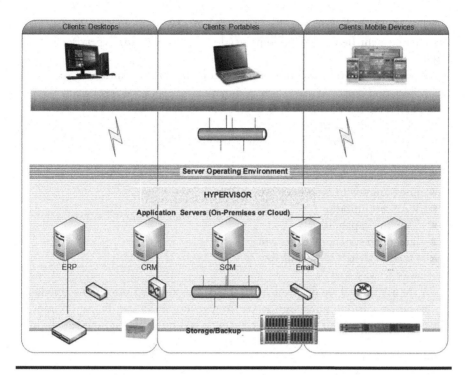

**Figure 4.6   Hyperconverged infrastructure.**

Hyperconverged infrastructure (HCI), which is based on a virtualization envir-onment, represents such hardware/software infrastructures that integrate server operating environment, virtualization technology, network environment, storage, and backup environment (Figure 4.6). From a business continuity perspective, the integration of data backup/recovery solutions is very important, not only standard tape-based or disk-based backup technologies but the advanced backup technologies as well (mirroring, snapshot, replication).

For instance, Microsoft's Windows Volume Shadow Service (VSS) is a technology included in the Windows OS environment that can be used for creating snapshots of data volumes, even when files are open. Several versions of this product are available for several versions of both desktop and server versions of the Windows operating system: Windows Server 2019 (2016, 2012, and 2008), Windows 10 (9, 8, and 7). In addition to snapshot technology, data replication can be used as well with moving whole servers to remote locations, not only a specific database or just data.

Some HCI vendors and their solutions are as follows:

- Dell EMC (VxRail)
- Nutanix
- HPE (SimpliVity)
- Datrium

All these HCI platforms are based on either VMWare or a Hyper-V virtualization environment (hypervisors). Some vendors offer their own hypervisor such as Nutanix (Acropolis).

Hyperconverged infrastructure solutions contain many features such as:

- Integrated hypervisor
- Distributed file system
- Data compression and data deduplication
- Built-in data protection
- Caching and tiering
- Integration with legacy systems
- WAN optimization
- Scale-out capabilities
- Integrated system management
- Ethernet switch for scaling out

In the traditional model, which was based on so-called three-tiered model, a business usually had to purchase a server from vendor A, a network from vendor B, and storage from vendor C. In the hyperconverged infrastructure model, all three components are well integrated and offered by a single vendor. All three components are managed by a unified system management solution.

In the traditional architecture, physical servers run a virtualization software (hypervisor), which manages virtual machines (VMs) created on those servers. Such a solution comprises direct attached storage (DAS), storage area network(SAN) or network attached storage (NAS).

In the converged and hyper-converged architecture, the storage is attached directly to the physical servers or to a controller running as a service. Bednarz (2019a) defined converged infrastructure as a preconfigured package of software and hardware in a single system for simplified management. The compute, storage, and networking components are discrete and can be separated. However, in a hyperconverged environment, the components can't be separated; the software-defined elements are implemented virtually, with seamless integration into the hypervisor environment. This allows organizations to easily expand capacity by deploying additional modules. Like a converged or hyperconverged infrastructure, a composable infrastructure combines compute, storage, and network fabric into one platform. But it's not preconfigured for specific workloads like a converged or hyperconverged infrastructure is.

WEEAM (2016) stated that to combat the need for near-constant maintenance, CIOs need to pioneer a new approach to managing their systems using intelligent data management practices that turn their organizations into a 24x7x365 available enterprise.

Gartner defined hyperconverged infrastructure (HCI) as a category of scale-out software-integrated infrastructure that applies a modular approach to compute,

| Table 3-1 | Data Center Architecture Spectrum | | | |
| --- | --- | --- | --- | --- |
| | *Traditional* | *Converged* | *Hyperconverged* | *Composable* |
| Complexity | High | Moderate | Moderate | Low |
| Time to value | Days, weeks, month | Days, weeks | Hours, minutes | Minutes, seconds |
| Flexibility | Moderate, but very complex | Moderate | Moderate | High |
| Scaling | Difficult | Moderate | Simple | Simple |
| Workloads supported | Physical, virtual, containers | Physical, virtual, containers | Virtual, containers | Physical, virtual, containers |

**Figure 4.7    Data center architectures. Scott, 2018.**

network, and storage on standard hardware, leveraging distributed, horizontal building blocks under unified management (Bednarz, 2018).

Scott (2018) presented a table showing the main features of traditional and modern architectures (Figure 4.7.).

A report provided by 451 Research demonstrated that improving performance availability is the dominant reason for establishing hybrid-multi-cloud-on-premises infrastructure in the digital era (451 Research Report, 2019).

In addition to the above-mentioned modern architectures/infrastructures, the new application paradigms such as: serverless computing, cloudless computing, utility computing, on-demand computing, software-as-a-service (SaaS), service-oriented architecture (SOA), grid computing, cloud computing, and green computing have been introduced in order to lower the total costs of ownership of IT infrastructures and improve both the efficiency and effectiveness of information processing.

Serverless computing is a model in which a cloud provider runs the server for a customer and manages the allocation of computing resources. The term "serverless" is a misnomer, in the sense that servers are still used, not within the boundaries of an organization but in the cloud provider's site. Violino (2019) notes that serverless computing is designed to automate infrastructure provisioning and eliminate the burden of server management. According to Ken Corless (Violino, 2019), for information technology (IT) administrators, serverless reduces the "request-response" cycle of ticket-based workloads and allows administrators to focus on higher-level tasks such as infrastructure design or creating more automation. His statement on this model is very interesting from both a server operating environment and a system administration perspective. He argues that

> The real promise of serverless, though, is having fewer people doing some of the mundane tasks of IT, such as software patching and backup.

[…] For IT administrators, serverless reduces the request-response cycle of ticket-based workloads and allows administrators to focus on higher-level tasks such as infrastructure design or creating more automation.

Another approach, called Cloudless computing, has been introduced as well; however, similar to serverless computing, the name is a misnomer. Hopkins (2019) noted that "Cloudless Computing doesn't make clouds go away. It just dissolves the walls between them, resulting in no discernible distinction between public-ness and private-ness".

## Server Operating Environment

A **Server operating environment** (SOE) consists of several components, namely: a) server, b) server operating system, c) serverware, d) applications, e) storage, f) network components. In short, it consists of server-based technologies and features that are used to install, implement, run, and manage application servers. These application servers are used to host most business applications, particularly those characterized as "business critical" or "mission critical". SOE can be installed "in-house" – "on-premises", by following the so-called "brick and mortar" model, within a traditional client-server architecture.

SOE can be implemented within the cloud-client model as well. In both cases, servers installed within the on-premises model or cloud model, are the most important components of such an environment that plays critical role in achieving high-availability and scalability ratios of business applications installed and implemented on these servers. Figures 4.8. and 4.9 demonstrate the roles of servers (SOEs) and system administration in enhancing business continuity and IT capability.

Figure 4.10. depicts the main framework in more detail by showing several types of continuous computing technologies that can be used in achieving continuous computing and business continuity. All these components represent major components of an always-on information system.

Continuous computing technologies are advanced information technologies for reducing downtime and enhancing uptime such as:

a) 64-bit processors, ECC/MEC, crash handling, redundant technologies (RAID/RAIM), fault tolerance, hot swappable components, automatic fail-over, storage-class memory (SCM), NAND flash memory, NVMe (non-volatile memory express), 3PAR Utility Storage technology, Non-Volatile DIMM (NVDIMM) technology, NVDIMM technology, HPE Persistent Memory;

b) application server features such as: VLDB, in-memory databases, crash-handing, application recovery, vendor-specific technologies such as: SAP HANA, Oracle MAA/RAC, and IBM HARD;

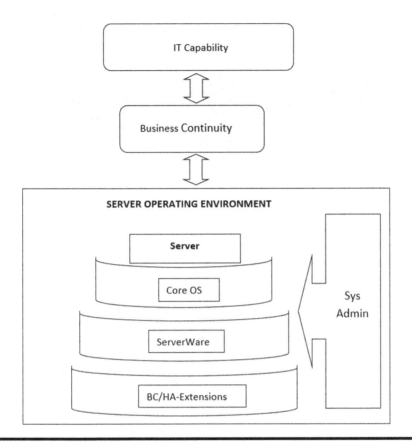

**Figure 4.8** **The role of servers and server operating environments and system administration in enhancing BC and ITC.**

    c) storage technologies such as: RAID, storage arrays, unified storage systems, online backup, shadowing, snapshooting, clustering, and virtualization;

    d) network technologies: SAN, NAS, virtual networks, software defined networking, redundant multipaths, IP multipaths, dual home links and so forth, software-defined WANs, intelligent network management tools, artificial intelligence/machine learning (AI/ML) for network management.

The main attributes of an always-on information system are as follows:

**Availability** is the ability of a server operating environment to provide services with a high percentage of system uptime, for example, 99.999%. The more "nines" in availability/uptime percentage, the higher level of availability is provided. Five or even six nines of server operating platform availability ratio means near-zero downtime and almost 100% business continuity.

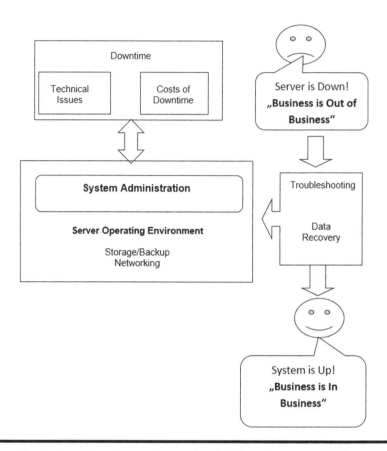

**Figure 4.9   System downtime and the role of SOE and system administrator.**

**Scalability** refers to the ability of a server operating environment to scale up and out by adding processors, memory, and computers.

**Reliability** basically refers to the capability of a server to minimize as much as possible system failures including fault tolerance capabilities. Several redundant components and advanced fault tolerant solutions are used.

A conceptual model has been developed, as shown in Figure 4.11, to illustrate the enablers of an always-on enterprise information system. As can be seen in Figure 4.11, different enablers of such an EIS overlap among each other. Therefore, all the enablers/tools should be integrated to achieve effective integration and management of all kinds of continuous computing technologies.

Continuous computing technologies comprise information technologies that are aimed at enhancing the availability, reliability, and scalability ratios of information infrastructure. The main component of such an infrastructure is an SOE as a

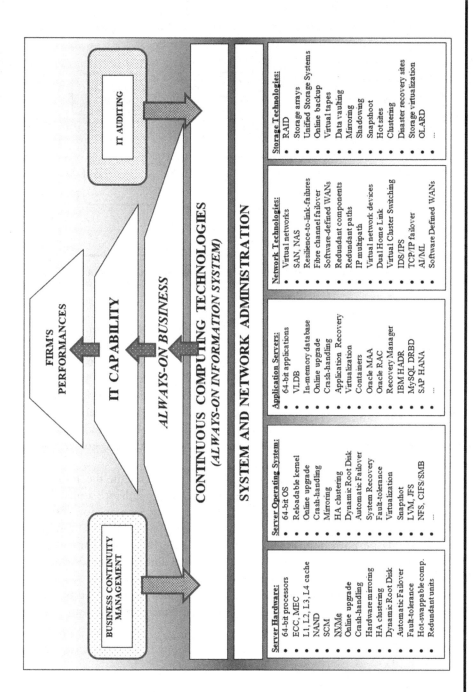

**Figure 4.10  Major enablers of continuous computing and always-on information system.**

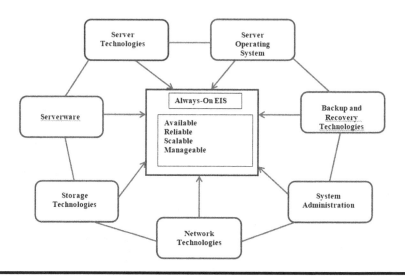

**Figure 4.11 A conceptual model to illustrate the concept and enablers of always-on EIS.**

collection of server, server operating system, application servers, network components, and storage components that are aimed at enhancing the ratios/dimensions of system uptime. Recently introduced technology called hyper-converged infrastructure (HCI) is a combination of these technologies provided by HCI vendors. (Figure 4.12).

Continuous computing technologies are explored here within an integrated IT-platform called the "server operating environment", which is considered a core technology layer of a continuous computing platform. It contains the technologies related to server hardware, server operating system, server applications, storage, and network technologies.

Modern server configurations are designed and configured in the form of integrated hardware platforms and implemented in order to enhance availability ratios. Some of the HA-enabling technologies include: multicore processors, ECC, MEC, L1, L2, L3, L4 cache, NAND, SCM, NVMe, Online upgrade, Crash-handling, Hardware mirroring, HA clustering, Dynamic Root Disk, Automatic Failover, Fault-tolerance, Hot-swappable components, Redundant units, memory double-chip spare, automatic deconfiguration of memory and processors.

Server platforms are run by server operating systems that are enhanced by several additional components (software modules) called serverware solutions. They include the following features:

■ 64-bit OS
■ Reloadable kernel
■ Online upgrade

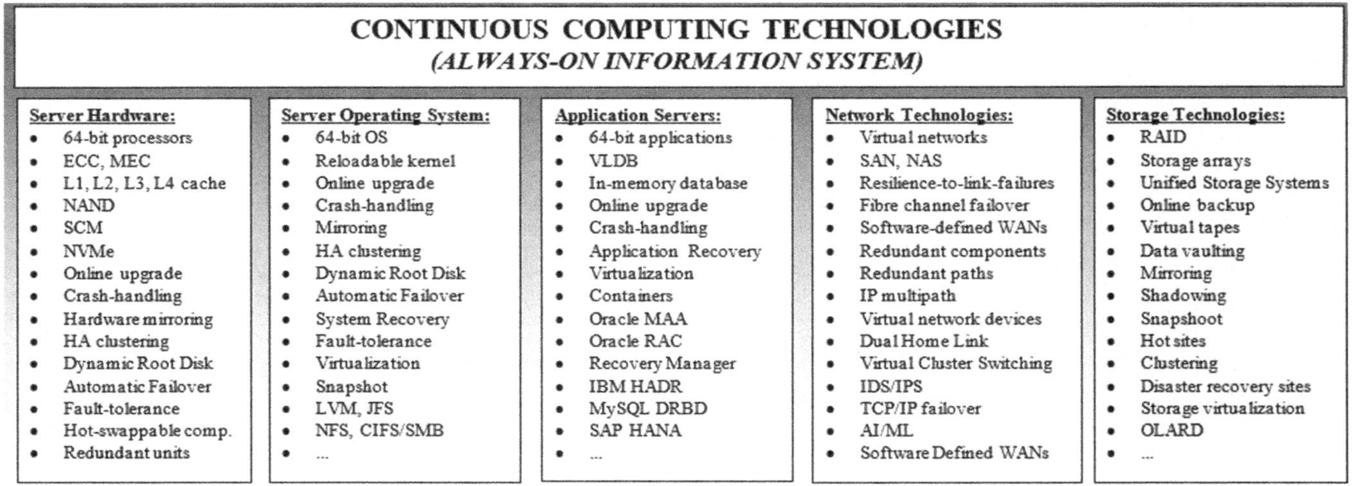

**CONTINUOUS COMPUTING TECHNOLOGIES**
*(ALWAYS-ON INFORMATION SYSTEM)*

**Server Hardware:**
- 64-bit processors
- ECC, MEC
- L1, L2, L3, L4 cache
- NAND
- SCM
- NVMe
- Online upgrade
- Crash-handling
- Hardware mirroring
- HA clustering
- Dynamic Root Disk
- Automatic Failover
- Fault-tolerance
- Hot-swappable comp.
- Redundant units

**Server Operating System:**
- 64-bit OS
- Reloadable kernel
- Online upgrade
- Crash-handling
- Mirroring
- HA clustering
- Dynamic Root Disk
- Automatic Failover
- System Recovery
- Fault-tolerance
- Virtualization
- Snapshot
- LVM, JFS
- NFS, CIFS/SMB
- ...

**Application Servers:**
- 64-bit applications
- VLDB
- In-memory database
- Online upgrade
- Crash-handling
- Application Recovery
- Virtualization
- Containers
- Oracle MAA
- Oracle RAC
- Recovery Manager
- IBM HADR
- MySQL DRBD
- SAP HANA
- ...

**Network Technologies:**
- Virtual networks
- SAN, NAS
- Resilience-to-link-failures
- Fibre channel failover
- Software-defined WANs
- Redundant components
- Redundant paths
- IP multipath
- Virtual network devices
- Dual Home Link
- Virtual Cluster Switching
- IDS/IPS
- TCP/IP failover
- AI/ML
- Software Defined WANs

**Storage Technologies:**
- RAID
- Storage arrays
- Unified Storage Systems
- Online backup
- Virtual tapes
- Data vaulting
- Mirroring
- Shadowing
- Snapshot
- Hot sites
- Clustering
- Disaster recovery sites
- Storage virtualization
- OLARD
- ...

**Figure 4.12** Continuous computing technologies.

- Crash-handling
- Mirroring
- HA clustering
- Dynamic Root Disk
- Automatic Failover
- System Recovery
- Fault-tolerance
- Virtualization
- Snapshot
- LVM, JFS
- NFS, CIFS/SMB
- …

In addition, these server platforms run application servers that are characterized by the following features/components:

- 64-bit applications
- VLDB
- In-memory database
- Online upgrade
- Crash-handling
- Application Recovery
- Virtualization
- Containers
- Oracle MAA
- Oracle RAC
- Recovery Manager
- IBM HADR
- MySQL DRBD
- SAP HANA
- …

Technologies used for data storage, backup, and data recovery include:

- RAID
- Storage arrays
- Unified Storage Systems
- Online backup
- Virtual tapes
- Data vaulting
- Mirroring
- Shadowing
- Snapshoot

- Hot sites
- Clustering
- Disaster recovery sites
- Storage virtualization
- OLARD
- ...

Several network technologies are used in order to minimize network downtime, such as:

- Virtual networks
- SAN, NAS
- Resilience-to-link-failures
- Fibre channel failover
- Software-defined WANs
- Redundant components
- Redundant paths
- IP multipath
- Virtual network devices
- Dual Home Link
- Virtual Cluster Switching
- IDS/IPS
- TCP/IP failover
- AI/ML
- Software Defined WANs
- ...

Moreover, on the DBMS level there exist a number of solutions aimed at enhancing availability ratios. Some examples of business continuity-oriented serverware solutions based on DBMS level include: Microsoft SQL Server's component called "SQL Server 2005 Always On Technologies" with features such as: database mirroring, failover clustering, database snapshots, snapshot isolation, peer-to-peer replication, log shipping, and online operations; Oracle's Maximum Availability Architecture (MAA); IBM's DB2 feature called HADR (high-availability, disaster-recovery); MySQL's Master/Slave Replication and Distributed Block device (DRBD) and MySQL Cluster.

## Enterprise Servers

From a historical perspective, several categories of computer systems that are used in business computing can be identified as follows:

a) mainframes
b) minicomputers

c) workstations
d) personal computers
e) enterprise servers
f) desktop computers
g) portable computers
h) mobile computing devices.

Supercomputers as a special class of computers are not listed here as they are mainly used for scientific purposes, but not in business computing.

Today, the mainframes and minicomputers from the sixties and seventies (e.g., IBM s360/390 and Digital VAX) have mainly been replaced by "enterprise servers". Unlike the term "mainframe", which is still used in some vendors' programs (e.g., IBM z13), the term "minicomputer" is not used anymore. However, even if a mainframe computer is used, it again plays the role of server in the client-server architecture, be it on-premises or cloud-based.

Tozzi (2018) revealed that:

■ 71 percent of Fortune 500 companies use mainframes.
■ Mainframes handle 87 percent of all credit card transactions.
■ 92 of the world's top 100 banks have continued to use mainframes.

Figure 4.13 shows the old-style IBM mainframe from the 1960s, while Figure 4.14 shows the Digital VAX minicomputer from the 1970s:

All computers that are in use in business computing today can be categorized into the following classes:

■ Enterprise Servers or simply "servers"
■ Workstations

**Figure 4.13   IBM mainframe S360. Wikipedia, https://en.wikipedia.org/wiki/ IBM_System/360.**

**Figure 4.14    Digital VAX – 11. Wikipedia, https://en.wikipedia.org/wiki/VAX-11.**

- Personal Computers
- Portable computing devices
- Mobile computing devices.

Modern server platforms consist of several components such as server hardware, server operating system, serverware, and application servers. They are expected to provide an SOE that must meet much more rigorous requirements than a standard desktop operating system can provide. Such platforms are of special interest for businesses that require "always-on" or "online-all-the-time" computing environments. Therefore, server and server operating systems that are characterized by "zero downtime" or "100 percent uptime" are very important for such businesses. However, despite all technology improvements in the last two decades, achieving "zero downtime" or "100% uptime" is still difficult; therefore, so-called "near-it" solutions are acceptable. Depending on the industry (financials, telecommunications, airlines, etc.), several models of the uptime percentage are seen in the real business world, for example, six-nines (99.9999%), five-nines, four-nines, and so on. Modern business admits that high-availability ratios are possible and desirable solutions; however, these are costly solutions. Figure 4.15 shows IBM System z as an example of a mainframe computer.

Server configurations are expected to be reliable, available, and scalable in the way that server-based applications installed on application servers, data servers, e-mail servers, Web servers, operate with high reliability-availability-scalability ratios. In addition, they provide several types of so-called serverware services such as web-hosting services, directory services, security services, remote access capabilities, and so on.

**Figure 4.15  Examples of today's mainframes – IBM System z. https://en.wikipedia.org/wiki/Mainframe_computer.**

How is a server different from a standard personal computer?

A personal computer or desktop computer is used to process, store, and disseminate data for personal purposes. It can be used as a stand-alone (desktop or portable) device and as a client device within a client-server information architecture. These are multitasking and single-user operating platforms run by desktop operating systems. They are used to access server-based applications and run client/desktop applications such as Microsoft Office and other personal productivity tools.

On the other side, enterprise servers run server-based applications that need to be accessed from dozens, hundreds, thousands, hundreds of thousands, even several millions of end users. From a business continuity perspective, when a personal computer (stand-alone or client computer) goes down for any reason, this affects only one user. However, when a server shuts down, this affects all end users that are connected to that server. Therefore, server configurations are expected to be available on a continuous basis, and be reliable and scalable enough. In short, they must be:

a) much faster with regard to data processing;
b) much more reliable, scalable, and available than a PC;
c) much more secure than a PC;
d) able to run business-critical applications.

In addition, servers should have the following features:

a) Fully integrated and high-availability oriented system architecture: 64-bit processor, symmetrical multiprocessing, and shared-memory architecture, very large memory, support for non-uniform memory access (NUMA architecture), built-in resilience to failures, interconnect architecture, networking architecture, increased levels of L1, L2, L3 cache memory, support for error correcting code (ECC) that can repair errors resulting from a corrupted bit.

b) A server operating system designed for symmetrical multiprocessing, hardware- and software-based fault tolerance, virtualization and clustering, kernel-level cache and application pools, system and operational robustness, workload management, support for online reconfiguration.

c) Powerful system administration, including online management, remote system administration and management, and online and remote backup.

d) Support for database management system that includes VLDB (very large database) support capabilities.

e) Support for middleware products and enterprise application integration.

An **enterprise server**, by definition, is a computer system that runs core IT operations of the whole enterprise or its subsystem within a client-server platform (be it with a so-called on-premises model or a "cloud-based model") Most enterprise-wide business applications installed on enterprise servers are called "business-critical" or "mission-critical" applications. Most widely used enterprise servers today are:

a) mainframe servers,
b) proprietary servers,
c) commercial UNIX-based servers,
d) free UNIX-based servers
e) Linux-based servers
f) Intel/AMD processors-based servers, and
g) Apple Macintosh servers.

Some examples of proprietary servers are shown in Figures 4.16–4.18.

Enterprise Servers can be purchased, installed, configured, implemented, and used as:

a) application servers,
b) database servers,
c) print servers,

    d) e-mail servers,
    e) web servers,
    f) e-business servers, and
    g) firewall servers.

**Figure 4.16    Alpha Server (HP/Compaq/DEC).**

**Figure 4.17    IBM AS 400.**

**Figure 4.18 Sun-Oracle server.**

All business applications can be classified according to business "criticality":

a) Front-end server applications, such as: application servers, e-commerce servers, firewall servers, portal servers.

b) Mid-tier servers: ERP, SCM, CRM applications.

c) Data-tier servers: large database servers, enterprise-wide ERP systems, enterprise-wide business intelligence solutions, and so on.

Most frequently used server configurations today are as follows:

■ Mainframe servers such as IBM z servers.

■ Commercial UNIX-based servers – various RISC-based platforms developed by IT vendors such as IBM, HP, and Sun (Oracle) running commercial versions of a UNIX operating system: IBM-AIX, HP-HP-UX, and Oracle Solaris.

■ Free UNIX servers running a FreeBSD operating system.

■ Linux-based servers – various configurations running Linux distributions (Red Hat, SUSE Linux, Debian, Mandrake, etc.).

■ Proprietary server platforms – servers that run proprietary operating systems developed for proprietary processors (e.g., HP's OpenVMS-based servers).

■ Intel/AMD processor-based servers using Intel's or AMD's server processor-based configurations. These servers are usually run by a Windows Server or Linux operating system.

■ Apple Macintosh servers running the macOS Server operating system.

Business requirements toward a specific server configuration are mainly bound to overall performances of the server configuration.

Typical server configurations include several dozens, hundreds, even thousands of gigabytes of RAM and several hundreds of TB in external memory space. Within this class, three subclasses can be identified:

a) high-end servers
b) mid-range servers
c) entry-level, workgroup, departmental or small business servers

High-end servers (mainframe servers, some proprietary systems, and UNIX-based servers) are characterized by

a) very high processing speed;
b) very high levels of reliability, scalability, and availability;
c) support for several thousand concurrent users;
d) VLM and VLDB support (Very Large Memory, Very Large Data Base);
e) multi-processor and multi-node support; and
f) powerful "fault-tolerance" capabilities.

In addition, servers can be classified according to a number of processors/nodes/cabinets installed:

a) single-processor
b) multi-processor/single-node
c) multi-processor and multi-node.

Servers can be made as multi-node, cabinet, and multi-cabinet configurations.

**Blade servers**, or server blades, are new server configurations designed a couple of years ago based on the concept of sharing some hardware resources (devices). Blade servers include more computer power within a smaller space than traditional server configurations. This feature has made blade servers a more attractive option when trying to integrate server applications, consolidate servers, balance data processing workload and its optimization, and cut costs (see Figure 4.19).

## *Server Configurations of Major Server Vendors*

Major server vendors such as IBM, HP, Oracle, and Dell, offer several models of server configurations according to business requirements.

Models are classified according to the following:

a) business requirements
b) operating system platform
c) processor technology

**Figure 4.19   HP Proliant blade enclosure (full of blades), with two 3U UPS units below. http://en.wikipedia.org/wiki/Blade_server.**

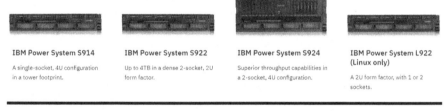

| IBM Power System S914 | IBM Power System S922 | IBM Power System S924 | IBM Power System L922 (Linux only) |
|---|---|---|---|
| A single-socket, 4U configuration in a tower footprint. | Up to 4TB in a dense 2-socket, 2U form factor. | Superior throughput capabilities in a 2-socket, 4U configuration. | A 2U form factor, with 1 or 2 sockets. |

**Figure 4.20   IBM small servers. www.ibm.com/it-infrastructure/servers/ small-enterprise.**

For instance, **IBM** (www.ibm.com) has a number of server configurations with regard to

a) business needs (high-end, mid-range, entry-level servers);
b) processor (proprietary POWER, Intel processors, AMD processors); and
c) operating system (z/OS, AIX, Linux, Windows Server).

Today, IBM offers the following server configurations with regard to the operating system that they use (Figure 4.20):

a) Small Enterprise Servers for AIX and Linux (POWER9-based Power Systems)
b) Large Enterprise Servers (Figure 4.21)
c) IBM Mainframes (Figure 4.22)

**Hewlett-Packard** (www.hpe.com) offers several models of servers (Figure 4.23 and Figure 4.24).

IBM z14 dual frame, side view | IBM z14 dual frame, front view | IBM z14 single frame, front view | IBM z14 single frame, side view

**Figure 4.21    IBM large enterprise servers. www.ibm.com/us-en/marketplace/z14.**

IBM z14                          IBM z13                          IBM z13s

**Figure 4.22    IBM mainframes. www.ibm.com/it-infrastructure/servers/ mainframes.**

Rack servers          Tower servers          HPE Synergy          Hyperconverged Systems          Converged Systems          Blade Servers and Systems

**Figure 4.23    HP servers. www.hpe.com/emea_europe/en/servers.html.**

## HPE mission-critical server portfolio

HPE Superdome Flex          HPE Integrity Superdome X          HPE Integrity MC990 X          HPE Solutions for SAP HANA

**Figure 4.24    HP mission critical servers www.hpe.com/emea_europe/en/ servers/mission-critical.html.**

HP's portfolio of server operating systems includes the following:

a) HP-UX 11i
b) OpenVMS
c) NonStop
d) Tru64 UNIX
e) Windows Server
f) Linux

**Oracle** (www.oracle.com) has several server configurations that operate Sun SPARC and UltraSPARC processors, and run the Solaris or Linux operating system.

**Dell** (www.dell.com) has a line of servers, including several models such as: rack servers, blade servers, tower servers, and rack infrastructure-based servers.

**Apple** has its own line of server products based on the macOS server operating system.

In addition to their proprietary processors, almost all server vendors offer servers based on Intel (i3, i5, i7, i9, Xeon E7, Itanium) and/or AMD processors (Ryzen, Ryzen Threadripper, Athlon, for desktops/laptops and EPYC, Opteron for server configurations). Intel announced the end of life for the Itanium processor line in January 2019. These servers in most cases run the Windows Server or Linux operating system; however, some other operating systems can be installed as well (e.g., Novell NetWare, Sun Solaris).

PC-like servers from Intel and AMD can also be configured with regard to the following classifications:

a) Enterprise servers
b) Small business servers
c) Workgroup servers
d) Departmental servers
e) Entry level

All these servers can be configured in a way that they include one, two, or more processors. Intel and AMD are two main players in this market.

## Choosing A Server for Business Continuance

Server selection is an activity that has to provide answers to a number of questions depending on the purpose of the server. Purchaing a server that will be used for a web server or an e-mail server is not a difficult issue. However, when selecting a server for mission-critical applications, a systems approach should be used. The process starts with the identification of objectives (Why do we need servers? What is the purpose of servers?). Then follows an identification of the main components and resources of the server platform as well as the components of an SOE.

What follows is a list of questions that have to be considered (answered) from a business continuity perspective.

1. Number of users. How many employees do we have? What will be the number of users (named users)? How many concurrent users?
2. Application portfolio. What kind of applications will be implemented?
3. Type of infrastructure: on-premises or cloud-based?
4. Server type. What type of server (file, e-mail, print, Web, e-commerce, etc.)?
5. Number of servers. How many servers do we need? Are we going to opt for tower servers or blade/rack mount servers?
6. Availability requirement. Will the server be used for mission-critical applications? Do we need an option of guaranteed uptime in the service-level agreement?
7. Scalability requirement. What kind of data traffic do we expect; in the beginning and later? Do we need a scalable server?
8. Reliability and redundancy. Do we need redundant servers and/or redundant server locations?
9. High-performance computing requirements. How fast data processing do we need? What kind of processors? How many processors?
10. Memory requirements (RAM). How much memory we need (RAM)? Do we need fault-tolerant RAM technology? Should we opt for in-memory database technology?
11. Memory requirements (external). How much external memory space we need? What kind of HD controller (SCSI, SATA, etc.)? Which RAID system, network attached storage, storage area networks?
12. Advanced technologies for business continuity. Do we need a system that supports hot-swappable technology, mirroring technology, snapshot technology, virtualization?
13. Server operating system. Which server operating system will be used? Will it be based on one of the Linux flavors, Windows server-based, UNIX-based, or proprietary OS?
14. Backup. What kind of backup technology?
15. Data recovery. Identify RPO and RTO.
16. What kind of security system will be implemented?
17. Network infrastructure – LAN, WAN. How many Ethernet cards on the server do we need?
18. System management; system administration. Do we have a system administrator for selected server OS platform?
19. SOS support. What industry support exists for selected operating systems?
20. What is the viability of the server and server OS vendor?

Each of these questions can be defined in more detail. For instance, when server operating system selection is considered, the following dilemmas are present:

a) Commercial or open-source OS platform
b) Windows Server or Unix
c) Windows Server or Linux
d) Unix versus Linux
e) If Unix, which Unix: commercial or free-open source (e.g., FreeBSD); if commercial, which vendor (HPE, IBM, Oracle, Dell, etc.)
f) If Linux, which Linux (Red Hat, SUSE, Debian, etc.)
g) If a multi-platform approach is selected, which integration platform will be used (SAMBA, etc.).

## Conclusions

Servers and server operating systems are offered today as integrated server operating environments that include not only standard server operating system features but also additional components called serverware. These components are aimed at enhancing the capabilities in terms of availability, reliability, and scalability of application servers. Several platforms are analyzed in this chapter in order to present a framework for selecting the platform from a business continuity perspective.

## Discussion Questions

1. Define the major client-server infrastructure layers and components.
2. Identify the main critical points within the client-server architectures with regard to business continuity.
3. Think about a company you know very well. What would be a model of client-server architecture for that company?
4. Explain the role of server operating systems within the client-server architecture.
5. How can server operating platforms be used strategically?
6. Describe the major continuous computing drivers of the server operating platform
7. How can server operating platforms be used strategically?
8. What is the strategic advantage (if any) of those companies that opted for an open source platform?
9. Why are 64-bit technology and VLM/VLDB technologies important from a business continuity perspective?
10. Make an assessment of DBMS-based business continuity-oriented solutions of major DBMS vendors.

# References

The 451 Research Report. (2019). The Holistic Approach to Multicloud for Digital Operations, Retrieved from www.cio.com/playlist/the-cloud-innovators/collection/cloud-strategy-and-migration/article/the-holistic-approach-to-multicloud-for-digital-operations

Alsultanny, Y.A. (2014). Assessment of e-government weak points to enhance computer network security, *International Journal of Information Science, 4*(1), 13–20.

Bajgoric, N. (2010), Server Operating Environment for BusinessContinuance: Framework for Selection, *Int. J. Business Continuity and Risk Management, 1*, (4), 317–338.

Balabko, P., Wegmann, A. (2006). Systemic classification of concern-based design methods in the context of enterprise architecture, *Information Systems Frontiers, 8*, 115–131.

Bednarz, A. (2018). Hyperconverged Infrastructure Gets Its Own Gartner Magic Quadrant, *Network World*, March 16. Retrieved from www.networkworld.com/article/3263646/hyperconverged-infrastructure-gets-its-own-gartner-magic-quadrant.html

Bednarz, A. (2019a). What Is Composable Infrastructure? Retrieved from www.network world.com/article/3266106/what-is-composable-infrastructure.html

Bednarz, A. (2019b). What Is Hyperconvergence?, *Network World*, February 2. Retrieved from www.networkworld.com/article/3207567/what-is-hyperconvergence.html

Goethals, F.G., Snoeck, M., Lemahieu, W., Vandenbulcke, J. (2006). Management and enterprise architecture click: The FAD(E)E framework, *Information Systems Frontiers, 8*, 67–79.

Hopkins, C. (2019). The Cloud Goes "Cloudless", Retrieved from www.hpe.com/us/en/insights/articles/cloudless-1906.html

Jonkers, H., Lankhorst, M.M., Doest, H.W.L., Arbab, F., Bosma, H., Wieringa, R.J. (2006). Enterprise architecture: Management tool and blueprint for the organization, *Information Systems Frontiers, 8*, 63–66.

Kim, J., Lee, J., Han, K., Lee, M. (2002). Businesses as buildings: Metrics for the architectural quality of internet businesses, *Information Systems Research, 13*(3), 239–254.

Scott, D.L. (2018). *Composable Infrastructure for Dummies*, HPE Special Edition, John Wiley & Sons.

Tozzi, C. (2018). Mainframe Statistics That May Surprise You. Retrieved from https://blog.syncsort.com/2018/06/mainframe/9-mainframe-statistics/

Turban, E., Rainer, R.K., Potter, R. (2005). *Introduction to Information Technology*, Wiley.

Versteeg, G., Bouwman, H. (2006). Business architecture: A new paradigm to relate business strategy to ICT, *Information Systems Frontiers, 8*, 91–102.

Violino, B. (2019). How and Where to Use Serverless Computing. Retrieved from www.idginsiderpro.com/article/3390116/how-and-where-to-use-serverless-computing.html

WEEAM White Paper. (2016). IT Guide to Build Converged and Hyper-Converged Infrastructure. Retrieved from www.veeam.com/wp-building-converged-infrastructure.html

# Chapter 5

# System Administration and Business Continuity

## Background

Server operating systems that are used to run server configurations are implemented today mainly as "integrated server operating environments", the environments that include not only a core server operating system such as UNIX, Linux, or Windows Server, but several server applications and extensions for fault tolerance, disaster tolerance/recovery and other high-availability/reliability/scalability features as well. In addition, newly introduced hyperconverged infrastructure solutions encompass storage and networking solutions.

In previous chapters, we mentioned so-called downtime points at which an application server or network may go down and make application/s and users go offline. These situations in modern e-business produce negative financial effects. Depending on the type of business and the level of mission/business criticality of applications, the duration of downtime means different numbers in downtime costs for different industries.

From system management/system administration and network management/ network administration perspectives, well-educated, skilled, and experienced system or network administrators are capable of resolving the problems that occur on servers, server operating systems and networks, in cases of server shutdown, operating system crash, and network disconnectivity. By using numerous system administration tasks, operations, and troubleshooting techniques, they can significantly reduce recovery time (system recovery time) from days to hours, or from hours to minutes (RTO – Recovery Time Objective and RPO – Recovery Point Objective).

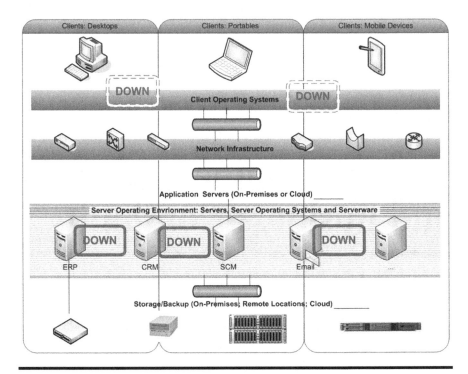

**Figure 5.1   Operating systems in IS infrastructure – downtime points: layers.**

System administration tasks and operations are essential in ensuring server availability as many issues on a server and server operating system may cause server unavailability. If those issues are resolved quickly by system administrators, downtime is shorter, the RTO is shorter, and consequently the negative effects of system unavailability are minimized. The same applies for network administration and resolving the issues related to Internet/network disconnections caused by, for instance, network adapter failures, broken network configuration files and/or processes, DNS configuration errors, physical disconnections in cabling systems, and so on.

Business-critical applications such as messaging systems, ERP, CRM, SCM, BI, are implemented on enterprise servers that are run by server operating systems (Figure 5.1). Therefore, the availability, reliability, and scalability of these systems are of extreme importance for modern organizations (Figure 5.2).

System administration skills are crucial in modern business computing as skilled system administrators are able to fix the crashes and other issues related to servers and server operating systems and consequently minimize downtime. Resolving the hardware and systems software issues on enterprise servers in terms of several troubleshooting operations is very important in reducing downtime and system recovery time. System

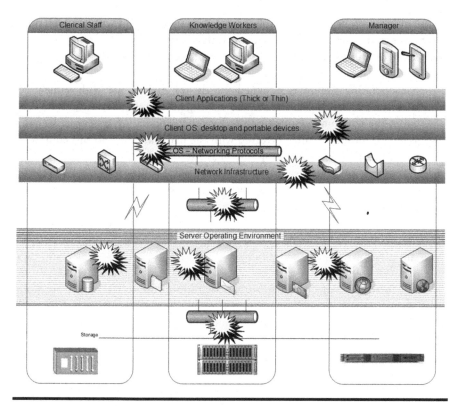

**Figure 5.2** **Operating systems in IS infrastructure – downtime points: business functions.**

administrators play an important role in keeping application servers up and running, and ensuring troubleshooting solutions when the system goes down. IDC (2009) noted that by adopting industry best practices and compliance regulations (e.g., ITIL, CobiT), companies can lower annual downtime by up to 85%.

## Operating Systems in E-Business Era: The Three Perspectives

Tanenbaum (2009) considered operating systems from their two basically unrelated functions: providing application programmers a clean abstract set of resources instead of the messy hardware ones and managing these hardware resources. According to this approach, operating systems are seen as: a) an extended machine, and b) a resource manager. Silberschatz et al. (2007) compared an operating system to a government in the way that the operating system, like a government, performs no useful function by itself. It simply provides an environment within which other programs can do useful work. They defined the operating system from a) user and b) system (computer) perspectives. In the case of the user's view,

> the operating system is designed mostly for ease of use with some attention paid to performance and none paid to resource utilization. From the computer system's point of view, the operating system is the program most intimately involved with the hardware. [...] In this context, we can view an operating system as a resource allocator.

These are two basic views of operating systems as they are studied in most computer science and computer engineering programs.

An attempt is made in (Bajgoric, 2008) to identify a "business perspective" of operating systems. The main reasons for adding the third view – a business perspective – are as follows:

a) All three types of operating systems that are in use today (server operating systems, desktop operating systems, mobile operating systems) have their impacts on the costs of business computing in a way that businesses select from either commercial or open-source versions of OSs.

b) Modern applications are installed on enterprise servers (on-premises or cloud-based) that are operated by server operating systems. So-called business-critical applications are of extreme importance for modern businesses, particularly for those operating on a continuous or "follow-the-sun" basis.

c) If, for any reason, a server operating system crashes and mission-critical data or applications become unavailable for some time, this causes negative financial effects for a business.

The business perspective of server operating systems contains a set of attributes that mainly relate to their availability, reliability, and scalability, although this class of operating systems has some other business dimensions as well. These are license costs, maintenance costs, update/upgrade costs, and support costs. Unlike desktop operating systems and mobile operating systems that are used on client devices, where the user's perspective (viewpoint) is the most important dimension with regard to how user-friendly operating systems are, server operating systems are less considered from the user's perspective and much more from a business point of view. In other words, the user-friendliness of an operating system (ease of use) is much more important on desktop computers and portable-mobile devices than on server systems. However, server operating systems are expected to have a much stronger "business dimension" with a number of features that relate to high-availability, reliability, and scalability ratios, in other words, continuous computing (see Figure 5.3 and Figure 5.4). The computer's view is important for all computer platforms, with regard to processing speed and computer performances in general; however, the

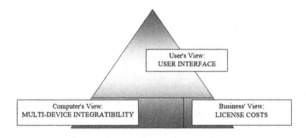

**Figure 5.3  OS views triangle – case of desktop and portable operating systems.**

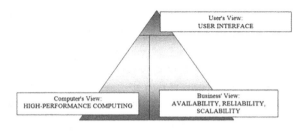

**Figure 5.4  OS views triangle – case of server operating system.**

computer's view is of critical importance on server platforms as well. It has a strong relation to the business view of server operating systems, as hardware configuration strongly impacts the overall server's performances.

The most prevalent importance of the business perspective in the case of server operating systems (Figure 5.4) can be identified as follows:

a) Servers are used for storing server-based applications, particularly mission-critical applications. The availability and scalability of these applications are determined by RAS features of both server hardware and server OS.

b) They have a number of services set on the "on" mode (open, active) after installation, which opens the door for possible attacks that may cause system and application unavailability.

c) They host several configuration files that can be broken and/or misused (e.g., /etc/passwd file, /etc/hosts file, allow/deny access files on Unix/Linux), which again may result in system/application unavailability.

The most important dimension is that of downtime, which is by definition a state of a computer when it is "out of use" or doesn't provide services to clients (Figure 5.5.). Even though client computers (desktop and portables) may also experience "system is down" situations, server downtime is of much more importance in modern business (Figure 5.6).

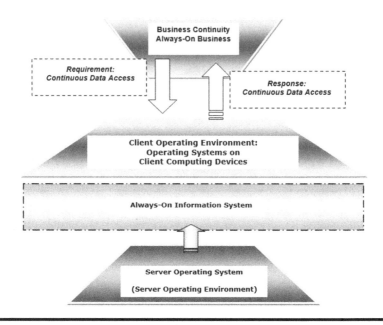

**Figure 5.5** SOE (server operating environment) and COE (client operating environment).

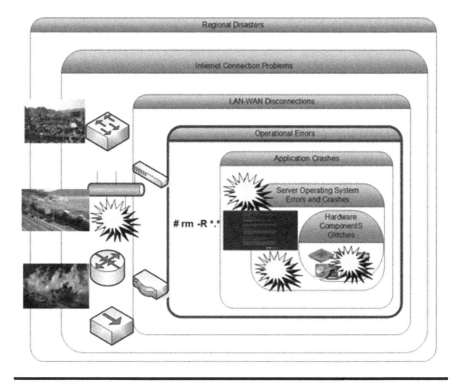

**Figure 5.6** Operating systems in IS infrastructure: the downtime points.

As already indicated in Chapter 2, downtime has two dimensions: technical and cost (Figure 5.7).

Vendors of servers and server operating systems provide integrated solutions for fault tolerance/disaster tolerance, hardware mirroring, hot spared discs, high-availability storage systems, clustering, and redundant units. They are expected to enhance their OS platforms in order to support embedded high-availability and fault tolerant hardware capabilities. Figure 5.8 demonstrates a holistic perspective of the server operating system and system administration with regard to availability, business continuity, and IT capability.

Conway et al. (2019) noted that in the modern world, system management requirements fall into the following main categories:

a) Heterogeneous workloads (floating point-based simulation, integer-based analytics)
b) The movement from synchronous applications to asynchronous workflows
c) Rapid growth in average system sizes and component counts
d) Heterogeneous processing elements (CPUs, coprocessors/accelerators)
e) Heterogeneous environments (on-premise data centers, public/private/hybrid clouds)
f) Reliability/resiliency at scale
g) Power efficiency and power awareness ("power steering")
h) Cyber security

## Server Operating Environment for Continuous Computing: Major Enablers

The operating environment that facilitates modern business computing is a server operating environment which encompasses several server technologies and features that are necessary for efficient and effective business-critical applications (Figure 5.9). A server operating system represents a core component of a server operating environment, which includes server, server operating system, data storage, and networking technologies. This class of operating systems, with their performances related to availability, reliability, and scalability, is crucial for modern businesses as most of them operate in an e-business environment.

In addition to business applications, servers host several operating system-related critical configuration files that can be misused, corrupted, deleted, or changed, such as: /etc/passwd, /etc/hosts, allow/deny access files on Unix/Linux. Moreover, the servers usually have a number of services set to "on" mode (open, active) after its initial installation, which opens the door for possible attacks. Figures 5.10 and 5.11 demonstrate the roles of server, server operating system, server operating

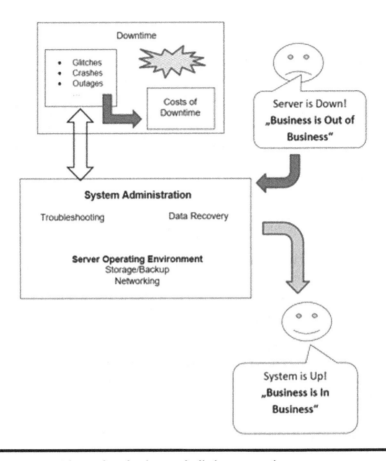

**Figure 5.7   SOS in modern business – holistic perspective.**

environment, and system administration in a modern client-server or cloud-server architecture.

An implementation framework to illustrate major SOS continuous computing technologies in the form of enablers of continuous computing is shown in Figure 5.12.

The continuous computing technologies are explored here within an integrated IT platform called a "server operating environment", which is identified as a core technology layer of a continuous computing platform for business continuity. It contains the technologies related to server hardware, server operating system, server applications, and, in a broader sense, storage and network technologies. The managerial aspect is represented through system and network administration activities and business continuity management. System and network administration represents a set of operations on the server, server operating system, and network, including the role of system and network administrators in ensuring business continuity.

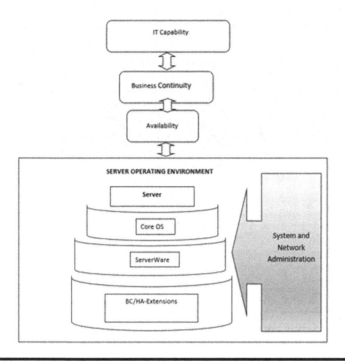

**Figure 5.8** SOS and system administration in modern business – holistic perspective.

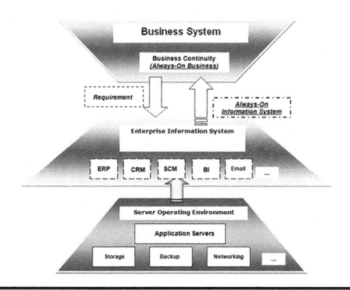

**Figure 5.9** A conceptual model to illustrate the role of server operating environment in enterprise information systems.

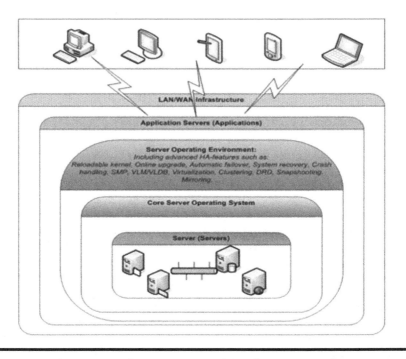

**Figure 5.10    Server operating system: core OS and server operating environment.**

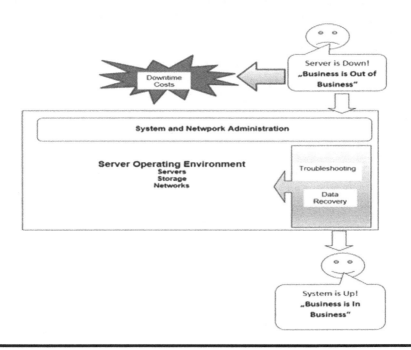

**Figure 5.11    Server – server operating environment – system administration – downtime.**

Modern server configurations are designed and configured in the form of integrated hardware platforms and implemented in order to enhance availability ratios. Some of the HA-enabling technologies include: 64-bit processors, multicore processors, L1/L2/L3/L4 cache, ECC, MEC, memory double-chip spare, automatic deconFigureuration of memory and processors, hot-swappable components, fault-tolerance, and redundant units. Server platforms are run by server operating systems that are expected to provide high ratios in terms of availability, reliability, and scalability, by supporting the following features: automatic failover, system recovery, reloadable kernel, online upgrade, crash handling, SMP, VLM/VLDB, virtualization, and the like. Modern server operating systems provide several additional components (software modules) called serverware solutions, in addition to the core operating platform. Technologies used for data storage, backup, and data recovery play a crucial role in data management in the form of a secondary layer, in addition to primary data storage (hard disk). The technologies that are used include both local storage and backup technologies such as RAID, tape, virtual tape, D2D, DAS, and off-site technologies (online backup, data vaulting, mirroring, shadowing, snapshoot, hot sites, clustering, disaster recovery sites, storage virtualization). Moreover, on the DBMS level there exist a number of solutions aimed at enhancing availability ratios such as: database mirroring, failover clustering, database snapshots, snapshot isolation, peer-to-peer replication, log shipping, and online operations. Several advanced network technologies are used in order to minimize network downtime, such as: resilience-to-link-failures, network virtualization, virtual application networks, fibre channel failover, software defined networking, redundant components, redundant paths, IP multipathing, virtual network devices, Dual Home Link, Ethernet Ring protection, Bi-directional forwarding detection, Virtual Cluster Switching, Firewall, IDS/IPS, and Malware/SPAM filtering. In addition to standard continuous computing technologies, IT vendors have developed new technologies such as snapshoot mirroring, data vaulting, virtual tape backup, online backup, and so on.

Table 5.1 illustrates some server issues or messages that reflect the problems that may occur on enterprise servers and typical troubleshooting-like activities performed by system administrators to resolve them. These problems/issues are listed from a business continuity perspective, meaning that most of them may cause some sort of unavailability of data, application, or the whole application server. That means system downtime and consequently lost customers, lost prospective customers, unavailable data for decisions, in short, some sort of financial losses.

Sometimes servers may go down due to mistakes and/or fault system operations done by system administrators. Some of them are listed below:

a) Setting too simple passwords that are easy to compromise.
b) Setting too complex passwords that lead end users to write down their passwords.

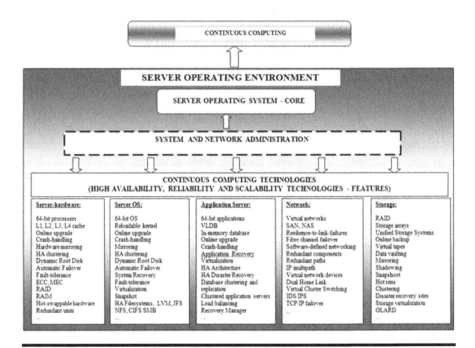

**Figure 5.12  Server operating environment: enablers of continuous computing.**

c) Sometimes strong passwords (too complex) are even worse than weak passwords if found on a piece of paper. However, weak passwords can be broken from anywhere.

d) Password reset policies.

e) Not implementing additional protection of /etc/passwd files on Unix/Linux server.

f) Settings on network protocols (TCP/IP, NetBIOS, IPX/SPX, WINS, ...).

g) DNS settings (Domain Name Server).

h) Using non-standard ports.

i) Bypassing firewall.

j) Problems with /etc/hosts file.

k) Expiration of security certificates.

System administrators ("Super Users" or "Root Account/Users") have the highest administrative privileges, which include complete and unchecked data access rights. These IT professionals can do whatever they want to, with regard to all data, all applications installed, and all users. Their unlimited privileges are often considered the biggest internal threats. Therefore, these privileges must be implemented in accordance with compliance regulations such as FDCC, Sarbanes–Oxley, PCI,

**Table 5.1  System Administration: Typical Problems and Sys-Admin Actions**

| Problems/Issues/Messages: | Sys-Admin's Action: |
| --- | --- |
| Application server is down | Checking hardware and server operating system |
| Application server unreachable | Checking network card/settings on server |
| Network is down/unreachable | Checking connections/settings on LAN/WAN |
| Broken configuration file and server malfunctioning | Recovering the file |
| Broken process and server malfunctioning | Restarting the process |
| Processes causing malfunctioning and/or slowdown | Killing/Ending processes |
| Users causing system/network slowdown | Logging out/disconnecting users |
| Network disconnection | Diagnosing and resolving network issues |
| Patch/Update/Upgrade issues | OS-patching/update/upgrade w/o shutdown |
| Application loads | Managing server application loads |
| Failure of primary server | Migrating applications to secondary server |
| Storage Failure | Replacing storage device and data recovery |
| Slow server (Server is slowing down) | Monitor server status, processes and user activities |
| Server hangs or freezes | Configuration error, Hardware issue, System overload, ... |
| ... | |

HIPAA, and GLBA. Several solutions such as Fine-Grained Privileges and Role-based Access Control can be applied, depending on the server operating platform. This "super-user account" is considered critical in modern business as, for instance, a disgruntled system administrator can destroy all data, as can be seen from the story cited by Tynan (2013):

> All the data files were gone, the database was gone, and the ERP software was nowhere to be found. It turned out a disgruntled IT contractor had enacted revenge by wiping the garment maker's servers. [...] It was a $10 or $12 million company, and they probably lost $2 million as a result of this.

According to IDC's White Paper (2009), by adopting industry best practices compliance regulations (e.g., ITIL, CobiT), companies can lower annual downtime by up to 85%. IDC (2014) stated that "The management and administration cost associated with server environments has grown to eclipse costs in other categories. Many customers report that the personnel cost to maintain their server installed base consumes the majority of their IT budgets".

Modern server configurations are based on the following three technologies that are critical for continuous computing and consequently for always-on business:

a) Fault tolerant RAM – RAM memory technologies such ECC (Error Correcting Code).
b) Redundancy – redundant technologies; the servers have redundancy built in (redundant technology components) in order to overcome so called single points of failure.
c) Hot-swap technology – the components are hot-swappable; in case of failure, they can be swapped without shutting down the servers.

With regard to storage and backup, in addition to traditional disk-based storage and tape-based backup, modern solutions include storage area networks, network attached storage, storage based snapshots, mirroring (onsite – offsite), replication (onsite and offsite), and archiving (onsite, offsite, cloud-based).

Taken together in the form of integrated server operating environments, modern servers and server operating systems provide several high-availability–oriented features. Some of them are listed below:

- Hardware mirroring
- Software mirroring
- Journalized File System for high reliability and fast recovery
- JFS snapshot technology
- System recovery image
- LVM, VxVM, LVM/Mirrordisk, LVM Snapshots, Online JFS
- Hot spared disk
- Dynamic Root Disk (DRD)
- Clustering technologies
- SSHA (Single System High Availability) Online-Deletion of NICs
- Rules-based failover
- Node recovery with Relax and Recov
- NIC failover
- Server Message Block (SMB) 3.0
- Transparent Failover and Multichannel features
- Failover Clustering
- Hybrid physical and virtual high-availability clusters
- Clustered Logical Volume Manager

- Cluster Failover Manager
- Cluster-aware file system and volume management
- High-availability clustering
- Flexible, policy-driven clustering and continuous data replication
- Storage-based fencing that eliminates single point failure.
- Support for DRBD (Distributed Replicated Block Device)
- Database Mirroring
- Online Corruption Repairs
- NUMA-aware scalability
- Rolling upgrade capabilities
- Failback configuration
- Live patching
- Dynamically assigning and reassigning server storage
- Support for Fibre Channel and iSCSI storage area networks
- Support for shared disk systems
- Cluster-aware file systems
- Network load balancing
- Support for clustered SAMBA

# Business Continuity-Oriented System Administration Features of the Main SOS Platforms

Table 5.2 lists key vendors (key players) in the operating systems arena. In the section that follows the table, we summarize five server OS products: HP's HP-UX, IBM's AIX, Microsoft's Windows Server, Oracle's Solaris, and SUSE Linux with regard to their main OS-features and advanced BC/HA-features.

Table 5.3 lists key vendors (key players) in the server operating systems arena:

The most widely used commercial UNIX platforms are: HP's HP-UX, IBM's AIX, Oracle's Solaris, while the most widely used Linux servers are:

1) Red Hat Enterprise Linux (RHEL) Server
2) Ubuntu Server
3) Oracle Linux
4) Amazon Linux
5) CentOS Server
6) ClearOS Server
7) SUSE Linux Enterprise Server (SLES)
8) Open SUSE
9) Debian
10) Fedora

**Table 5.2 Key Vendors (Players) in the Operating Systems Arena**

| Vendor | Desktop/ Client OS | Mobile/ Client OS | Server OS |
|---|---|---|---|
| IBM (www.ibm.com) | | | Proprietary: zOS, OS/400 (IBM i), AIX Linux: RedHat (RHE) Support: Windows Servers |
| HP (www.hpe.com) | | | Proprietary: HP-UX, OpenVMS Support: RedHat, SUSE, Ubuntu and Windows Server |
| Microsoft (www. microsoft.com) | Windows | Windows Phone | Windows Server |
| Oracle (www.oracle. com) | | | Solaris Support: Linux, Windows Server |
| Apple | OS X | iOS | OS X Server |
| Google | | Android | |
| Free/Open source Linux | Red Hat, Ubuntu, Debian, SUSE, ... | | Red Hat, Ubuntu, Debian, SUSE, ... |
| Free/ Open source UNIX | | | FreeBSD |

The most widely used free Unix server OS are:

1) FreeBSD
2) MenuetOS
3) NetBSD
4) OpenBSD

In order to demonstrate the characteristics of a server operating platform that contains several continuous computing technologies for building an always-on enterprise information system, the following five SOS platforms are analyzed: HP's HP-UX, IBM's AIX, Oracle's Solaris, Windows Server, and SUSE Linux. The main features of these server operating system platforms are listed in Table 5.4 in the form of a SWOT analysis.

**Table 5.3    Key Vendors in the Server Operating Systems Arena**

| Vendor | Server OS | Current Status |
|---|---|---|
| IBM (www.ibm.com) | Proprietary: zOS, OS/ 400 Proprietary UNIX: AIX Support: Windows Server, Linux RHE | z/OS still supported AIX still supported OS/400 renamed to i5/OS and IBM i |
| HP (www.hpe.com) | Proprietary UNIX: HP-UX, Proprietary: OpenVMS Support: RedHat, SUSE, Ubuntu and Windows Server | OpenVMS and HP-UX still supported |
| SGI (www.hpe.com) | Proprietary UNIX: IRIX | SGI acquired by HP in 2016. IRIX discontinued in 2006. |
| Microsoft (www.microsoft. com) | Windows Server | |
| Oracle (www.oracle.com) | Proprietary UNIX: Solaris Support: Linux, Windows Server | Sun acquired by Oracle in 2010 Solaris discontinued in 2018. |
| Apple (www.apple.com) | OS X Server | |
| Linux community (www.linux.org) | Ubuntu, RedHat, Debian, SUSE, … | |
| FreeBSD www.freebsd.org) | | |

In addition to the SWOT analysis provided in Table 5.4, in the section that follows, we go a step further in explaining the "S" component (Strength) of these SOS platforms, with regard to their business continuity and system administration perspectives considered through additional high-availability, reliability, and scalability features and system administration utilities. The data for these three cases have been collected mainly from vendors' websites.

All these features represent a set of capabilities of the server operating environment that are aimed at enhancing the levels of availability, reliability, and scalability of application servers and the whole information system. It includes not only operating system-related features but also the server hardware, network infrastructure, storage systems, and solutions for system administration.

**Table 5.4  SWOT Analysis**

| | HP HP-UX | Microsoft Windows Server | SUSE Linux | IBM AIX | Oracle Solaris |
|---|---|---|---|---|---|
| Strengths | • Stable UNIX platform<br>• 35 years in use<br>• Integrated with HP servers<br>• HA features<br>• HA Features of System Administration | • Strong integration with Microsoft Back Office<br>• Strong Application Base<br>• Rich Set of App. Dev. Tools<br>• HA features<br>• HA Features of System Administration | • Open platform<br>• Scalability (available for IBM System z)<br>• HA features<br>• HA Features of System Administration<br>• Strong partnerships with SAP and VMW | • Stable UNIX platform<br>• 35 years in use<br>• Integrated with IBM server line (POWER)<br>• HA features<br>• HA Features of System Administration<br>• The only Unix which is not discontinued | • Stable UNIX platform<br>• 27 years in use<br>• Sun-Oracle Servers<br>• Integration with Oracle and MySQL DBMS<br>• integration with Java platform<br>• HA Features of System Administration |
| Weaknesses | • Runs only on HP servers<br>• Vendor lock-in<br>• License costs<br>• TCO<br>• App. Dev. Environm.<br>• Discontinued in 2019 | • License costs<br>• TCO<br>• Costs of application servers<br>• Costs of application development tools | • Application Development Environment<br>• Vendor viability<br>• Maintenance and support lifetime<br>• Pricing confusion | • Runs only on IBM servers<br>• Proprietary OS<br>• Vendor lock-in<br>• License and update costs<br>• TCO<br>• App. Dev. Environm. | • Runs only on SPARC<br>• Proprietary OS<br>• Vendor lock-in<br>• License and update costs<br>• TCO<br>• App. Dev. Environm.<br>• Discontinued |

*(Continued)*

**Table 5.4 (Continued)  SWOT Analysis**

|  | *HP HP-UX* | *Microsoft Windows Server* | *SUSE Linux* | *IBM AIX* | *Oracle Solaris* |
|---|---|---|---|---|---|
| Opportunities | • Cloud technologies<br>• Virtualization<br>• Containers<br>• Mission-critical systems(Fortune 500) | • Cloud technologies<br>• Virtualization<br>• Containers<br>• Decline of commercial UNIX | • Cloud technologies<br>• Virtualization<br>• Containers<br>• Decline of commercial UNIX | • Cloud technologies<br>• Virtualization<br>• Containers<br>• Mission-critical systems (Fortune 500) | • Cloud technologies<br>• Virtualization<br>• Containers<br>• Mission-critical systems (Fortune 500) |
| Threats | • Linux<br>• Other Commercial UNIX (AIX, Solaris, …)<br>• Free UNIX (Free BSD)<br>• Proprietary Server OS (Open VMS, z/OS, …)<br>• Windows Server | • Linux<br>• Commercial UNIX (AIX, HP-UX, Solaris, …)<br>• Free UNIX (Free BSD)<br>• Proprietary Server OS (Open VMS, z/OS, …)<br>• OS X Server<br>• … | • Linux versions (RedHat, Ubuntu, …)<br>• Commercial UNIX (AIX, HP-UX, Solaris, …)<br>• Free UNIX (Free BSD)<br>• Proprietary Server OS (Open VMS, z/OS, …)<br>• Windows Server<br>• … | • Linux<br>• Other Commercial UNIX (HP-UX, Solaris, …)<br>• Free UNIX (Free BSD)<br>• Proprietary Server OS (Open VMS, z/OS, …)<br>• Windows Server<br>• … | • Linux<br>• Other Commercial UNIX (AIX, HP-UX)<br>• Free UNIX (Free BSD)<br>• Proprietary Server OS (Open VMS, z/OS, …)<br>• Windows Server<br>• … |

With regard to storage, backup, and recovery, in addition to standard server operating system features, several features and technologies are included within the enhanced server operation environment, such as: automatic detection and auto conFigureuration of storage devices, SAN – agile addressing, resilience-to-link failures, native multi-pathing, immense scalability, load balancing, deferred path recovery, device data repository, Fibre Channel failover optimization, online disk replacement, performance improvements, support for storage array snapshots and clones, support for striped mirroring providing increased availability, no single point of failure-separate controllers/power supplies, disk mirroring, online backup, root disk mirroring, split brain avoidance for high-availability, FlexNetwork architecture, software defined networking, Federated software-defined networking, network virtualization, virtual application networks, NFS v3, NFS v4, redundant NFS server, and client side failover.

# System Administration and Business Continuity: Basic and High-availability Features of Some Server OS Platforms

As already stated, in order to demonstrate BC/HA-related features of server operating systems, these five OS platforms are selected: HP's HP-UX, IBM's AIX, Oracle's Solaris, Microsoft's Windows Server, and SUSE Linux. The data for these cases has been collected from the vendors' websites.

In order to demonstrate some basic system administration features, the following three server operating systems are presented: a) HP's HP-UX (www.hpe. com), as an example of commercial UNIX, b) Microsoft's Windows Server (www. microsoft.com), and c) SUSE Linux (www.suse.com). What follows is a selection of screenshots taken on these three OS platforms. Basic system administration skills include several activities related to server and SOS settings and administering server operations. Below are some screenshots showing some commands or GUI-based operations on HP-UX, Windows Server, and SUSE Linux. We provide just few examples of standard system administrator tasks without going into detail when standard system administration is considered. (See figures 5.13–5.18).

In addition to standard system administration commands and utilities, every modern server operating system platform includes a set of additional features developed and implemented in order to enhance the availability, reliability, and scalability ratios.

Some of the business continuity/high-availability–oriented technologies, security features, and system management options of HP-UX, Windows Server, SUSE Linux, IBM's AIX, and Oracle's Solaris operating systems are briefly explained below.

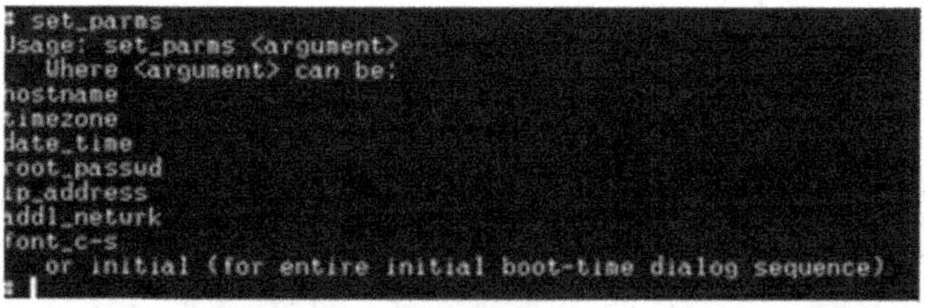

```
# set_params
Usage: set_params <argument>
    Where <argument> can be:
hostname
timezone
date_time
root_passwd
ip_address
addl_neturk
font_c-s
    or initial (for entire initial boot-time dialog sequence)
#
```

**Figure 5.13   Setting system parameters on HP-UX.**

```
# ifconfig lan0
lan0: flags=863<UP,BROADCAST,NOTRAILERS,RUNNING,MULTICAST>
      inet 193.140.207.25 netmask ffffff00 broadcast 193.140.207.255
#
```

**Figure 5.14   Getting the status of network adapter on HP-UX.**

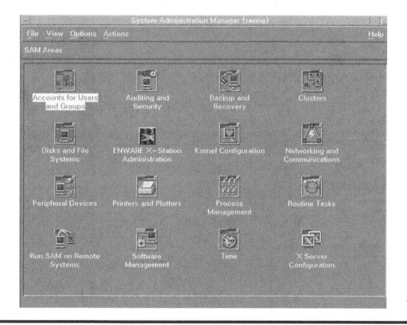

**Figure 5.15   SAM (system administration manager) on HP-UX.**

**Figure 5.16    System administration utilities on Windows server.**

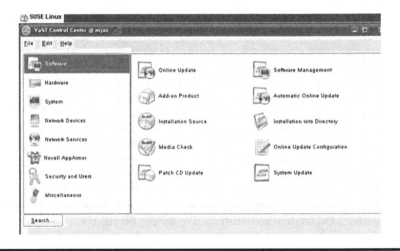

**Figure 5.17    SUSE Linux YaST interface for system administration.**

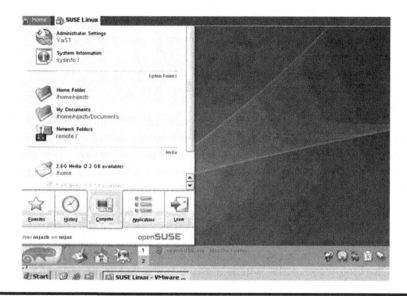

**Figure 5.18   SUSE Linux on Windows Server via VMWare.**

HP-UX HA features are described first and in more detail, while similar solutions for other OS platforms are briefly listed. It should be noted here that all commercial UNIX vendors provide similar HA features within their integrated server operating platforms. The situation is similar with Linux versions. However, a detailed comparative analysis of all available platforms is always suggested before the purchase decision. In addition, it is also worth checking the recent analyses provided by IDC, Gartner, and other consulting companies.

## HP-UX Server Operating Environment

Hewlett-Packard offers a range of server operating features for its UNIX-based server operating system – HP-UX 11i (www.hpe.com):

1) HP-UX 11i Foundation Operating Environment – HP-UX core.
2) HP-UX 11i Enterprise Operating Environment.
3) HP-UX 11i Mission Critical Operating Environment.
4) HP Virtual Server Environment Suite for HP-UX 11i.
5) HP Serviceguard Storage Management Suite for HP-UX 11i.

The latest release, HP-UX 11i v3, puts an emphasis on the following features:

a) Support for scalability. HP-UX 11i v3 supports an extensible range of systems, scaling up from the entry-level to the high-end servers.

b) Support for reliability and availability. With the HP-UX 11i v3 release, the Serviceguard high-availability (HA) software is now shipping as an integrated part of the mission-critical version of the HP-UX 11i v3 release.

c) Support for high availability. HP-UX 11i v3, along with HP Serviceguard, addresses this business requirement by minimizing unplanned downtime.

In addition to most commonly used system administration utilities, HP-UX supports an additional set of advanced technologies, tools, routines, and utilities that can be used in order to ensure higher levels of availability (see Table 5.5). Most of them are supported by HP's advanced system administration commands, features, and modules for high availability, including integrated high-availability suites such as: Ignite-UX, Bastille, and HP Serviceguard. Some of them related to availability are extracted and listed below:

- Creating the system recovery image by using the command make_recovery.
- Checking whether the system recovery image has to be recreated: check_ recovery.
- Hardware mirroring as a method of providing high availability by duplicating data on redundant hard drives.
- Software mirroring – making identical copies of data on several locations, by using features such as: Logical Volume Manager (LVM), Veritas Volume Manager (VxVM), LVM/Mirrordisk, LVM Snapshots, and Online JFS.
- Hot spared disk – a disk that is reserved for swapping with a broken disk that has no mirrored data.
- Data encoding performed by a hard disk array controller when a disk drive fails.
- High-availability Storage Systems. These systems as typical hardware redundancy technology are based on using two SCSI buses including hot-pluggable disks.
- High-availability monitors that work on detecting the problems on disks, network devices, and other system resources, and alerting the system administrator to correct the problem.
- Dynamic Root Disk (DRD) – a feature that provides the ability to clone an HP-UX system image to an inactive disk. DRD utility can be used for rebooting the system during "off-hours", in order to reduce system downtime.
- Clustering technologies such as: Extended Distance Cluster, Cluster for Oracle's RAC Database, Metrocluster, Continental Cluster.
- HP Serviceguard Extensions for SAP: Hot Standby for liveCache – failover and disaster tolerance capabilities for enhancing uptime of the SAP ERP suites.

With regard to the role of system administration and server operating platforms in enhancing business continuity, the following features of server operating platforms are important:

**Table 5.5   HP-UX High-Availability Features**

| *HP-UX v. 11.11v 3 – High-Availability Features* |
|---|
| • Journalized File System for high reliability and fast recovery |
| • JFS snapshot technology |
| • System recovery image |
| • Hardware mirroring |
| • Software mirroring |
| • Hot spared disk technology |
| • Data encoding |
| • High-availability storage systems |
| • High-availability monitors |
| • Dynamic Root Disk |
| • Clustering |
| • HP Serviceguard Extensions for SAP |
| • Compartments |
| • Fine-Grained privileges |
| • Role-based Access Control |
| • Bastille as a security tool |
| • Built-in native multi-pathing and load balancing |
| • Automatic detection and auto configuration for new storage devices |
| • Resilience to link failures |
| • OLARD (online addition, replacement, deletion) of I/O interfaces. |
| • Device data repository (DDR) name generation. |
| • Fibre Channel failover optimization. |
| • etc. |

a) Veritas' VxFS JFS/Online JFS – Journaled File System is particularly important on HP-UX and other Unix/Linux server platforms as it provides fast file system recovery in case of system failures and the ability to perform a number of administrative tasks online. JFS is a recommended file system for high reliability, fast recovery, and online administrative operations. JFS snapshot is a new technique that allows the system administrator to capture the file-system state at a moment in time (without taking it off-line and copying it), mount that file-system image elsewhere, and back it up.

b) Several HP-UX features (e.g., Journaled File System for fast file system recovery, hardware mirroring, software mirroring, data encoding), commands (e.g., fsck, lvcreate, make_recovery, check_recovery), tools (e.g., JFS snapshot, Bastille), utilities (Compartments, Fine-Grained privileges), and additional packages (e.g., Ignite-UX, Bastille, and HP Serviceguard) that can be used in assuring system uptime and high-availability ratios are explained as well. In addition, HP's "Serviceguard Extensions for SAP" – failover and disaster tolerance capabilities are used for enhancing uptime of the SAP ERP suites.

c) High-availability Monitors are used for detecting the problems on disks, network devices, and other system resources, and alerting the system administrator to correct them. High-availability Storage Systems, being typical hardware redundancy technology, are based on using two SCSI buses and connectors, power supply units and fans, and hot-pluggable disks. Dynamic Root Disk provides the ability to clone an HP-UX system image to an inactive disk; it can be used for rebooting the system during the "off-hours", an operation that may reduce system downtime. HP-UX hardware mirroring as a method of providing high availability by duplicating data on redundant hard drives and software mirroring – to make identical copies of data on several locations, by using features such as: Logical Volume Manager (LVM), Veritas Volume Manager (VxVM), LVM/Mirrordisk, LVM Snapshots, Online JFS.

The newest release of HP-UX11i v.3 offers a set of security technologies that can provide greater access control. These technologies include:

a) Compartments – some applications are isolated into what is called a "compartment" in order to prevent catastrophic damage to the server as a whole.
b) Fine-Grained privileges – a new approach in setting root-based privileges that grants processes only those privileges needed for a specific task.
c) Role-based Access Control – enables non-root users some root privileges for specific tasks.
d) Bastille is a security tool that is used to enhance the security of the HP-UX operating environment.

The latest release of HP's UNIX operating system – HP-UX 11i v3 (www.hpe. com) – puts an emphasis on the following features:

a) Support for high reliability and availability, by using features such as: HP Serviceguard, Online patching, and Dynamic Root Disk.
b) Extensions for Serviceguard such as Serviceguard for SAP and Serviceguard · for RAC, supporting rapid deployment of Serviceguard-enabled application solutions.
c) Support for scalability with an extensible range of systems, scaling up from volume servers (servers that are priced at less than $25,000) to 64-socket, 128 core Superdome systems at the high-end enterprise range (servers priced at more than $500,000).

In addition to most commonly used system administration utilities, HP-UX supports advanced technologies, tools, routines, and utilities that can be used in order to ensure higher levels of availability. Most of them are supported by HP's advanced system administration modules for high availability, including integrated and dedicated high-availability suites such as: Ignite-UX, Bastille, and HP Serviceguard. Some of them are listed below:

- Creating the system recovery image by using the command make_recovery.
- Checking whether the system recovery image has to be recreated: check_ recovery.
- Hardware mirroring as a method of providing high availability by duplicating data.
- Software mirroring, by using features such as: LVM, VxVM, LVM/Mirrordisk, LVM Snapshots, Online JFS.
- Hot spared disk – a disk that is reserved for swapping with a broken disk.
- Data encoding performed by a hard disk array controller when a disk drive fails.
- High-availability Storage Systems.
- High-availability monitors.
- Dynamic Root Disk (DRD) – a feature that can be used for rebooting the system during "off-hours", in order to reduce system downtime.
- Clustering technologies.
- HP Serviceguard Extensions for SAP such as Hot Standby for liveCache – failover and disaster tolerance capabilities for enhancing uptime of the SAP ERP suites.

The newest release of HP-UX11i v.3 offers a set of security technologies that can provide greater access control. These technologies include:

- Compartments – some applications can be isolated into what is called a "compartment" in order to prevent catastrophic damage to the server as a whole.
- Fine-Grained privileges – a new approach in setting root-based privileges that grants processes only those privileges needed for a specific task.
- Role-based Access Control – enables non-root users some root privileges for specific tasks.
- Bastille is a security tool that is used to enhance the security of the HP-UX OS.
- Supports SSHA (Single System High Availability) Online-Deletion of NICs. Improves system and network availability.
- High-availability NFS environments
- Client-side Failover Support
- HA database support
- Virtualized environment high availability
- Mission-critical high availability to lower cost storage.
- High availability and disaster recovery (HPE Serviceguard)
- High availability (HPE Serviceguard Extension for SAP–SGeSAP)
- HPE Serviceguard Toolkit for Oracle Data Guard
- Storage availability
- High availability (single system)
- High availability (SAP® integration)

Like HP-UX, both IBM AIX and Oracle Solaris as two commercial/proprietary UNIX platforms also include several HA features. Some of them are listed below, while full lists of those features can be found on their websites (www.ibm.com, www.oracle.com), respectively:

> www.ibm.com/it-infrastructure/power/os/aix
> www.oracle.com/solaris/solaris11/

## IBM AIX Server Operating Environment

Some of the HA-features of IBM AIX serve operating system include are shown in Table 5.6.

## Oracle Solaris Server Operating Environment

A list of some HA-features of Oracle's Solaris is shown in Table 5.7.

In addition to Solaris, Oracle supports Oracle Linux Server and SunOS.

## Windows Server Operating Environment

Microsoft's server operating system "Windows Server", particularly with the latest version – 2019, provides several features related to continuous availability. Some of them are listed below and in Table 5.8:

■ Recovery procedures and assistance for high IT service uptime and recovery from a wide range of failure scenarios for servers, clusters, and servers across datacenters.

**Table 5.6　IBM AIX High-Availability Features**

| |
|---|
| • Logical Volume Mirroring (LVM). |
| • Host mirroring |
| • HyperSwap – Continuous availability protection against storage failures through |
| • Oracle Real Application Clusters (RAC) |
| • Active-Active Sites solutions. |
| • PowerHA SAP liveCache HotStandby |
| • Enhanced HA management support in SAP environments. |
| • Capacity optimized failovers through Capacity on Demand (CoD) exploitation. |
| • The Encrypted File System function in the cluster |
| • PowerHA SystemMirror for both planned and unplanned outages. |
| • … |

*Source*: www.ibm.com/us-en/marketplace/powerha/details

**Table 5.7   Oracle Solaris High-Availability Features**

| *Oracle Solaris – High-Availability Features* |
|---|
| • Oracle Solaris cluster for application and database availability<br>• Oracle real application clusters (RAC)<br>• Oracle clusterware<br>• Agent BUILDER<br>• HA Oracle agent<br>• Load balancing<br>• Fault detection,<br>• Disaster recovery<br>• Failover zone features<br>• Oracle Solaris zones<br>• … |

*Source*: www.oracle.com/solaris/solaris11/

- Server Message Block (SMB) 3.0, Transparent Failover, and Multichannel features
- Windows NIC Teaming provides transparent NIC failover
- Windows Server Failover Clustering
- Hyper-V live migration, and Hyper-V Replica.
- Windows Server 2012 Cluster Failover Manager
- Support for SQL Server Always On
- Support for Database Mirroring
- Support for the concept of Always On Availability Groups for SQL Server
- System Center's Data Protection Manager
- Online Corruption Repairs isolates and repairs file system corruption while the volume is online and unaffected portions of the file system remain available
- Active-Active File Server Clusters provides transparent failover across server clusters by moving file server clients without any service interruption.
- Hyper-V Replica provides active-active clustering of any workload across datacenters by replicating a virtual machine from one location to another.
- Supports NUMA-aware scalability for NUMA-aware applications
- NIC failover
- Online Corruption Repairs
- Always On Dashboard
- Rolling upgrade capabilities
- Windows Azure Backup for reliable offsite data protection
- Shielded Virtual Machines
- failback conFigureuration
- Host guardian service (HGS)

Windows Server's HA-features are listed in Table 5.8.

**Table 5.8  Windows Server High-Availability Features**

| *Windows Server – High-Availability Features* |
|---|
| • High-availability features |
| • HA Features of system administration |
| • Recovery procedures and assistance for high IT service uptime and recovery from a wide range of failure scenarios for servers, clusters, and servers across datacenters. |
| • Server Message Block (SMB) 3.0, Transparent Failover and Multichannel features |
| • Windows NIC Teaming provides transparent NIC failover |
| • Windows Server Failover Clustering |
| • Hyper-V live migration, and Hyper-V Replica. |
| • Windows Server 2012 Cluster Failover Manager |
| • Support for SQL Server Always On |
| • Support for Database Mirroring |
| • Support for the concept of Always On Availability Groups for SQL Server |
| • System Center's Data Protection Manager |
| • Online Corruption Repairs |
| • Active-Active File Server Clusters provides transparent failover across server clusters by moving file server clients without any service interruption. |
| • Hyper-V Replica provides active-active clustering of any workload across datacenters |
| • Supports NUMA-aware scalability for NUMA-aware applications |
| • NIC failover |
| • Online Corruption Repairs |
| • Always On Dashboard |
| • Rolling upgrade capabilities |
| • Windows Azure Backup for reliable offsite data protection |

(www.microsoft.com/en-us/cloud-platform/windows-server)

## *SUSE Linux Operating Environment*

The SUSE Linux operating platform provides additional high-availability features by including the "SUSE Linux Enterprise High Availability Extension" as an add-on product to the SUSE Linux Enterprise Server 12 (SLES 12). The SUSE Linux Enterprise High Availability Extension supports OpenAIS – the Open Source initiative's Service Availability Forum Application Interface Specification (see features listed in Table 5.9). This extension platform includes the following features:

- Btrfs (B-tree file system)
- Btrfs-based snapshoots
- Live patching features
- Cluster-aware file system and volume management
- Hybrid physical and virtual high-availability clusters

**Table 5.9    SUSE Linux High-Availability Features (www.suse.com; www.suse.org)**

| *SUSE Linux HA Features* |
|---|
| • Btrfs (B-tree file system) |
| • Btrfs-based snapshoots |
| • Live patching features |
| • Cluster-aware file system and volume management |
| • Hybrid physical and virtual high-availability clusters |
| • Clustered Logical Volume Manager 2 |
| • Active/active and active/passive conFigureurations |
| • Support for DRBD (Distributed Replicated Block Device) |
| • Support for KVM and Xen, the leading open source virtualization hypervisors. |
| • Corosync/OpenAIS messaging layer |
| • Pacemaker High-Availability features |
| • Pacemaker Cluster Resource Manager for continuous monitoring and managing server |
| • Dynamically assigning and reassigning server storage |
| • Support for Fibre Channel and iSCSI storage area networks |
| • Support for shared disk systems |
| • Cluster-aware file systems |
| • Network load balancing |
| • Support for clustered SAMBA |
| • installing the HA Extension on top of SUSE Linux Enterprise Server |
| • cluster setup |
| • conFigureuration of a Distributed Replicated Block Device |
| • IP Load Balancing |
| • Support for Relax and Recover (ReaR) for creating disaster recovery images. |

- Clustered Logical Volume Manager 2
- Active/active and active/passive conFigureurations
- Support for DRBD (Distributed Replicated Block Device)
- Support for KVM and Xen, the leading open source virtualization hypervisors.
- Corosync/OpenAIS messaging layer
- Pacemaker High Availability features
- Pacemaker Cluster Resource Manager for continuous monitoring and of managing server
- Dynamically assigning and reassigning server storage
- Support for Fibre Channel and iSCSI storage area networks
- Support for shared disk systems
- Cluster-aware file systems
- Network load balancing
- Support for clustered SAMBA

- High-availability clustering
- Flexible, policy-driven clustering and continuous data replication
- Setup, administration, management, and monitoring
- Continuous data replication
- Cluster-aware file system and volume management
- Virtualization aware
- Corosync and OpenAIS
- Pacemaker is a highly scalable cluster resource manager
- Rules-based failover for automatic and manual transfer of a workload to another cluster outside of the affected area.
- Mixed clustering of both physical and virtual Linux servers to boost flexibility while improving service availability and resource utilization.
- HAProxy
- Cluster Join enables effortless cluster setup and expansion of existing clusters
- Storage-based fencing that eliminates single point failure
- Cluster Bootstrap
- Metro area clusters – failover across data center locations as far as 30 kilometers apart.
- Geo clustering delivers failover – protects against regional disruptive events.
- Distributed Replicated Block Device (DRBD)
- Node recovery with Relax and Recov

In addition, several HA-oriented system administration tools are added into the "YaST" – SUSE's system administration GUI-based tool, such as:

- Installing the HA Extension on top of SUSE Linux Enterprise Server
- Cluster setup
- ConFigureuration of a Distributed Replicated Block Device
- IP Load Balancing
- Support for Relax and Recover (ReaR) for creating disaster recovery images.
- Powerful unified interface, HAWK (High Availability Web Konsole)
- Access control lists align cluster management with your processes and policies
- Cluster-wide shell improves the effectiveness of managing cluster nodes by enabling the execution of commands across all nodes using the PSSH command.
- History explorer allows interactive access to cluster logs. It displays and analyzes actions taken by SUSE Linux Enterprise High Availability Extension.
- Cluster test drive allows users to simulate a failover situation before an actual disaster happens, making sure of the configuration and resource allocation prior to production.
- Resource agents for open source applications such as Apache, IPv6, DRBD, KVM, Xen, and Postgres; resource agents for popular third-party applications such as IBM WebSphere, IBM DB2, VMWare, and SAP.

■ Clustered Samba (CTDB) can be made highly available and scalable using multiple nodes and can transparently failover through cluster-wide locking. CTDB resources are automatically added and synced to Active.

# Business Continuity-Oriented Operating Systems Course

Operating systems are traditionally taught as part of the undergraduate or graduate curriculum of computer science/computer engineering university programs. On the other side, in business schools, operating systems are in most cases briefly mentioned/covered as part of basic/introductory courses such as Business Computing, Intro to Information Systems, Business Informatics, Information Systems, and Business Information Systems. However, as modern e-businesses today rely on their information infrastructures, in other words, on the availability and scalability of their business information system infrastructures, the importance of server operating platforms becomes evident as those platforms determine the availability and scalability of e-business platforms. The roles of servers and server operating systems are becoming critical with regard to business-critical applications. Simply put, many businesses in the digital age go "out of business" due to the downtime caused by several factors on the server side in the client's server architecture including the one related to server operating system crashes. Therefore, there is a need for teaching operating systems, particularly server operating systems, in business programs as well.

What follows is a framework for designing such a course in a business information systems or even business administration program.

Course title(s): Operating Systems: A Business Perspective; System Administration for Business Continuity, System Administration for High Availability

Course contents:

## *Lectures*

■ Modern business; business continuity and continuous computing
■ Downtime and uptime
■ Financial aspects of system downtime
■ Server and server OS in modern business computing
■ Server platforms
■ OS concepts: a short introduction
■ Server operating systems and Server operating environments
■ Availability, Reliability, Scalability
■ Virtualization technologies
■ System administration
■ HA Features of Server OS

- Comparing Server OS platforms
- Client OS issues (desktop/portable devices)

## *Practical/Problem Sessions*

- Administering desktop OS (Windows, MacOS, Linux)
- Using server OS (Windows Server, HP-UX, SUSE Linux)
- Administering server OS (Windows Server, HP-UX, SUSE Linux)
- Remote Administration
- Working with VMWare
- SAMBA: Windows/UNIX-Linux Integration
- JFS and Cluster-aware FS
- Backup and Recovery
- Patching, Updating, Upgrading
- Installing and administering HA-features of server OS
- Mirroring and Snapshot
- HA Monitors

Based on the previous course contents, the following topics are identified in the course syllabus:

1. OS – Business Perspective: Real-life stories showing the costs of downtime accross industries.
2. The role of server OS and system administration in continuous computing and business continuity.
3. Short intro on modern computer system configurations with a focus on enterprise servers.
4. Introduction to OS concepts/functions, covering the topics of process management, scheduling, memory management, file systems, user management, networks, and so on.
5. Exploring the types of modern operating systems; focusing on server operating systems. Selection of SOS.
6. Positioning the system administration as part of IT management.
7. System administration of modern OS platforms with a focus on administering server OS. Practical–problem sessions covering system administration of a) desktop OS: Windows, MacOS, Linux and b) server OS platforms: Windows Server, HP-UX, SUSE Linux. Virtualization concept and technology; practical on using VMWare.
8. Extending SOS to the concept of "server operating environment" by adding Business Continuity/High Availability features. HA features of selected SOS platforms.
9. Comparative analysis of most widely used SOS platforms.
10. Client OS–business issues (operating systems of desktop/portable devices)

The course is delivered over 14–15 weeks, five hours of class contact per week (a three-hour lecture and two-hour problem session). With regard to learning outcomes, after completing the course, the students will be able to:

1. Understand how modern business depends on IT platforms, servers, and server operating systems;
2. Understand how business computing platforms, mainly application servers, affect financial performance and the whole business;
3. Understand terms such as: downtime, uptime, availability, reliability, scalability, system administration, backup and recovery, and so on.
4. Recognize the role of server operating systems for "stability" of business application platforms in terms of availability, reliability, and scalability;
5. Understand main operating system functions on an introductory level;
6. Identify the role of system administration in achieving higher levels of system uptime;
7. Gain practical experience in system administration on the most widely used server platforms;
8. Recognize the role of advanced features of some modern server operating systems related to business continuity and high availability.

An overview of the course contents with regard to learning outcomes is shown in Table 5.10.

**Table 5.10   Course Contents versus Learning Outcomes**

| No | Topic | Learning Outcomes |
|----|-------|-------------------|
| 1. | OS – Business Perspective | 1 |
| 2. | The role of server OS and system administration in continuous computing and business continuity. | 2, 3 |
| 3. | Short intro on modern computer system conFigureurations with focus on enterprise servers. | 3, 4 |
| 4. | OS concepts and main OS functions | 4 |
| 5- | Exploring the types of modern operating systems | 4, 5 |
| 6. | Positioning the system administration as part of IT-management | 5, 6, 7 |
| 7. | System administration of modern OS platforms | 6, 7 |
| 8. | Extending SOS into the concept of "server operating environment" | 7, 8 |
| 9. | Comparative analysis of most widely used SOS platforms | 6, 7, 8 |
| 10. | Client OS – business issues | 1 |

Course assessment is based on the following scheme:

- Midterm (In-class, 25%) – Computer conFigureurations, OS concepts and functions.
- Class participation and discussion (10%, teamwork): Modern OS – business perspective.
- PS (25%) – Administering Windows-desktop, UNIX/Linux, Windows Server, VMWare.
- Final (In-class, 40%) – UNIX (HP-UX) and Windows Server system administration (commands/routines); the role of OS in business continuity.

## System Administration and DevOps

The paradigms of software development and implementation are continually changing, which inevitably affects the availability of information systems and the job of the system administrator. Since the advent of various agile methodologies (XP, Scrum, Lean software development, Kanban, etc.) starting in 2010, many organizations have been implementing the DevOps software development method that has appeared as an upgrade to agile methodologies. In this section, we will discuss DevOps and its impact on business continuity and system administration.

DevOps is a combination of cultural philosophies, practices, and tools that increase an organization's ability to accelerate application delivery to production: developing and improving products faster than organizations using traditional software development and infrastructure management processes. This speed enables organizations to serve their customers better and be more efficient in the market (Amazon, 2019).

John Willis created the CAMS model (Culture, Automation, Measurement, and Sharing) to describe his thoughts on DevOps central values:

- **Culture:** DevOps strives to solve business problems that occur when people create and manage complex systems. In this respect, DevOps is also a method for managing social issues, although it is a technological solution. Even with the advent of more innovative tools and advanced computer technology, the software development process depends on elements of human culture. Its practitioners need to create an open communication environment in which shared goals and understanding between all participants are particularly crucial for project success. Project-oriented teams are formed around results to avoid prioritizing individual skills or siloing functions.
- Automation: DevOps is not just about tools or task automation with software. That is, automation is at the core of DevOps value, and this is key to using agile development practices, including continuous integration and continuous

delivery. To enable continuous deployment, DevOps encourages automation. In the DevOps method, it is crucial to prioritize problem-solving leveraging automation and to ensure that quality is everyone's responsibility. Automating tests and forcing rapid response to issues raised by the customer, came about from the acceptance of the idea that there is always something to go wrong and recognized the inherent instability in these complex systems. DevOps focuses on the continued use of automation to create stress and encourage partial failures of complex distributed systems, leading to improvements and accelerations in production.

■ Measurement: To determine whether DevOps is continuously improving processes, team members need to collect and analyze data. This obligation applies to measuring business process data as well as development, testing, and operations data. One of the primary metrics involves the mean time to recovery (MTTR) of a product or system failure. There are many other measurement objects: How long does it take to get the right people? Is this the correct information to avoid bottlenecks? How long does it take to navigate the whole life cycle from development-to-deployment? How often are problems repeated? What is the current state of employee satisfaction? Measuring and encouraging the right behavior is a core value of DevOps. Measurement evaluation and testable behavior drive learning and consistent improvement – two critical aspects of DevOps culture.

■ Sharing: Willis recognized this value in the form of a feedback process in the DevOps cycle, where participants share ideas and solve problems. Sharing is a core value of DevOps, as the development and operation staff share traditionally separate team functions. At DevOps, teams embrace the idea that everyone participates in building and deploying applications and make sure it meets customers' and businesses' goals. Sharing means being transparent and evaluating the results and data of all teams. Figure 5.19 illustrates the DevOps process.

Amazon recognizes the following DevOps process parts:

## Plan and Track

Identify and monitor work using practices and processes such as Kanban boards and agile methodologies. When the work is visually monitored, participants have a clear insight into the capacity of the development team and can better plan and prioritize tasks and avoid work in which teams are only firefighting with problems.

## Develop

The code is written using a modern version control system like Git, so it is continuously and securely integrated into the main branch.

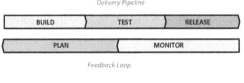

**Figure 5.19  DevOps process. Amazon, 2019.**

## Build and Test

Adding code to a Git or other version control system starts the automated build process. The code is tested and verified, ensuring that bugs are caught early in development – when they are fresh in the development team's mind and cheaper to repair. This process of building and testing automation is called continuous integration (CI). The application can be deployed after successful build and integration, enabling continuous delivery (CD) – the ability to deploy into production at any time.

## Deploy

Once tested and validated, any change is ready for deployment to the production environment. In the case of continuous delivery, final production deployment is a manually controlled business decision. With continuous deployment, the entire process from coding completion to deployment in production is automated.

## Monitor and Operate

Once the application is live in production, monitoring delivers performance and usage information of an application. Application teams can use immediately, rich diagnostic information supplied by the monitoring subsystem for proactive and fast action to keep the app highly available. Monitoring helps in reducing customer problems and gathering data to make informed business decisions about future development. With automated compliance policies using infrastructure as code and policies as code, the organization will ensure that applications they deploy to production, use desired state conFigureurations that are aligned with security best practices. (Amazon, 2019)

# DevOps Implementation and Impact on the Availability of an Information System

In this section, the IT pieces known as building blocks of the DevOps process are briefly presented. We explain terms such as: Continuous Integration, Continuous Delivery, Microservices, Infrastructure as Code and give some examples of tools

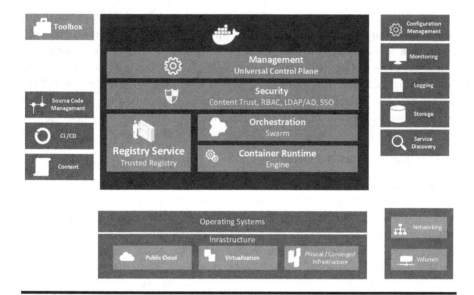

**Figure 5.20    Example of enterprise architecture based on Docker containers.**

used in a particular phase. Figure 5.20 represents an example of a new enterprise IT architecture based on Docker.

## *Continuous Integration*

Continuous integration is a software development practice in which developers regularly merge their code changes into a central repository, followed by automated builds and tests. The key goals of continuous integration are to find and resolve errors as quickly as possible, to improve the quality of software, and to reduce the time required to check and complete new software updates.

## *Continuous Delivery*

Continuous delivery is a software development practice where code changes are automatically built, tested, and prepared for release. It extends to continuous integration by incorporating all code changes into the test and/or production environment after the build phase. When continuous delivery is done correctly, developers always have a code that has gone through a standardized test process before release.

## *Microservices*

Microservice architecture is a design approach for building an application as a set of small services. Each service operates in its own process and communicates with other services through a well-defined interface using a lightweight mechanism, usually an HTTP-based application interface (API). Microservices are built around business cases; each service is designed for one purpose. Different frameworks or programming languages can be used to write microservices. Microservices can be deployed individually, as a single service or as a group of services. In the DevOps model, the release of a new version of the microservice does not depend on the administrator; instead, it is the result of an automated process.

## Infrastructure as a Code

Infrastructure as a code is a practice in which infrastructure is assigned and managed using code and software development methods, such as version control and continuous integration. The cloud API model allows developers and system administrators to interact with the software infrastructure and scale, rather than manually setting up and conFigureuring resources. Therefore, engineers can interact with infrastructure using code-based tools and upgrade infrastructure like how they treat application code. Code-defined, infrastructure, and servers can be implemented quickly using standardized templates, updated with the latest patches and versions, or can be duplicated in a repeatable manner.

## Configuration Management

Developers and system administrators use code to automate the operating system and host configurations, operating tasks, and more. Using code makes configuration changes reproducible and standardized. It frees developers and system administrators from manually configuring operating systems, system applications, or servers. Figure 5.21 illustrates a snippet from the Ansible, which is one of the most used configuration tools.

With infrastructure as code and automated configuration management, organizations can monitor and enforce compliance dynamically and regardless of system size. The infrastructure described by the code can, therefore, be monitored, verified, and reconfigured in an automated manner. This allows organizations to manage resource changes and ensures that security measures are implemented correctly in a policy-compliant way. This will enable teams within the organization to work faster as mismatched resources can be automatically flagged for further investigation or even automatically returned to compliance.

## DevOps Tools

To find suitable DevOps tools, we did some Internet research and combined it with practical experience. Below is the list of the widely used DevOps tools.

**Figure 5.21   An Ansible playbook example.**

## Infrastructure Automation

Amazon Web Services (AWS), Microsoft Azure, and Google Cloud: Being a cloud service, you do not need to be physically present in the data center. Also, they are easy to scale on-demand. There are no up-front hardware costs. It can be conFigured to provision more servers based on traffic automatically.

Docker: Docker is a containerization technology. Containers consist of all the applications with all of their dependencies. These containers can be deployed on any machine without caring about underlying host details.

## Configuration Management

Chef, Puppet, Ansible: It is a useful DevOps tool for achieving speed, scale, and consistency. It can be used to ease complex tasks and perform conFigureuration management. With these tools, the DevOps team can avoid making changes across ten thousand servers. Instead, they need only to make changes in one place, which is automatically reflected in other servers.

### Deployment Automation

Jenkins: This tool facilitates continuous integration and testing. It helps integrate project changes more efficiently by quickly finding issues as soon as a built is deployed.

### Log Management

Splunk: This is a tool that solves issues like aggregating, storing, and analyzing all logs in one place.

### Performance Management

App Dynamic: This is a DevOps tool that offers real-time performance monitoring. The data collected by this tool helps developers debug when issues occur.

### Monitoring

Nagios: It is also essential to make sure people are notified when infrastructure and related services go down. Nagios is one such tool for this purpose, which helps DevOps teams find and correct problems.

### Continuous Deployment

Kubernetes: Google develops Kubernetes as an open-source container orchestration tool. It is used in continuous deployment and auto-scaling of container clusters. It increases fault tolerance, load balancing in a container cluster.

### Testing

Selenium: Selenium is an open-source, automated testing framework. Selenium is used majorly to automate the testing of web applications (Guru99, 2019; Intellipat, 2019)

### When Not DevOps

DevOps should not be used in critical applications such as banks, power plants, and other essential facilities. Such applications need strict access controls to the production environment, detailed change management rules, data center access, and control rules.

## The Impact of Modern Software Architectures on System Administration – Sysadmin 4.0

The question arises: How do all these new paradigm shifts affect the system administrator profession?

The workload is moving from an on-premise data center to the public cloud, even inside on prem data center architecture changes from traditional (cluster of servers, Virtualization, SAN storage) to the hyperconverged and private cloud-based. Hybrid cloud architectures are also available as a solution for capacity management and availability problems. Backup and DR are also moving to the cloud, and containers are becoming increasingly ubiquitous. The role of a system administrator, as we know it, is undergoing a significant transformation due to digitalization and the cloud. It was a role for those who did all the installation, backup, and so on, and owned the complete IT infrastructure. Starting from the last decade of the twentieth century, the system administration job has been beginning to change by introducing virtualization, proactive monitoring, smart switches, and so on.

Infrastructure as Code and software-defined Data Centers blur the border between the roles of system administrator and developer. The developer is now able to establish the necessary infrastructure without the help of an administrator. The developer is also empowered to deploy a new version of an application without submitting a ticket for a system administrator.

The most significant limitation of traditional IT infrastructure is scaling. It was important that the server size and capacity planning was done correctly before the project started. In the past, if the system did not meet the SLA response time or it was under capacitated processors or storage systems, the only option was to order new hardware and wait for the purchase completion. To be on the safe side, IT managers used to order more equipment than optimal.

Sysadmins 4.0 needs to be a team player, not an introverted and shy person as he used to be. He needs to have both communication and planning skills as well as technical skills. From a technical point of view, he needs, as soon as possible, to dig into learning: public cloud system administration, private cloud technology stacks (e.g., RedHat OpenStack), scripting and service and configuration automation tools, and to be able to deploy tens or even hundreds of servers with a "single click" in a consistent manner. An administrator who has all those skills can be a leader in the DevOps process inside an organization

In the end, instead of a conclusion, we will paraphrase an *Information Week* article from 2017.

> No matter what percentage of IT will take place virtually and/or within the cloud over the next few years, IT infrastructure will always be a necessity. The cloud server is still a piece of hardware in the end. The server will also be connected to the physical network, and there will be a server room for a while. And the assets of these devices must be managed. If necessary, several administrators, instead of several dozen, might be centrally located in the data center, and maintain complete infrastructure, but the workforce is still irreplaceable.

Also, there will still be a large number of legacy systems in the coming years. Just think about the old ERP solutions that are managed locally and, in many cases, are too inflexible to move to the cloud.

Generally, cloud or no cloud, enough IT infrastructure will remain on site. The scope of system-administrator tasks is shifting from classic server management to managing local clients, networks, surveillance cameras, and IoT devices. IoT will especially expand exponentially in the coming years and must be operated and maintained (Balan, 2017).

## Conclusions

System administration is considered one of the main factors and operational activities that help in managing application servers from a business continuity perspective. Server operating systems must be considered from a business perspective: therefore, standard system administration features and activities on server platforms are today enhanced by additional components that are aimed at improving availability and scalability ratios of application servers. DevOps framework helps from that perspective as well.

## Discussion Questions

1. What is the difference between standard system administration and integrated system management?
2. Explain the requirement related to applications availability and integratability.
3. Make an assessment (Internet survey) of the following UNIX platforms: AIX, HP-UX, and Solaris with regard to their features of integrated system administration.
4. Make an assessment (Internet survey) of the following proprietary server operating platforms with regard to their high-availability features: OS/390 (z/OS), OpenVMS, and OS/400 (IBM i).
5. Make an assessment (Internet survey) on the availability and salary ranges of UNIX, Linux, and Windows Server system administrators.
6. Why might a system administrator affect the IT infrastructure?
7. Explain the main duties of a system administrator.
8. Briefly discuss the issue of "disgruntled system administrator".
9. What new IT job profiles help a business continuity project in a company?
10. How is server management software differentiated from the main system administration utilities?

# References

Amazon. (2019). Cloud Solutions | Vetted, Technical Reference Architecture | AWS. Retrieved September 1, 2019, from https://aws.amazon.com/solutions/?ncl=f_cc&solutions-all. sort-by=item.additionalFields.sortDate&solutions-all.sort-order=desc

Bajgoric, N. (2008). Operating Systems: A Business Perspective, in: Wah, B.W. (ed.), *Wiley Encyclopedia of Computer Science and Engineering*, Wiley, 2045–2059.

Balan, S. (2017). RIP, Systems Administrator, Welcome DevOps – InformationWeek. Retrieved September 1, 2019, from www.informationweek.com/devops/rip-systems-administrator-welcome-devops/a/d-id/1329208

Conway, S. et al. (2019). The Business Value of Leading-Edge High Performance Computing: 2019 Update, March 2019. Retrieved from: www.hpe.com/us/en/resources/solutions/hyperion-hpc-value.html

Guru99. (2019). DevOps Tutorial: Complete Beginners Training. Retrieved September 1, 2019, from www.guru99.com/devops-tutorial.html#13

IDC White Paper. (2009). Reducing Downtime and Business Loss: Addressing Business Risk with Effective Technology, IDC, August 2009

IDC White Paper. (2014). DevOps and the Cost of Downtime: Fortune 1000 Best Practice Metrics Quantified. Retrieved from www.idc.com/getdoc.jsp?containerId=253155

Intellipat. (2019). Top DevOps Tools 2019 – The Best DevOps Software – Intellipaat. Retrieved September 1, 2019, from https://intellipaat.com/blog/top-devops-tools/

Silberschatz, A., Galvin, P.B., Gagne, G. (2007). *Operating System Concepts with Java*, Wiley.

Tanenbaum, A.S. (2009). *Modern Operating Systems*, Prentice Hall.

Tynan, D. (2013). Fatal distraction: 7 IT mistakes that will get you fired. Retrieved September 14, 2020 from: www.infoworld.com/article/2612027/fatal-distraction--7-it-mistakes-that-will-get-you-fired.html

# Enhancing Availability and Business Continuity: Methods, Techniques, and Technologies

## Background

As a starting point in this chapter, we compared the prevailing industry standards in the BCM/DRM[1] field. There are two reasons for this approach. First, it is more secure to follow established rules than start from the ground up. Second, in some phases, our business continuity management system (BCMS) will be subject to an external audit, and they usually conduct an audit relying on a standard (COBIT, NIST, ISO). In this book, we consulted the following standards:

- National Institute of Standards and Technology (NIST) Special Publication 800–34, Rev. 1, *Contingency Planning Guide for Federal Information Systems,* which provides instructions, recommendations, and considerations for US federal information system contingency planning.
- *Control Objectives for Information and related Technology* (COBIT ®) – specifically COBIT 2019, developed by the Information Systems Audit and Control Association (ISACA), which prescribes using generally applicable and accepted good practices.
- Information technology – Security techniques – Information security management systems – Requirements (ISO/IEC 27001:2013, IDT) and Information

technology – Security techniques – Code of practice for information security controls (ISO/IEC 27002:2013, IDT)
- Societal security – Business continuity management systems – Requirements (BS ISO 22301:2012) and Societal security – Business continuity management systems – Guidance (ISO/DIS 22313).

In Table 6.1 we show what those standards prescribe or recommend about business continuity

We also consulted ISO 27031, which provides guidance to business continuity and IT disaster recovery professionals on how to plan for IT continuity and recovery as part of a more comprehensive business continuity management system (BCMS). ISO 27031 describes a management system for ICT readiness for business continuity and has a focus on IT disaster recovery instead of on business continuity as a broader concept.

In this chapter, we describe the main elements of a BC plan, consulting standards mentioned above, as well as other relevant sources.

Before we start, we would like to, once again, explain the difference between a business continuity plan (BCP) and a disaster recovery plan (DRP) because the two terms are often used interchangeably, and many people, especially from the business side, do not know the difference.

Business continuity plan (BCP): Documented procedures that guide organizations to respond, recover, resume, and restore to a pre-defined level of operation following a disruption. The BCP is not necessarily one document, but a collection of procedures and information.

A disaster recovery plan (DRP) consists of a set of procedures and supporting information that enables an organization to restore its IT services (e.g., applications and infrastructure) as part of an overall business continuity plan (BCP) (Byrum et al., 2016)

If we use plain language, then we can say that the purpose of a BCP is to guide an organization on how to **recover critical business processes in** case of a disruption. At the same time, the main goal of DRP is to lead an organization on how to recover **Information Technology (and telecom) services.**

One more thing needs clarification since there is no unified approach among professionals and practitioners. Does DR plan activation necessarily mean relocation to an alternate site? If we are following the NIST definition shown in Table 6.2, it does.

In the other sources, we cannot find any concrete suggestions on whether Disaster recovery assumes relocation of IT operations or not. So according to the ISO definition

- ICT disaster recovery is the ability of the ICT elements of an organization to support its critical business functions to an acceptable level within a predetermined period following a disruption and

**Table 6.1  Comparison between BCM/DR Standards**

| NIST 800–34 | ISO 22301/ 22313 | COBIT 2019 | ISO 27001/27002 |
|---|---|---|---|
| Develop the contingency planning policy; Conduct the business impact analysis (BIA); Identify preventive controls; Create contingency strategies; Develop an information system contingency plan; Ensure plan testing, training, and exercises; and Ensure plan maintenance. | Business continuity program management Embedding competence and awareness Understanding the organization Selecting business continuity options Developing and implementing a business continuity response ( Exercise and testing | DSS04.01 Define the business continuity policy, objectives, and scope. DSS04.02 Maintain business resilience. DSS04.03 Develop and implement a business continuity response. DSS04.04 Exercise, test, and review the business continuity plan (BCP) and disaster response plan (DRP). DSS04.05 Review, maintain and improve continuity plans. DSS04.06 Conduct continuity plan training. DSS04.07 Manage backup arrangements. DSS04.08 Conduct post-resumption review. | The organization shall determine its requirements for information security, continuity security, and the continuity of information security management in adverse situations, for example, during a crisis or disaster. The organization shall establish, document, implement, and maintain processes, procedures, and controls to ensure the required level of continuity for information security during an adverse situation. The organization shall verify the established and implemented information security continuity controls at regular intervals in order to ensure that they are valid and effective during adverse situations. |

**Table 6.2  NIST 800–34 Definitions**

| Plan | Purpose | Scope | Plan Relationship |
|---|---|---|---|
| Business Continuity Plan (BCP) | Provides procedures for sustaining mission/business operations while recovering from a significant disruption. | Addresses mission/business processes at a lower or expanded level from COOP MEs. | Mission/business process-focused plan that may be activated in coordination with a COOP plan to sustain non-MEFs. |
| Continuity of Operations (COOP) Plan | Provides procedures and guidance to sustain an organization's MEFs at an alternate site for up to 30 days, mandated by federal directives. | Addresses MEFs at a facility; information systems are discussed based only on their support of the mission essential functions. | MEF focused plan that may also activate several business unit-level BCPs, ISCPs, or DRPs, as appropriate. |
| Crisis Communications Plan | Provides procedures for disseminating internal and external communications; means to provide critical status information and control rumors. | Addresses communications with personnel and the public, not information system-focused. | The incident-based plan often activated with a COOP or BCP, but may be used alone during a public exposure event. |
| Critical Infrastructure Protection (CIP) Plan | Provides policies and procedures for the protection of national critical infrastructure components, as defined in the National Infrastructure Protection Plan. | Addresses critical infrastructure components that are supported or operated by an agency or organization. | A risk management plan that supports COOP plans for organizations with critical infrastructure and key resource assets. |

**Table 6.2 (Continued)   NIST 800–34 Definitions**

| Plan | Purpose | Scope | Plan Relationship |
|---|---|---|---|
| Cyber Incident Response Plan | It provides procedures for mitigating and correcting a cyberattack, such as a virus, worm, or Trojan horse. | Addresses mitigation and isolation of affected systems, cleanup, and minimizing loss of information. | Information system-focused plan that may activate an ISCP or DRP, depending on the extent of the attack. |
| Disaster Recovery Plan (DRP) | Provides procedures for relocating information systems operations to an alternate location. | Activated after major system disruptions with long-term effects. | Information system-focused plan that activates one or more ISCPs for recovery of individual systems. |
| Information System Contingency Plan (ISCP) | Provides procedures and capabilities for recovering an information system. | Addresses single information system recovery at the current or, if appropriate, alternate location. | Information system-focused plan that may be activated independently from other plans or as part of a more significant recovery effort coordinated with a DRP, COOP, and/or BCP. |
| Occupant Emergency Plan (OEP) | Provides coordinated procedures for minimizing loss of life or injury and protecting property damage in response to a physical threat. | Focuses on personnel and property particular to the specific facility, not mission/business process or information system-based. | An incident-based plan that is initiated immediately after an event preceding a COOP or DRP activation. |

■ an ICT disaster recovery plan is a clearly defined and documented program, which recovers ICT capabilities when an outage occurs (ISO/IEC 27031, 2011).

ISACA defines the same terms as follows:

■ Disaster recovery – activities and programs designed to return the enterprise to an acceptable condition. The ability to respond to an interruption in services by implementing a disaster recovery plan (DRP) to restore an enterprise's critical business functions.
■ A disaster recovery plan (DRP) – A set of human, physical, technical, and procedural resources to recover, within a defined time and cost, an activity interrupted by an emergency or disaster (ISACA Glossary, 2019).

We can find a similar definition on the Business continuity institute's web page (BCI Glossary, 2019).

So, in this book, we will use a standard definition where Disaster recovery **does not imply automatically moving to an alternate location**. We can see from Table 6.2, that this definition matches with the NIST definition of the Information security contingency plan (ISCP).

Even though a majority of experts and web sources agree that a contingency planning process consists of the steps presented in Figure 6.1, we will keep our focus on actions, where according to our knowledge and experience, an organization should invest significant effort.

## Business Impact Analysis (BIA) and Assessing Downtime Impact

In this chapter, we explain how to conduct BIA and assess the impact of system downtime. According to ISO 22300, Business impact analysis (BIA) is a process of analyzing activities and assessing the effect that a business disruption might have on them (BSI Standards 2012). BIA is a vital part of a business continuity planning process. In this step, an organization must make an inventory of essential business functions and related applications and other resources needed to run those processes. The main goal of the BIA is to correlate system components with business activities and, based on that analysis, determine the effects of potential disruption. Figure 6.2 shows the results of Enterprise Strategy Group (ESG) research from 2017. We can see that indirect losses like "Loss of customer confidence" or "Damage to brand identity" concern companies to a great extent. To be able to provide adequate BIA, it is crucial to estimate and quantify in financial terms, the damage caused by downtime even for those impacts that are hard to predict.

## Approach to Business Continuity Planning

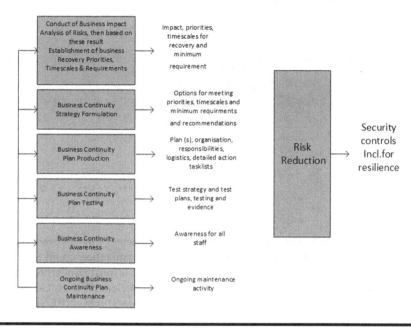

**Figure 6.1  Business continuity planning process according to ISO/IEC 24762(ISO/IEC, 2008).**

There are many standards for Business continuity management and the DR process (BCI institute, ISO 22301, ISO 22031, NIST 800–34, COBIT), but there is no single standard for BIA. When conducting BIA, it is essential to think about all possible scenarios, not only catastrophic ones (like fires, earthquakes, or similar disasters) because most downtime is caused by hardware failure, human error, and software errors, and only 5% are related to natural disasters.[2]

As an example of good practice, we will give examples of NIST 800–34 that distinguish three main steps in conducting BIA:

1. **Determine mission/business processes and recovery criticality.** Mission/ Business processes supported by the system are identified, and the impact of a system disruption to those processes is determined **along with outage impacts and estimated downtime.** The downtime should reflect the maximum time that an organization can tolerate while still maintaining the mission.

2. **Identify resource requirements.** Realistic recovery efforts require a thorough evaluation of the resources needed to resume mission/business processes and related interdependencies as quickly as possible. Examples of resources that

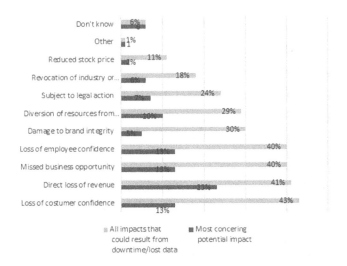

**Figure 6.2 Which of the following impacts to your organization could result from application downtime or lost data? Which impact is most concerning for you? (response from 174 organizations from North America, Western Europe, Asia Pacific, and Latin America with 250–2,499 employees) (ESG, 2017).**

should be identified include facilities, personnel, equipment, software, data files, system components, and vital records.

3. **Identify recovery priorities for system resources.** Based on the results from the previous activities, system resources can be linked more clearly to critical mission/business processes and functions. Priority levels can be established for sequencing recovery activities and resources (Swanson, Lynes, Swanson, & Gallup, 2010).

ISO 27313 assumes the following steps

1. **Identifying the activities that support the delivery of the organization's essential products and services;**
2. **Assessing the potential impacts over time of disruptions resulting from uncontrolled, non-specific events on these activities**. When assessing effects, the organization should primarily consider those relating to its business aims and objectives and its interested parties;
3. **Estimating how long it would take for the impacts associated with disruption of the** organization's activities to become unacceptable;
4. **Based on the assessment and considering other relevant factors**, setting prioritized time frames for resuming the organization's activities at a specified minimum acceptable level;

5. **Taking into account the prioritized time frames**, identifying relevant dependencies and supporting resources, including suppliers, outsource partners, and other interested parties (ISO 22313, 2012).

Since both standards have the same steps (step one from NIST 800–34 contains phases 1–3 from ISO 22313), we are going to discuss BIA steps according to NIST 800–34.

## Determine Mission/Business Processes and Recovery Criticality

As we can see from Figure 6.3, leading activities in this step are:

- Identifying key business processes. Critical business processes are not only customer-facing processes like sales, customer services, and so on, but also required support processes like an IT help desk that should provide IT support, facilities management who takes care of the power supply, compliance, legal, and others.
- Also, in this step, an organization needs to assess the impact of downtime. NIST 800–34 does not prescribe any methodology for quantifying downtime loss. In other sources, one can find different methods for a loss quantification, but the most common loss types considered in BIA are (Ibrahimović, Turulja, and Bajgorić, 2017)
  - loss of income from possible sales, obtained as the average income from services per hour;
  - loss of productivity calculated as the average affected labor expenditure per hour;
  - loss incurred in the process of service recovery;
  - loss of revenue from clients who have left the organization because of system unavailability; and
  - loss of income from customers who did not come to the organization because of system unavailability (word of mouth).

The simplest method for a loss calculation is to us the following formula:

$$\text{Cost of an IT Outage} = (To + Td) \times (Hr + Pr) + Oc^3$$

where:

- To – represents the outage duration,
- Td – represents the time needed to recover all data (from the backup media and manual entry from the last backup)
- Hr – productivity obtained as the average affected labor expenditure per hour

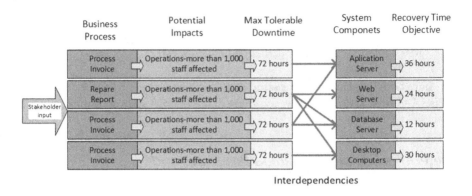

**Figure 6.3   BIA process according to NIST (Swanson et al., 2010).**

- Pr – Loss of income from possible sales, obtained as the average income from services per hour
- Oc – represents all other possible costs, including goodwill cost (from losing customers), legal/compliance costs, and similar costs. Since there is no exact formula to determine this cost component, the method to estimate it uses historical data.

Based on financial impact, all critical business functions can be grouped in impact categories. An organization can adopt a multipoint scale (e.g., Severe – above 1,000,000 USD, Moderate – financial loss between 200,000 and 1,000,000 USD, and Low impact for damage less than 200,000 USD). Figure 6.3 illustrates BIA process according to NIST.

- The next step would be to define maximal tolerable downtime (MTD)[4], Service delivery objective (SDO),[5] and Recovery point objective (RPO) for each vital business function. According to the results of the above-mentioned ESG research shown in Figure 6.4, almost half of the "high priority" business functions have MTD of less than 15 minutes. It is also worth noticing MTD as a term used in the BIA process because this term is much easier to understand for business matter experts than RTO, which is often used.
- In this step, an organization maps all identified essential business functions to IT systems and applications that support those functions. For every application, the Recovery Time Objective is determined. Recovery time for an application is shorter than MTD because application recovery is only part of the business process recovery, as is shown in Figure 6.5. The second part is Work Recovery Time (WRT). WRT is the maximum tolerable time that is needed to verify the system and/or data integrity and reenter missing data and prepare other prerequisites to resume affected business functions. When all systems

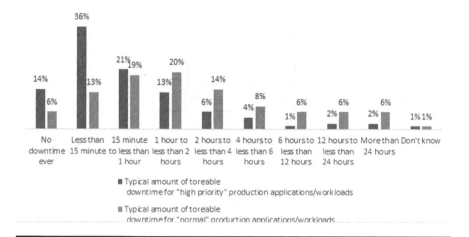

**Figure 6.4** **What is the amount of downtime your organization can tolerate from servers before they decide "failover/recover" to a BC/DR secondary site or service provider? (Percent of respondents, N = 320) (ESG, 2017).**

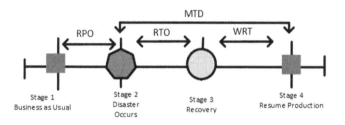

**Figure 6.5** **Relations between MTD, RTO, and WRT (Virtualization24x7, 2015).**

affected by the disaster are verified and/or recovered, the environment is ready to continue production again,

## *Identify Resource Requirements*

In this step, an organization needs to make a comprehensive list of the resources necessary to support critical business functions identified in the previous step. The list should include applications and all required hardware, software, network, people, vendor, and other resources. Table 6.3 represents an example of a resource list.

## *Identify Recovery Priorities for System Resources*

According to NIST 800–34, identifying recovery priorities for system resources is the last step of BIA. Since at this point an organization has all needed inputs: criticality

**Table 6.3  The Resource List**

| System Component | OS/Platform | Hardware Requirements | Staff Requirements | Network Requirements | Dependent on | Backup Method |
|---|---|---|---|---|---|---|
| CRM application | Cloud/SaaS | none | Network admin | Active internet connection | - | Cloud backup |
| Payroll | Virtualized Windows 2016 Standard | Two core processor 16 GB of RAM 250 GB | System admin | Connection to the Active directory | Active directory | Remote replication Disc backup |

of business functions, maximum tolerable downtime, recovery point objective, and financial impact of outage for them, as well as a list of the applications required to run those processes and their correlations and dependencies. it is a straightforward process to finish this task.

## Application Impact Analysis (AIA)

It is often the case that the BCP process does not start as prescribed by standards. Instead, the Information security department (or even worse, the IT department) gets the task of building DR procedure. In that case, it is almost impossible to conduct BIA as described above, and the BCP team can estimate RTO and RPO according to their knowledge of business processes (which is often enough) or conduct an application impact analysis. In the AIA process, business matter experts are asked how application downtime would affect their operations and if there are any manual workarounds they can use to continue the process in case of an application outage. According to those answers, IT prioritizes applications and sets RPO and RTOs.

## Risk Assessment

Most of the standard BCP methodologies have risk assessment as an essential step in a business continuity planning process. Some standards (mostly American) prescribe this step before BIA, and some put this step after BIA (Sikdar, 2017). ISO 22301 and ISO 22301 suggest conducting this step after BIA and recommend using the ISO 31000 set of standards in performing it. This assumes a "full-blown" risk management process, which starts with an assets inventory (in our case, this step has already been done in BIA), identifying vulnerability and threats for each asset, assessing probability, and then building a plan to mitigate those risks. From a resource and time standpoint, the risk analysis process is very resource-intensive and time-consuming. NIST 800–34 does not recognize this risk assessment step as a separate activity. Instead, it states, "Rather than just working to identify and mitigate threats, vulnerabilities, and risks, organizations can work toward building resilient infrastructure, minimizing the impact of any disruption on mission essential functions". We support the opinion that it is much better to concentrate organizational resources on building the resilience of the systems and components needed to support critical business processes, identified in BIA, and being prepared to minimize risk consequences regardless of the type of incident that could happen. A high-level risk analysis is used as a secondary driver (e.g., identify single points of failure for critical systems that should have redundancy based on business impact).

## Concluding Remarks from Practice

Sometimes it is hard to get business management's interest in any involvement in the BIA process, and it is perceived as an IT task. That does not have to mean that BIA should not be completed, however. IT (or any other employee with BCP manager role) can make the first BIA draft and then go to the business unit managers and ask them for their feedback. This could be one method to get their input since it is always easier to edit something that is already prepared than create something from scratch. Even weak estimates are far better than a blank sheet.

## Designing an Optimal BC Solution

In this chapter, we will explain, from an IT point of view, which techniques and designs can be used in designing a BC plan and which tools and methods could help finding an optimal one.

When designing a BC/DR solution, it is vital to know that BC plans are not intended only to cover extraordinary incidents, but that the main goal of BCM is to enhance information system availability. That means that BCP should have an impact on day-to-day activities and be embedded in operational procedures. The significant part of the BCP plan is to help in building a resilient primary IS site and its components. In the first part of this chapter, we discuss technologies that can help prevent an outage. In the second part of this chapter, we explore possibilities for an alternate (DR) site and present the advantages and disadvantages of various alternatives. Figure 6.6 shows the components of a comprehensive BC solution.

Before we dive into technical solutions, it is vital to have in mind the costs of their implementation. In the previous chapter, we explained how to calculate the

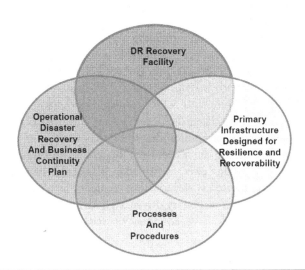

**Figure 6.6   Components of a holistic BC solution.**

financial impact of an outage. If we know how significant investment (using total cost of ownership – TCO over at least a three-year period as a measure) is needed to implement preventive control, we can compare it with loss reduction over the same period, to know if that investment is justified. Often one investment can improve the availability of several key business processes. The BCP project manager, working with business units management, should determine the optimum investment point to prevent outage and achieve required MTD, RTO, RPO, and SDO by balancing the cost of system inoperability against the cost of necessary resources and desired availability level of IS and its overall support for critical mission/business processes In Figure 6.7, we have illustrated the method of finding the optimal investment level in BC/DR technology.

The best strategy to deal with disasters is to reduce the chance of the incident happening. That means that an organization should implement adequate prevention measures. The primary technique to increase IS availability from a technological standpoint is to eliminate single-point failures wherever possible. Thus, an organization buys equipment with redundant components (processors, network cards, power supplies, etc.) and makes clustered configuration on the server, network, and storage level. Chapter 4 has more details about the high-availability server, network, and storage configurations, as well as virtualization technologies and vendors. High-level risk analysis combined with information security, BCM, and IS governance standards, and previous academic and practice research could be input for the selection of those measures.

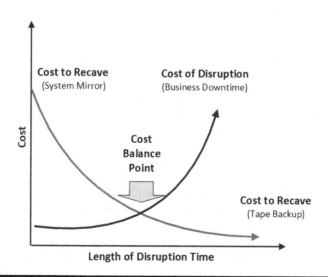

**Figure 6.7 Comparison between the cost of remediation and an outage duration according to NIST Sp-800–53 (NIST, 2014).**

## Bayesian Belief Networks (BBN) in Operational Risk Management, Information Security, and Availability Modeling

One of the possible options is to use Bayesian belief networks (BBN) to analyze the potential impact of various factors on the availability of information systems.

BBN has been widely used in operational risk management, information security, and availability modeling. Raderius, Narman, and Ekstedt (2009) presented a case study using "extended influence diagrams" combined with an architectural metamodel as the IS availability modeling tool. Hinz and Malinowski (2006) suggested a BBN model for assessing the risk of IT infrastructure. They got the model parameters using interviews with experts. Weber and Suhner (2001) used influence diagrams for the economic analysis of IS availability. Neil, Häger, and Andersen (2009) addressed the operational risk of IT infrastructure in financial institutions and proposed a methodology for representing it with a BBN model. Wei, Wang, Yang, and Liu (2011) developed an integrated framework for efficient IT services management based on BBN. Sommestad and Ekstedt (2009) created a model for the analysis of the cybersecurity of different architectural solutions based on the extended influence diagram. Cemerlic Yang, and Kizza (2008) proposed a BBN-based system for intrusion detection systems (IDS). Simonsson, Robert, and Johnson (2008) suggested a model for measuring IT governance efficiency based on BBN. Lande, Zuo, and Pimple (2010) modeled "critical information systems" using BBN. Zhang, Cope, and Heusler (2009) presented an innovative model for IS availability improvement, based on the BBN, in which the data for the CPT were obtained from the system logs. Different models based on BBN were presented in the area of software reliability (Dejaeger & Verbraken, 2012; Gran, 2002; Yu, Zheng, & Qian, 2009), and management of software development projects (Fenton, Hearty, Neil, & Radliński, 2010; Fineman, 2010; Radliński, Fenton, & Neil, 2007). Hu et al. (Hu, Zhang, Ngai, Cai, & Liu, 2013) proposed a model using Bayesian networks with causality constraints (BNCC) for risk analysis of software development projects. Feng, Wang, and Li (2014, p. 1 ) noted that "with the increasing organizational dependence on information systems, information systems security has become a very critical issue in enterprise risk management". They developed a Bayesian network model to simultaneously define the risk factors and their causal relationships based on the knowledge from observed cases and domain experts. Garvey, Carnovale, and Yeniyurt (2015) used a Bayesian network approach for developing a model of risk propagation in a supply network. Sharma and Routroy (2016) applied a Bayesian belief network to provide a framework for information risk analysis in a supply chain by presenting causal relationships among various information risks. Lauría and Duchessi (2007) suggested a methodology for building information technology (IT) implementation by using Bayesian network from client-server survey data. Their article demonstrates how to use the Bayesian network approach to predict the attainment of IT benefits, given specific implementation characteristics. Lauria and Duchessi (2006) showed how to create a Bayesian belief network (BBN) from real-world data on IT implementations. Li and Sun (2011) listed the Bayesian network as one of the models for business failure prediction (BFP). Gupta and Kim (2008) proposed linking Bayesian networks to structural equation modeling (SEM).

To summarize, Bayesian belief networks are a well-established method in IT management, particularly when it comes to security, risk, and availability management. It has been suggested that the main advantage of BBN is that they make it easier to understand and communicate with business users, as statistical and qualitative data are combined, and the causal structure of the process is graphically modeled (Neil, Marquez, & Fenton, 2008).

## Application of BBN for Availability Analysis

In this chapter, we explain how to use Bayesian belief networks in availability analysis, particularly to find variables (factors) with the most significant influence on system availability.

Availability is measured by the ratio of the time in which the system was available and the total time in which system is supposed to be running according to service level agreements:

$$\text{availability} = \frac{\text{System uptime}}{\text{System uptime} + \text{System downtime}} \quad (6.1)$$

Ibrahimovic and Bajgoric (2016) introduced a formula for complex systems availability calculation. They defined overall system availability as the average availability of each service weighted by a factor of the importance of service as represented by the Equation 6.2.

$$A = \frac{\sum_i A_i * k_i}{\sum_i k_i} \quad (6.2)$$

In this formula, $A$ represents overall system availability, $A_i$ is the availability of service $s_i$, and $k_i$ is a coefficient signifying the importance of service $s_i$.

For calculating availability of a particular service, it is vital to consider the service operating time, defined in the service level agreement, as well as the number of end users affected by the service interruption as represented by Formula 6.3.

$$A_i = \frac{t_i}{t_i + T_i * \dfrac{N_i}{n_i}} \quad (6.3)$$

$t_i$ is the total time that service $s_i$ was available under service level agreement, $T_i$ is the total time for which the system was unavailable, $n_i$ is the total number of the service users, and $N_i$ is the number of service users who experienced service interruption during time $T_i$.

## Bayesian Network

BBNs are graph models that combine graph theory and probability theory. Bayes' theorem is used for inference propagation so that the probability distribution can be quantified for each node if given the likelihood of an initial node and conditional probability table (CPT) for all nodes. For two events $A$ and $B$, Bayes' theorem states:

$$P(A|B) = P(B|A)\ P(A)/\ P(B) \tag{6.4}$$

In a Bayesian network, the full joint probability distribution of the modeled variables $X_1, \ldots, X_n$ can be expressed compactly using the chain rule of probability as follows:

$$P(X_1, \ldots, X_n) = \prod_{i=1}^{n} P(X_i | \text{Pa}(X_i)) \tag{6.5}$$

Pa $(X_i)$ designates the parents of $X_i$ in the directed acyclic graph (DAG). Thus, an entry in the full joint distribution is expressed as the product of the appropriate elements of the CPTs in the Bayesian network.

Although Bayesian networks significantly reduce the number of parameters, which must be determined to represent the full joint probability distribution, the number of parameters in the model remains one of the major bottlenecks of this framework. The most widely applied solution to this problem is the Noisy-OR model (Pearl, 1986). The Noisy-OR model gives a causal interpretation of the interaction between the parent node and the child node. It assumes that all causes (parents) are independent of each other regarding their ability to influence the variable effect (the child). The Noisy-OR model also assumes that the presence of any one of the causes $X_i$ by itself can be enough to cause the effect $Y$. Given these assumptions, the Noisy-OR model provides a logarithmic reduction in the number of parameters required for the construction of the CPT. Mathematically, the following holds:

$$p_i = P(y \,|, \bar{x}_1, \bar{x}_2, \ldots, x_i, \ldots, \bar{x}_n) \tag{6.6}$$

with $x_i$ designating that causal factor $X_i$ is present and $\bar{x}_i$ that it is absent. In other words, $p_i$ is the probability that the effect Y will occur when causal factor $p_i$ is present, and all other causal factors modeled are absent. However, the presence of the cause $X_i$ in a Noisy-OR model does not *guarantee* that effect $Y$ will happen. In practical models, there will always be additional factors not accounted for in the model.

To solve that weakness of the Noisy-OR model, Henrion (1989) introduced the concept of a *leakage* or background probabilities that allow modeling the effects of a combination of factors that are not explicitly included in the model. Introducing $p_0$ as a leak probability, the probability of y given that a subset $Xp \subseteq \{X_1, ..., X_n\}$ of antecedent causes are present, can be expressed as:

$$P(y|X_p) = 1 - (1 - p_0)\prod_{i:X_i \in X_p} \frac{(1 - p_i)}{(1 - p_0)} \tag{6.7}$$

However, the general concern is the availability of an entire park of systems, with a known prior availability baseline, for example, 99.5%. The Bayesian model, therefore, needs to be rescaled to reflect this prior availability. Such a rescaled model can be used for reasoning about which best practice solutions to apply to increase availability further. Franke, Johnson, König, and Marcks von Würtemberg (2012) rescale the model with a rescaling factor α applied to all $p_i$:

$$A(X_p) = 1 - P(y|X_p) = (1 - \alpha p_0)\prod_{i:X_i \in X_p} \frac{(1 - \alpha p_i)}{(1 - \alpha p_0)} \tag{6.8}$$

where $A(\mathbf{X}_p)$ is the availability of a given system lacking the best practice factors listed in the vector $\mathbf{X}_p$.

## Variables

Ibrahimović and Bajgoric (2016), based on Franke, Johnson, König, and Marcks von Würtemberg (2012) have identified that if an organization brings practices into the following 13 fields on the best practice level, it could significantly improve availability on an information system:

**Physical environment** is about the data center's location and equipment. By the ITIL definition (Taylor, Vernon, & Rudd, 2007), "data center" can refer to the primary data centers, regional data centers, server rooms, and other facilities that accommodate the communications and server equipment. However, in the empirical part of their article, all companies have a centralized infrastructure, so only main data centers are treated.

One crucial component of the resilient primary site is proper data center design. The first component that needs to be adequately designed is the building (or server room itself). To protect equipment from fire and temperature from outside, it should be EN 1047 compliant, which means that the temperature inside the room will now exceed 70 degrees Celsius for the certified period. It also must be smoke-, dust-, and water resistant to the IP67 level, which could guarantee that if there is fire or flood outside, equipment would be undamaged.

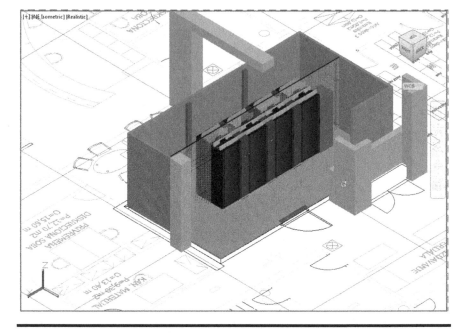

**Figure 6.8   A small data center scheme.**

It is vital to have an adequate cooling system, enough electrical power supply, and automatic fire protection, which preserves computer equipment undamaged, as well as other systems (light, alarms, video control, access control, smoke detector, and water detectors). Figure 6.8 represents an illustration of a small data center design.

To be sure that a data center is adequately equipped, it is good practice to adopt at least Tier III according to Uptime institute standard.

- Tier I: lacks redundant IT equipment, with 99.671% availability, maximum of 1729 minutes annual downtime
- Tier II: adds redundant infrastructure – 99.741% availability (1361 minutes annually)
- Tier III: adds more data paths, duplicate equipment, and that all IT equipment must be dual-powered (99.982%, 95 minutes annually)
- Tier IV: all cooling equipment is independently dual-powered; adds fault-tolerance (99.995%, 26 minutes annually)

In Figure 6.9, we show a possible redundancy solution for a cooling subsystem.

**Availability requirements management** represents the availability requirements that the information system should achieve, defined at the stage of system design and

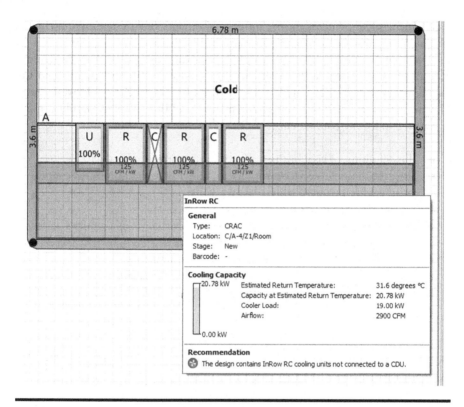

**Figure 6.9** Cooling system is designed to keep working even if one of the in-row units went out.

planning. Enterprise systems can vary significantly in their availability requirements (Cai, 2008).

The shortcomings that exist at this stage may be painful to correct in later stages. This is especially true for systems requiring continuous operations. Bauer (2010) distinguishes between two types of requirements on system availability:

- High-level requirements that determine Service level agreement (SLA) on service availability
- Detailed requirements defining the design and test scenarios for system testing

High-level requirements need to answer three questions: Which downtime cases are covered (planned, unplanned)? Do we cover only the complete downtime of the system, or do partial downtimes also count? What is the requirement for the availability of the system at an annual level, expressed in percentages? The detailed requirements are classified in one of four categories: behavioral requirements (behavior requirement), requirements on the number of outages (failure rate), requirements on system response (latency requirements), the likelihood of interruptions.

Defining Availability Management, ITIL says "that the goal of the management of availability is to ensure the agreed level of service availability according to the requirements of the business side, taking into account the efficiency of investments" (Taylor, Vernon et al., 2007). The requirements on ITIL availability should contain at least the following components:

- The definition of vital business processes supported by IT service[6]
- The definition of a service error, that is, under which conditions the service is considered to be unavailable
- Business impact analysis and risk analysis
- Quantitative request for availability, that is, which level of a service's performance degradation a business can tolerate
- Required periods in which the service must be available
- The relative importance of availability in different periods
- Requirements on system security
- Requests to backup and recovery services

Further, ITIL recommends that all purchases and/or development of the IT services and applications should be based on their ability to satisfy the required service availability parameters.

These requirements for availability directly affect the design and acquisition (development) of system components, and it can be concluded that if the requirements are not well defined, it will significantly affect system availability.

A system administrator has a crucial role in availability requirements definitions because he is included in the design (or purchase) part and can guide business users in defining requirements since he knows possible technical solutions.

**Operations management** includes managing operations or processes such as event management, incident and problem management, service requests, access control, and so on. No matter how well you plan and design the information system, issues in operations can have a considerable impact on the availability of the system. According to Microsoft (MOF-Operations Service Management Function), operations management has the following objectives:

- Ensure the execution of the necessary activities for the successful execution of all identified IT services within the contractual parameters
- Reduce the time that employees spend on reactive work
- Minimize service interruptions and time in which service is not a responding
- Perform periodic and ad-hoc IT operational tasks efficiently and effectively.

According to the ITIL definition (S. Taylor, Cannon, & Wheldon, 2007), operations include the following processes:

- Event management – represents the monitoring of all events in the system to identify and respond to all unusual activities
- Managing incidents and problems – to establish suddenly unavailable services in a short time, or restore the level of service in contracted frames to reduce the impact on business. Managing problems, on the other hand, aims at finding and eliminating the cause of incidents, and taking preventive activities that prevent future incidents.
- Managing requests for services – This category of operations includes solving requirements that pass through the desk service and can be fulfilled without a change formal request for (replacing standard computer equipment, etc.)
- Access management is dealing with enabling the use of information resources and services to authorized users while preventing access to unauthorized users. Practically, it means handling user accounts and access rights upon request of the Human Resources Management Department.

According to ITIL, the processes are managed through the following functions:

- Service desk – Service desk represents the central location where service users report incidents, submit service requests, and change requests
- Technology management – The purpose of this function is to provide and maintain technology for normal operations and service development.
- Operations management – This function is responsible for the proper operation of daily tasks according to the prescribed performance.
- Application Management – Within this function, application management is performed throughout the entire life cycle.
- Connection with other stages of the service lifecycle – such as change management, business continuity management, financial management, and similar.

When we look at the objectives, processes, and functions explained above, we can see that the best practices in performing operations can have a significant impact on the availability of the service. Again, system administrators have an important role in operations management since they are responsible for technology management, operations management, and parts of application management (deployment of service), and link to the other stages (especially a business continuity stage).

**Change management** encompasses managing changes according to the ITIL framework; "the introduction, modification or removal of approved, maintained or basic hardware, network, software, application, environment, system, desktop or associated documentation" (Taylor, Lacy, & MacFarlane, 2007).

The ITIL in several places emphasizes the connections of change management with the system availability, so when it lists the reasons why management of changes is essential, as one of the reasons it states, "minimizing influence and business interruption". Further specifying the characteristics of weak change management points to "sudden interruptions". Also, as one of the measures to measure the change management, ITIL states "the number of interruptions, incidents, problems/errors, unsuccessful changes" (Taylor, Lacy et al., 2007, p. 64).

To establish an efficient change management mechanism, ITIL prescribes the establishment of standardized processes, adapted according to the size and nature of the organization. In a process design step, it is necessary to consider the following:

- Creating a culture with zero tolerance for unauthorized changes
- Harmonization of change management processes with the business needs, project and change management process of the stakeholders
- Priorities for change, for example, innovation versus preventive versus defective versus corrective changes
- Determining responsibility for changes through the service life cycle
- Separation of duties in the change management process
- Establishment of a single change control function aimed at reducing the likelihood of conflicting changes and potential disruption in the production environment
- Prevent access to a production environment for people who are not authorized to implement the change
- Integration with other services management processes, monitoring the implementation of changes, detecting unauthorized changes, and identifying incidents arising from changes
- Select the time to implement changes – procedures for approvals of changes outside the prescribed time
- Assessing the performance and risk of any changes having an impact on the level and availability of the affected service
- Measuring the performance of the process, for example, efficiency and effectiveness (Taylor, Lacy et al., 2007)

A sysadmin role in a change management process is significant. He is usually in charge of the change implementation and establishing a monitoring system for change implementation and securing systems to prevent unauthorized changes.

**Backup** as "an additional copy of production data, created and kept especially for recovery of lost or corrupted data" (Gnanasundaram & Shrivastava, 2012), is widely used to lower RTO and RPO and improve IS availability, by implementing both traditional and advanced technologies (Castagna, 2013; Gartner, 2011). Introducing a backup variable is intended to determine to what extent best practices in this area affect the increase in the availability of the system. This issue is even more impressive because, thanks to the relatively affordable WAN and MAN connections, continuous data protection (CDP) is increasingly entering into production use.

The research that *Storage* magazine conducted in autumn 2012, in which 702 storage managers participated (Castagna, 2013), showed that the use of disk-to-disk backup is on a massive increase. Although data storage technology, in terms of speed, is not progressing at the same rate as CPU and memory solutions, large-capacity hard drives are enabling a change in basic assumptions in the implementation of backup solutions. Moreover, it can be noted that more and more companies are turning to a cloud-based backup, especially for e-mail backup.

In a survey conducted by IDC Research (Gantz & Reinsel, 2011) in 2011, the amount of data has reached 1.8 ZB. In similar research from 2018 (Reinsel, Gantz, & Rydning, 2018) the global amount of data was estimated at 33 ZB. Data "explosion" directly influences the requirements on the amount of data to be backed up. New technologies and practices, such as virtualization, cloud, containerization, and hyper-converged infrastructure, need new backup tools and techniques. Hence, the two main priorities for storage managers are deduplication, which reduces the requirements for storage space (and network resources if deduplication is done on the client-side), and the introduction of a 10 GB Ethernet connection that will significantly increase the speed of transmission backup data over the network.

Another important conclusion that can be drawn from the same research is that a large percentage of the company does not do any backup of end-user devices. Also, an important issue, especially in an environment with low-bandwidth WAN connections, is to back up data from remote branches.

ITIL recognizes three purposes of backup: As part of protection against loss of data, corruption of data and as part of the IT plan for service continuity.

Best practices include:

■ Creating processes and procedures to ensure that the data has been successfully backed up, including determining the responsibility for backups and establish monitoring, logging, and a notification system for the backup process. Employees responsible for a backup must be adequately trained to be able to manage the process.

■ It is necessary to ensure that backups are valid and tested, and that they can be successfully restored, which requires the ranking of the importance of data and the procedure in such a way that the most critical data is first backed up and restored. One should be sure that there is enough time to complete the backups of all the vital business data and understand the time it takes to restore this data in case of loss or corruption. It is also necessary to regularly test equipment, media, and processes.

■ Provide security for backup media. In general, this means that one copy of the backup media is kept in a logical and physically secure backup location. It also means that the backup does not contain viruses and other malware, spam, and irrelevant data or files.

■ Regularly review the risks related to the backup/restore process, procedures, and technologies to be sure that the backup process is compliant with changes occurring in business and environment.

■ Proper disposal of the backup media after completion of use, ensuring that it is physically destroyed

In small and medium organizations, a sysadmin is the owner of the entire backup process. Larger organizations have dedicated backup admin roles inside the sysadmin department.

**Storage redundancy** was considered from two aspects: data redundancy (Bakkaloglu, Wylie, Wang, & Ganger, 2002) and storage redundancy – technologies such as direct-attached storage (DAS), network-attached storage (NAS), or storage area networks (SAN). Data redundancy means the application of methods by which data is encoded and distributed to more independent data storage units to increase resilience in case of malfunctions and malicious attacks (Bakkaloglu et al., 2002). The techniques applied to this purpose include redundant array of inexpensive disks (RAID), local, and remote data replication. The complete architecture of the data storage system should contain redundant paths from the server to the disks where the data is stored. These include redundant controllers, redundant network components that transmit data between servers and data storage systems (switches and network cards/HBA). Whether it is local disks or disks that are part of a data storage system, all disks should be configured in the RAID array.

RAID systems can help in the event that one or more disks in array fail, but when designing RAID arrays, one needs to consider the speed of data restores to the replaced drive in the RAID series. Restore time for large-capacity disks could be significant depending on RAID level and disk I/O performance. During rebuild RAID, single parity RAID arrays do not protect data and have significantly decreased performance. Shroeder (2007) demonstrated in a survey conducted on a sample of 100,000 disks that the probability of a second disk failing during a rebuild is higher than predicted using the exponential distribution.

Best practices should be applied in the adequate architecture of a data storage system. During the design phase, the following questions should be asked: Should direct-attached storage (DAS), network area storage (NAS), or storage area networks (SAN) be used? Should we take into account all relevant criteria when choosing solutions? Are the best practices applied when selecting a type of SAN connection (iSCSI vs. FC)? Each of these approaches has its pros and cons, as shown in Table 6.4.

From the availability standpoint, the impact of the development of virtualization technology on data storage-type selection should be considered. In recent years it has been possible to make a "live" migration of virtual machines in the "shared nothing" architecture (Microsoft 2013) between nonclustered servers, meaning that failover configurations are not required for high-availability Hyper-V virtualization (although this remains the preferred method). Also, in the new Hyper-V 3.0 architecture, it is possible to use shared directories (SMB 3.0) instead of the "block-based" data storage system (Microsoft 2013a) and to perform replication on another Hyper-V Host on the virtual machine level.[7]

All these changes in the virtualization world significantly affect the process of selecting data storage technologies, suggesting that it is possible to achieve a high level of resilience using these technologies (live migration and replications) without investing in costly and complex data storage systems.

**Table 6.4  Comparison of Data Storage Technology (www.nasi.com/storage_networking-comparison.php)**

| Technology | Advantages | Possible Faults |
|---|---|---|
| IP SAN/iSCSI Storage Area Network | ■ Wide compatibility<br>■ Uses an existing network infrastructure<br>■ Lower costs and TCO<br>■ Data security<br>■ Reserve App Space<br>■ The system is also available during maintenance and upgrade<br>■ Cluster architecture allows for simple upgrades and thus reduces the need for significant initial investments<br>■ Uses standardized technology, so no additional training is required from the administrator | ■ Performance is still not at the level of SAN-based Fiber Optic technology<br>■ Not designed for graphics or video streaming<br>■ Enters extra load on LAN infrastructure, which may be a problem if the LAN does not have an adequate capacity |
| Fiber Storage Area Network | ■ Best Performance<br>■ Great scalability<br>■ Shared storage resources organized in pool<br>■ Ability to add capacity | ■ The most expensive<br>■ Requires specialist knowledge skills<br>■ Interconnections limited to 10 km<br>■ Problems connecting devices from different manufacturers |
| NAS Network Attached Storage | ■ Easy to install and manage<br>■ Less complicated than SAN technology<br>■ Allows file sharing and capacity between different operating and file systems<br>■ Enables the acquisition of data storage systems independently of the purchase of another computer equipment | ■ Less performance than SAN<br>■ When utilization of the capacity of NAS filer exceeds 90%, the device becomes a bottleneck and SPOF<br>■ Databases are not supported, only file transfer. |
| DAS Direct Attached Storage | ■ Suitable for tiny data-storage requests or hardware of the old generation<br>■ The system is usually part of the server | ■ Nonefficient space allocation<br>■ Adding space means adding a server<br>■ May require an interruption in operations when upgrading<br>■ Cannot share resources |

Replication can be performed at the server level, the data storage system where changed data storage blocks are copied to the different storage devices, the network level, or at the application level where the transactions from the primary system, using the log shipping mechanism, are transferred to the backup system. The best results from the availability standpoint are achieved when the data is replicated, at the same time, both locally and on a remote location (Gnanasundaram & Shrivastava, 2012).

There is also more and more data redundancy in the "cloud" and not only on the personal level (Dropbox, SkyDrive, Google Drive, etc.), and the use of data replication in the cloud, for increasing availability, takes momentum on the enterprise level.

ITIL recommends that all decisions related to redundancy should undergo a proper process of engineering requirements (S. Taylor, Vernon et al., 2007).[8]

In addition to the technical part of ITIL, best practices include process activities and a clear definition of responsibility for the following processes:

■ Policy definition and procedures for data storage
■ Naming conventions, hierarchy, and decisions on data storage locations
■ Design, dimensioning, selection, acquisition, configuration, and operation of all data storage systems
■ Maintenance and support for all storage systems
■ A link to the Information Lifecycle management team to ensure that access control, data protection policies, and IT management procedures are obeyed (Taylor, Cannon et al., 2007)

As in the backup management case, in small and medium organizations the sysadmin, as a jack of all trades, must manage data storage systems too. In larger organizations, there are dedicated storage admins, and often storage admins for one type of storage (Nettap storage admin, EMC storage admin, etc.)

**Avoiding errors in internal applications** refers to applications used in the production environment, as well as in the process of the design, development, and introduction of new applications. The ability to target the software stability team is a difficult task because it is necessary at the same time to provide scalability in response to increasing the number of users, and constant changes in complex systems where changes in one part of the system (software, network, hardware) can affect the stability of applications that have not been altered.

From the standpoint of the system availability, it is necessary to control all processes in the application life cycle. The process can be controlled by various techniques for quality control ISO 9000, CMM (Capability Maturity Model), Spice (Software Process Improvement and Capability Determination-ISO/IEC 15504), and Bootstrap (Conradi & Fuggetta, 2002). The most famous and commonly applied is CMMI-DEV, which is a subset of the CMMI model. "CMMI® (Capability Maturity Model Integration ®)" is a model that contains best practices that help organizations improve their processes. This model assumes the realization

**Table 6.5   CMM for Software Preview (Paulk, 1998)**

| Level | Focus | Key Process Authorities |
|-------|-------|-------------------------|
| 5<br>Optimizing | *Continuous improvement of the processes* | Prevention of defects<br>Managing technological changes<br>Managing changes to processes |
| 4<br>Managed | *Quality of products and processes* | Quantitative Process Management<br>Software Quality Management |
| 3<br>Defined | *Engineering of processes and organizational support* | Focus on organizational processes<br>Define an organizational process<br>Training program<br>Integrated Software Management<br>Software Engineering<br>Coordination between groups<br>Review code from another team member |
| 2<br>Repeatable | *Project Process Management* | Manage requests<br>Plan software projects<br>Monito software projects<br>Management of externalized parts of the project<br>Software Quality Assurance<br>Manage software configurations |
| 1<br>Initial | *Competent Employees and Heroes* | |

of 22 processes and is divided into five levels of maturity, presented in Table 6.5. To achieve a certain level of maturity, the organization must implement all processes belonging to that level (and levels below).

The ITIL assumes that the procedure for introducing a new service respects the change management procedure.

If all production applications for an organization follow ITIL recommendations for the application support team, this would lead to a decrease in application error frequency:

- Identifying the knowledge and skills needed to manage and operate applications
- Launching training programs to develop and enhance application supporting skills and keep records of these training sessions.
- Designing and executing end-user training.
- Designing and conducting tests of functionality, performance, and management of IT services
- Modeling and forecasting application operations under increased load

■ Assisting in assessing risks, identifying critical services and dependencies between parts of the system, as well as defining and implementing countermeasures.
■ Managing vendor relationships for all applications that are not developed within an organization
■ Performing the problem management process and maintaining a database of known faults
■ Defining, managing, and maintaining attributes and interdependencies for all configuration items (CIs) in Configuration Management System (CMS)
■ Ensuring the updating and proper use of the system and operational documentation
■ Defining and maintaining applications' documentation in cooperation with development teams
■ Providing third-level support for applications-related incidents
■ Tracking errors in applications and patch management
■ Identifying opportunities to improve existing applications, from the perspective of functionality and manageability (Taylor, Cannon et al., 2007).

**Avoiding errors in external services** can improve system availability by efficiently managing several external services, such as data communication, application development, maintenance, and so on.

The main reasons why organizations are resorting to outsourcing are:

■ Insufficient resources to implement appropriate technology
■ Lack of professional staff
■ Solution implementation speed
■ Lower costs of implementing technological solutions

An organization that outsources IT services has the same types of operational risks as an organization that provides these services internally. With the right approach to outsourcing, an organization can significantly reduce operational risks by improving the availability and quality of systems and services. In addition to the benefits that can be achieved in the operational risk domain, there are the following risks:

■ The attitude of the organization's management toward addressing operational risk through outsourcing
■ Failure to build the necessary knowledge and skills within the organization
■ Management's belief that outsourcing resolves all IT-related issues

Before deciding to outsource some IT services or the entire IT department, the organization's management should take all necessary steps to protect the organization against potential operational risks. Services that are outsourced need to be fully controlled as if they were being performed within the organization. That is, before deciding on outsourcing, the organization must fully understand the functioning of the services being outsourced. Management must ensure that outsourced services are subject to fundamental risk management operations:

- Risk assessment
- Selection of service providers
- Contracts
- Controls
- Access to Information
- Planning of exit solutions[9]

When selecting a service provider, it is necessary to assess the potential, financial strength, reputation, and risk management of the potential partner before concluding the contract. The contract should clearly define the obligations of the contracting parties, the method of verifying the fulfillment of the responsibilities, and liability for possible damages resulting from non-performance of the contract.

Moreover, the impact of outsourcing on the organization's operations, legal obligations, reputation risks, costs, liquidity, and capital, and the effects on the internal reporting system should be considered. Externalization must not increase operational risks, nor may it reduce the organization's effectiveness in performing day-to-day operations.

ITIL requires the establishment of service level management (SLM) for all outsourcing cases, which includes:

- Identifying existing contractual relationships with external vendors. Verify that these contracts meet the revised business requirements. Renegotiate contract terms where necessary.
- Creating a service improvement plan that anticipates continuous monitoring and service level improvement
- Implementing monitoring and data collection procedures (both internal and external vendors should be covered by service monitoring as their performance must be evaluated and managed)
- Analyzing service performance against SLAs and target service levels defined in the service catalog
- Documenting and reviewing trends over time to identify the consistency of service levels (S. Taylor, Case, & Spalding, 2007)

The critical elements of a successful relationship with suppliers at ITIL are:

- A clearly written, well-defined, and well-managed contract
- Clearly defined (and communicated) roles and responsibilities of both parties
- Good relations and communication between the parties

- Well-defined service management processes on both sides
- A selection of suppliers who have achieved certification on internationally recognized certificates such as ISO 9001, ISO/IEC 20000, and so on.

**Network management** has a considerable impact on IS availability, and several technologies can increase network availability, for example, redundant network components, redundant security appliances, and redundant critical network services (DNS, DHCP, LDAP, RADIUS, IDP).

ITIL defines a network-managed process with the following tasks:

- Initial planning and deployment of new networks/network components, maintenance, and upgrades of physical network infrastructure.
- The third level of support for all network services, including network issues investigations, as well as a contract with external service providers when necessary. It also includes the installation and use of "sniffer" tools, which are used to analyze network traffic, to assist in resolving the incidents and problems.
- Maintenance and support for network operating system and middleware software, including patch management, upgrades, and so on.
- Monitor network traffic to identify errors or potential bottlenecks and performance issues.
- Reconfiguring or redirecting traffic to achieve better bandwidth or better traffic balancing – dynamic load balancing/policy routing rules.
- Network security (in collaboration with the Information Security Management Department), including firewall management, access rights, password management, and so forth.
- Assigning and managing IP addresses, domain name systems (DNS), and Dynamic Host Configuration Protocol (DHCP) servers
- Managing relations with Internet Service Providers (ISP).
- Implementation, monitoring, and maintenance of intrusion detection systems on behalf of the Department for Information Security Management. Responsibility for ensuring that there is no denial of service to legitimate network users.
- Updating the Configuration Management Database, as needed, documenting the status of configuration items (CIs) and their relations (S. Taylor, Cannon et al., 2007).

To achieve the required system availability level, in addition to increasing the availability of specific components, connections between the system components should have at least the same availability. This implies that all critical service servers should have redundant network interfaces that are connected to different distribution switches. All key switches, routers, and security devices must be redundant as well as all essential network services (DNS, DHCP, LDAP, RADIUS, IDP, etc.). In an ideal situation, such redundant devices should operate in active/active mode

Besides this aspect, which includes enhancing reliability by increasing availability and maintainability, ITIL recommends the service design should take care of the following elements

- Channel Diversity: Provide multiple diversified access channels so that service access goes through different channels and eliminates the existence of components whose outage results in a single point of failure.
- Network density: Adding additional access points to services, nodes, or terminals of the same type to increase network capacity with higher coverage density.
- The flexibility of connection (loose coupling): design interface based on public infrastructure, open-source technologies, and ubiquitous access points, such as mobile phones and Internet browsers, so that the marginal cost of adding a user is low (S. Taylor, Iqbal, et al., 2007).

In the smallest organizations, a sysadmin also plays the role of a network admin, but even in medium-sized organizations, the duties of a network admin and sysadmins are separated.

**Equipment and location of the DR data center** involve deciding on the location of the DR center and setting the DR teams concerning RTO and RPO parameters. This decision significantly affects the feasibility of a complete DR plan. On the one hand, it is necessary to make sure that the backup site is far enough from the primary, and that they do not share the same risks. On the other hand, it is necessary to make it possible, quickly (within the defined RTO) to transfer the DR team to the backup location if necessary, and that the replication of the data to the backup site takes place within limits defined by the RPO parameter. This decision should be made after a thorough risk analysis for the primary data center and a risk analysis for potential backup sites. All unacceptable risks for the primary data center must not simultaneously affect the backup location. The following factors should be considered when choosing a physical location for a secondary data center:

- Is it possible to make a connection between two locations such that both data centers are in the same storage area network (SAN)? Fulfillment of this requirement enables disk mirroring in the storage system and near-zero RPO without additional replication software.
- Do both sites share the same infrastructure services (primarily electricity, Internet connection, data services, and telephone service)? Could a single adverse event cause service interruption at both locations?
- Is the backup location near medical facilities? In addition to being able to access medical services quickly, this can also be significant from a communication point of view, since roads to medical facilities are first cleared in the event of snow or other incidents.

- Is the location anonymous (low-key)? It is generally right that the backup data center be in a building that is not too prominent, and that the location of the backup data center is not published unnecessarily.
- Is the backup location adequately sized? In addition to the backup data center being required to continue operations, space must also be provided for all necessary employees and for their equipment needed to set up and continue operating business processes at the backup location.

Ideally, the backup data center should have a permanent staff that works on data center maintenance and, in the event of an emergency, can immediately start the recovery process. Backup data center security should be considered in two aspects: whether the site is adequately secured and, whether the DR team has access to the DR center in the event of site activation.

**Resilient client/server** systems involve implementing advanced technologies such as failover, load balancing, clustering, virtualization, software as service (SaaS) that can significantly enhance availability ratios (Bauer, 2010; Calzolari, 2006; Liu, Deters, & Zhang, 2010; Marcus & Stern, 2003; Singh, 2009). Calzolari (2006) defines the following conditions that an application must satisfy to utilize failover cluster resources optimally:

- Have an easy way to start, stop, force stop, check status – usually via command-line commands or scripts, including support for running multiple instances of an application;
- Using a shared disk subsystem (Network Attached Storage (NAS) or Storage Area Network (SAN));
- Storing as much status information as possible in a persistent shared storage system (usually a database or file) – this information is used when restarting an application at another node to the last stable state before an error;
- Having built-in mechanisms to avoid data corruption after an application crash.

In addition to these concepts, to improve the availability of client-server systems, Liu et al. (2010) also recommend using: "explicit messaging, uniform interface, partitioning, self-management, and decentralized control" concepts. In his doctoral dissertation, Cai (2008) exposes the idea of proactive self-regulating dynamic optimization based on dynamic risk assessment.

From the aspect of the system availability, ITIL provides the following recommendations for client-server systems:

- The third level of support: The third level of support for all incidents on servers and/or server operating systems, middleware, and other applications that include system diagnostics and recovery. If necessary, this activity also includes communication with external suppliers.

- Security system: Access and permissions control within relevant server environments, as well as an appropriate system of physical security measures
- Capacity management process to achieve optimal bandwidth, utilization, and performance of available servers
- Defining system architecture
- Specification of standards for application development and management
- Design, testing, implementation, and maintenance of applications
- Monitoring and managing application performance (S. Taylor, Cannon, et al., 2007).

Additionally, it is necessary to have in place the right policies, procedures, and practices for deploying client-server applications from the test phase to production.

**Monitoring** systems, according to the ITIL definition, refers to the activity of observing a system to detect changes that occur over time. In the context of operations management (and service's availability) that includes:

- Using tools to monitor the status of critical system components and vital operational activities
- Ensuring alerts generation and distribution to a responsible person if defined conditions are met
- Ensuring that the performance and utilization of the component or system are within a specific range (e.g., disk space and memory usage)
- Detecting abnormal types or levels of activity in the infrastructure (e.g., potential security threats). Detecting an unauthorized change (e.g., unauthorized software installation)
- Ensuring adherence to organizational policies (e.g., inappropriate use of e-mail)
- Monitoring service results and ensuring that they meet the quality requirements
- Tracking information used to measure Key Performance Indicators (KPIs).

ITIL defines a control process as the process of managing the use or behavior of a device, system, or service. It is important to note, however, that just manipulating the device is not the same as controlling it. Control requires three conditions:

- The action must ensure that the behavior conforms to a defined standard or norm.
- Circumstances that trigger responses need to be specified, explicit, and confirmed.
- Action must be defined, approved, and appropriate for given conditions.

In the availability context, control implies the following:

- using tools to define the circumstances that represent normal operations or abnormal operations

- regulating the performance of a device, system, or service
- availability measurement
- starting corrective measures, whether they are automated (e.g., restarting the device remotely or running the script) or manual (e.g., informing supervisory staff about the status)

**Human resources management** is also critical for ensuring IS availability concerning the role of human resources in operations and service management. ITIL states that organizations often feel that buying or developing tools will solve all their problems, and that it is easy to forget that they still depend on the process, functions, and, most importantly, people, and recalls that as Grady Booch famously said "fool with the tool is still a fool". As skills and characteristics necessary for efficient and effective service management, regardless of the role one performs, ITIL recognizes:

- awareness of business priorities and goals
- awareness of the role of IT in enabling business
- skills needed to provide customer service
- awareness of what IT can deliver to the company, including the latest development
- competencies, knowledge, and information required to fulfill the role successfully
- ability to apply, understand, and interpret best practices, policies, and procedures.

The following attributes are required in many roles, depending on the organization and specificity of the role:

- Management skills – From the perspective of managing people and from the standpoint of overall process control
- Meeting management skills – Organize, lead, document and ensure follow-up to agreed actions
- Communicativeness – An essential element of all roles is to raise awareness of the running processes, to ensure the participation of all employees
- Articulation – Both in the domain of report writing as well as verbal
- Negotiation power – Required for several aspects, such as procurement and contracts
- Analytical – For analyzing metrics derived from activity (S. Taylor, Vernon et al., 2007).

When applying best practices in the domain, as well as other areas, contextual and organizational specificities must be considered. One cannot simply "google" the notion of "best practices in the field of IT human resources" and then apply it to

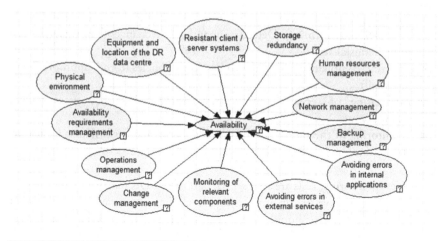

**Figure 6.10  Leaky Noisy-OR BBN model for IS availability analysis (Ibrahimovic & Bajgoric, 2016).**

one's organization. Some practices that fit a marketing agency may not be appropriate for an insurance company, and wholesaler practices may not apply to the hospital, and so on. In this respect, we can observe that most of the practices and policies publicly available on the Internet relate to educational and governmental institutions and may not apply to corporates.

Figure 6.10 shows the IS availability BBN Leaky Noisy-OR model based on 13 variables described above.

## BCP Management and Testing

This section deals with BCP testing, which is a vital part of the BCM lifecycle, and explains what options an organization has for BCP testing. It is imperative to have a monitoring mechanism to monitor primary and DR center systems components, servers and virtual machine status, network status, available disk space, and replication status. In a service operation context (and thereby providing service availability), ITIL implies:

- Using tools to monitor the status of critical system components and critical operational activities
- Generating notifications and distributing them to the responsible persons when defined conditions are met.
- Ensuring that the system's performance or component state is within a specified range (e.g., disk space and memory usage)

- Detecting abnormal activity types or activity levels in infrastructure (e.g., a potential security threat). Detecting unauthorized changes (e.g., unauthorized software installation)
- Ensuring compliance with the organizational policies (e.g., inappropriate use of e-mail)
- Monitoring of services' output and ensuring that they meet quality requirements
- Monitoring of the information used to measure key performance indicators (KPI) (Ibrahimović & Bajgoric, 2018)

Besides monitoring, tests are an essential part of BC/DR management. The purpose of the tests is to verify the preparedness level of an organization to implement a plan. Results of the test should be thoroughly analyzed and used as input for the planned improvement.

There are file levels of testing:

- Document review
- Walkthrough
- Simulation
- Parallel test
- Cutover test

**Document** review is a kind of test that is limited to documentation checking and assumes an analysis of recovery, operations, resumption plans, and procedures. It is performed by individuals, and as a result, it provides feedback to document owners.

**Walkthrough** review is performed by teams and consists of group discussion of recovery, operations, resumption plans, and procedures in forms of brainstorming and discussion. As a result, like the document review, it provides feedback to document owners.

A **simulation** assumes a walkthrough of recovery, operations, resumption plans, and procedures in a scripted "case study" or "scenario". It is performed by teams, and places participants in a mental disaster setting that helps them discern real issues more easily.

In a **parallel test,** an organization runs full or partial workload on recovery systems. It is performed by teams as scripted in BCP. A parallel test tests actual system readiness and accuracy of procedures. During this test, production systems continue to operate and support actual business processes.

A **Cutover test** goes one level above a parallel test and assumes that production systems are shut down or disconnected, and recovery systems take over the full actual workload. These kinds of tests induce the risk of interrupting real business but if carefully planned and executed, give confidence in the Disaster Recovery (DR) system.

From the frequency point of view, an organization must perform BCP /DR tests as often as possible (e.g., DR parallel test monthly, full BCP at least annually). It is also important that, besides scheduled inspections, an organization occasionally run undisclosed tests.

## Continuous Improvements

This part will explain how to maintain and keep BCP up-to-date, and how to work on constant improvement following internal IS changes, as well as global technological shifts.

To keep DR up-to-date, it is necessary to follow these events and modify BCP and DRP accordingly:

- Changes in business processes and procedures. Business procedures and processes are often subject to change. An organization introduces new products and services, and optimizes procedures (e.g., bank introduces factoring as a new service). It is good practice, prior to implementing change, to consider what it means from the BC aspect and to update BIA, RA, and BCP accordingly. Additionally, all BIA and RA should be reviewed on an annual basis
- Changes to IT systems and applications. If an application or operating system is upgraded on the primary side, the same version should be applied on the DR site (e.g., Oracle server version is upgraded from Oracle Database 11g to Oracle Database 18c)
- Changes in IT architecture – All changes in IT architecture on the primary site should be analyzed from the BC angle, and if the impact is positive, change is approved and should be applied on both sides (primary and DR). BCP documentation should be changed as well (e.g., replacing Hyper-V virtualization with VMware).
- Additions to IT applications – Whenever a new IT application is added, BIA and RA should be conducted, BCP and DRP updated, and DR center infrastructure updated (e.g., an organization introduces a mobile sales application)
- Changes in service providers – It is also essential that every change in service provider is adequately reflected in BCP and DRP (e.g., change of Internet link provider)
- Changes in organizational structure – Changes in organizational structures should be reflected in the BCP plan as well (e.g., splitting in the marketing and sales department may trigger changes in BC functional team)

Besides internal changes, an organization must follow technological advancement and update BCP accordingly. For example, an organization should follow a trend in SAN virtualization and explore benefits from a BC standpoint, and eventually propose implementation in a DR plan.

# Influence of Contemporary IS Architectures on BC/DR Solutions

This section considers the latest developments in the IT infrastructure field from a business continuity point of view. Primarily, we discuss software defined storage, hyperconverged infrastructure, and containerization impact on disaster recovery strategies.

We also show how an organization can use the cloud for backup and disaster recovery purposes.

## *Hyperconverged Infrastructure*

In recent years there has been a rise in the popularity of software defined infrastructure, which consists of virtualized compute, networking, and storage components. Those components are grouped into pools and enable full policy-based automated provisioning. Hyperconverged infrastructure (HCI) is a category of scale-out software-integrated infrastructure that applies a modular approach to compute, network, and store on standard hardware, leveraging distributed, horizontal building blocks under unified management (Gartner, 2019). Three software components make up a hyperconverged platform: storage virtualization, compute virtualization, and management. The virtualization software abstracts and pools the underlying resources, then dynamically allocates them to applications running in VMs or containers. HCI is based on the software virtualization layer on the top and commodity x86, servers that serve as compute and storage nodes. HCI vendors either build their appliances or they engage with system vendors that package the HCI vendor's software stack as an appliance. Additionally, an organization can make "do it yourself" HCI clusters. Figure 6.11 illustrates a typical hyperconverged infrastructure architecture.

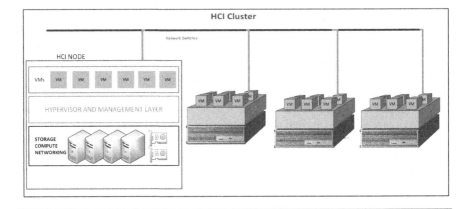

**Figure 6.11  A typical hyperconverged infrastructure architecture (Pott, 2018).**

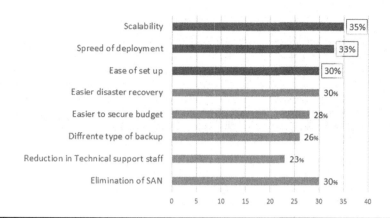

**Figure 6.12  Key motivators to deploy HCI, European storage survey 410 respondents (IDC, 2015).**

Figure 6.12 represents the results of IDC research from 2017, where one of the main reasons to implement HCI architecture is that implementing disaster recovery is easier than in classic datacenter architecture.

HCI platform is scalable, and it is possible to add computing or storage resources by plugging a new node into a cluster.

Since hyperconvergent systems have a virtualization component, compute nodes behave as a failover cluster, and storage is implemented using a virtualization layer as well, and there are multiple copies of data distributed among the storage nodes. This architecture enables workloads to be distributed among nodes, ensuring resilience in case of hardware failure. If an organization implements HCI in a metro cluster, then it is protected in case of a site or a rack failure. Hyperconvergence architecture is designed to eliminate all single points of failures and be resilient on any hardware failure, including failure of management nodes, which are implemented as active/active or active/passive clusters. Additionally, HCI systems have implemented snapshot technology, thus enabling backup and replication to alternate sites or cloud. Deduplication, which is a standard feature of HCI systems, makes all application migrations and replications easier since it drastically reduces the amount of data needed to be transferred.

On the other hand, since the storage level is virtualized, synchronous replication is much harder to implement.

Leading vendors in HCI, according to Gartner (2019), are Nutanix, VMware, DELL/EMC, and HPE/SimpliVity.

## Cloud Operations

Cloud computing can be explained in two ways. When someone thinks about the cloud, they primarily refer to the applications operated and managed on the

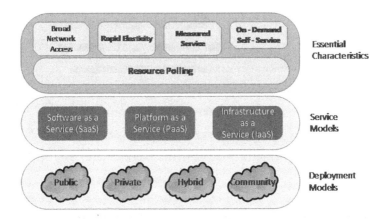

**Figure 6.13   NIST cloud service model.**

Internet using the commercial provider-controlled infrastructure. There are many cloud providers; the most popular are Amazon (AWS), Microsoft Azure, Google Cloud, and Salesforce's CRM. Nowadays, most businesses are using services from more than one cloud provider. Another meaning of the cloud refers to the way the cloud works: using virtualized resources, available and scalable on customer demand via automated procedures and scripts. There are no upfront costs and investments; the customer pays for what he uses. Figure 6.13 shows a generic cloud model.

There are three basic types of public cloud services: Infrastructure as service (IaaS), Platform as Service (PaaS), and Software as Service (SaaS). Besides these, with the appearance of serverless computing, Function as Service (FaaS) has emerged as a new cloud computing model.

IaaS public cloud providers offer storage and compute services on a pay-per-use basis. Additionally, it can provide a whole range of infrastructure services like databases, networking services, machine learning, application servers, analytics services, archive, deep storage services, and so on. The leader in this field is Amazon Web Services, followed by Microsoft Azure and Google Cloud Platform,

PaaS provides sets of services aimed at application development and hosting. The target population is a developer who can use different tools to build and host applications. Primary providers are Salesforce's Heroku and Force.com, and Microsoft with Flow, Forms, and Power Bi services.

The SaaS type of public cloud enables using the whole application using an Internet browser. The most popular services in this category are Office365, Google G Suite, Salesforce, and others.

FaaS is the cloud version of serverless computing, and it enables developers to write and use functions as service. Leading cloud providers in this area are AWS Lambda, Azure Functions, and Google Cloud Functions. A unique benefit of the

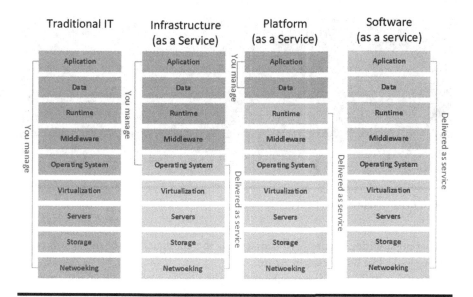

**Figure 6.14   Cloud service models (Chou, 2018).**

FaaS application is that they are billed using the pay-per-call model. Figure 6.14 illustrates cloud computing models.

Even though it looks like, by using any of the cloud architectures mentioned above, an organization transfers most business continuity-related risks, that is not the case. Depending on the model used, there are still different risks an organization needs to mitigate. BIA and business continuity plans are still unavoidable, but risk types may be different.

Two most significant risks to IS availability introduced by using the public cloud are:

- Cloud services are not always available
- Data protection is not included by default

Big cloud providers can have availability rates higher than 99.5%, which is better than most organizations can provide in their data center, but an organization must do its best to keep its services up. If an organization signs a standard Service level agreement with cloud providers, it can have a clause stating that it will get one week of free service for every day of the service unavailability. Most often, that is not enough, because every hour of a critical service outage can cause significant damage to an organization. To prevent that situation, most providers offer an option to buy a site recovery service. Site recovery service assumes that the virtual machines and service, which run in the primary data center, can be both recovered and started in a different data center automatically if a problem occurs. They also offer periodic DR

**Figure 6.15    Azure site recovery services.**

testing possibilities. Figure 6.15 shows what the configuration of the site recovery service looks like on Microsoft Azure.

An organization needs to configure a regular backup of all critical data and virtual machines it uses in the cloud. It protects from problems on the vendor side, as well as from mistakes in configuration, user errors, accidental deletion, and hacker attacks (especially ransomware). All cloud vendors offer backup features, and the organization must configure it appropriately.

Since most of the public cloud services use proprietary data storage formats, an organization should have a strategy on how to transfer those data back into its own data center or to another cloud provider in case of contract termination.

## Containers

Containers as part of IS infrastructure have gained popularity in recent years. This happened because of their ability to address the following practical problems:

- Easy and fast deployment from development to production. A container includes an application, all depended libraries, and a necessary configuration. Thus, when we decide to move the container from a development environment through a test to a production, there will be no surprises with missing libraries and changed config files.
- In contrast to virtualization, a container does not have a complete operating system but uses the OS kernel from the host system. That means that it is smaller in size, it boots almost immediately, and since it has a small footprint, one host can run many containers
- Since it has a small footprint, it enables application modularity. A monolithic application can be divided into microservices, each of which is deployed each in its own container.

In the real world, Docker (www.docker.com) is de-facto standard container technology. As an application for container management, Kubernetes is most prevalent. Still, some companies use Docker Enterprise Edition for container management (shown in Figure 6.16). There is also Red Hat's Open Shift Container Platform (now part of IBM) as an on-premises private platform as a service product. Open Shift is built around a core of application containers powered by Docker, with orchestration and management provided by Kubernetes on a foundation of Red Hat Enterprise Linux (Rubens, 2017).

From the business continuity point of view, the protection of container infrastructure needs to be part of BCP. Applications that run in containers are composed of multiple microservices and communicate with each other using various protocols, like REST, MQ, or TCP. Since containers are stateless, when service does not respond, it is enough to start another instance of the container, and an application continues running. A containerized application often uses persistent storage to keep data. It could be a file system or an SQL database. A good practice is that persistent storage is retained on the container host, and should be backed up as part of the host backup together with container repositories that contain container images. Since containers themselves are stateless, it makes no sense to back up a running container. Depending on required RTOs and RPOs, an organization might want to include container hosts in a replication process and make a replica in the cloud or an on-premise DR site.

## The Latest Development for Backup and Disaster Recovery Solutions

Disaster recovery (DR) has several components. The first is moving data from the primary data center to the secondary data center. Traditionally, this meant backing

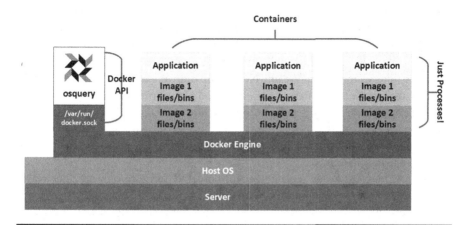

**Figure 6.16   Docker architecture.**

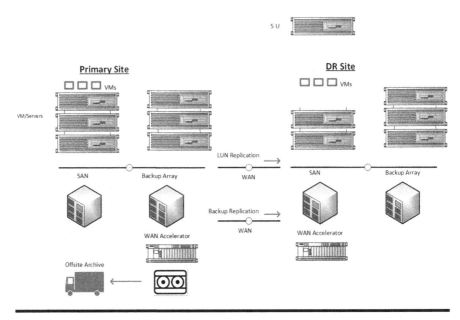

**Figure 6.17    Traditional data protection architecture.**

up data to tape and shipping tapes off-site. Alternatively, it might mean using replication software on the host, the array, or the disk backup appliance to copy data to a secondary site over a WAN intelligently. Many data centers used replication, but it had to be managed separately because the backup software was not integrated with it. So, the software had no way to verify that data was securely off-site (Crump, 2015). A typical traditional backup and DR architecture are shown in Figure 6.17.

In today's world, backup and DR tools are converging. Tape as a backup medium has been used less and less, and backup software uses modern technologies like snapshots, source, and target deduplication; compression; and WAN acceleration, which enables efficient backup replication to the disaster recovery site. Some backup products (like Commvault, Veeam, NetBackup) can make consistent application-aware snapshots on the primary storage array and replicate it to a secondary location. Almost every major backup software vendor supports conversion from a physical server to a virtual machine (P2V) and runs a backed-up virtual machine without a restore process. Modern backup software supports the DR management process, DR testing, and planning.

An organization needs separate backup and DR software only in cases where RTO and RPO for some applications are stringent (e.g., core banking system), and then the organization uses some replication technologies (continues data protection, application-level replication for database server or storage to storage synchronous or asynchronous replication) to transfer data to an alternate location. Even in that case, backup is still important, not so much for complete system recovery purposes, but for investigation and forensic purposes. When we are talking about the recovery of a high-volume transaction system like e-commerce, e-banking, or payment card processing, recovery from the backup or even snapshot is a very cumbersome process, because RPO for those systems is close to zero, and from the last backup or snapshot tens of thousands or more transaction need manual recovery.

## Backup to Cloud

Backup to cloud is gaining in popularity and replacing transferring the backup to the alternate site. A typical architecture is presented in Figure 6.18. Every cloud backup service provider must fulfill basic security and functional requirements:

■ Data must be encrypted during transit.
■ Data must be stored encrypted in the cloud via a state-of-the-art encryption protocol, such as 256-bit AES encryption.
■ The cloud service provider must support robust and enforceable authentication with features like password expiration and complexity (Castagna, 2012).

There are different options to send the backup to the cloud. The backup can be sent directly to the cloud without any interim storage on a customer site. Personal computer backup is the most common usage pattern in this scenario. The pure cloud backup option assumes that agents are installed on protected desktops and servers. This method is quick for setup and easy for maintenance, but is prone to bandwidth and latency problems since if many files are changed at once, it takes some time to perform backup directly to the cloud.

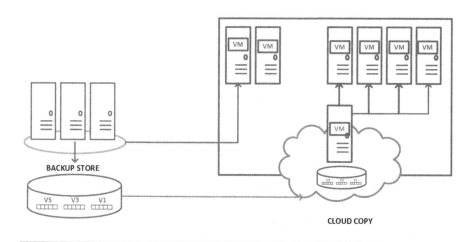

**Figure 6.18   Backup to cloud.**

To overcome bandwidth and latency issues, an organization can use a hybrid cloud backup option. In that option, backups are first stored to an on-premises disk or gateway, and after backup is completed, it is replicated to the cloud. An additional benefit of this approach is that the last few backups, kept on-premise, can be used in the restore process, instead of copying data from the cloud, which can be a very slow process. Hybrid cloud backups usually use source-side deduplication as well as features like block-level tracking and incremental forever backup, to be able to efficiently back up large files like e-mail archives or database files. In Table 6.6, we gave an overview of the advantages and disadvantages of various backup options. Table 6.7 contains a checklist that an organization should consider before deciding to run a backup to the cloud.

## DR Sites Planning

In a traditional IT world, depending on the results of BIA analysis, an organization chooses between cold, warm, hot, or mobile DR sites (see Chapter 3). That means that an organization must invest in DR center facilities and equipment. Figure 6.19 illustrates the relations between data protection technologies and RTO and RPO.

**Table 6.6  Backup to Cloud Options (Castagna, 2012)**

| Option | Advantages | Disadvantages |
|---|---|---|
| Managed service provider (MSP) | - Simplicity<br>- Cost-effective<br>- Few on-premises IT resource requirements | - Complete dependency on the MSP for all aspects of the backup<br>- Control is handed off to the MSP |
| Cloud-enabled backup applications | - Extends and supplements existing backup infrastructure and processes<br>- Except for backup data location, control remains with the customer<br>- Cost-effective | - Requires a cloud-enabled backup application<br>- Little impact on IT resource requirements |
| Cloud gateways | - Works with any backup application that supports backup to disks<br>- Extends and supplements existing backup infrastructure and processes<br>- Except for backup data location, control remains with the customer | - Introduction of an additional IT infrastructure component that needs to be managed<br>- Higher cost |

**Table 6.7    Backup to Cloud Checklist (Castagna, 2012)**

| Feature | Reason for Relevance |
|---|---|
| Encryption of data in transit and at rest in the cloud | Prevents access to the data by cloud service provider staff and other unauthorized users |
| SAS 70/SSAE16 Type II compliance of the cloud service provider | Ensures the service provider has reliable IT controls in place; a must-have for public companies and industries with additional regulatory requirements |
| Data deduplication | Reduces storage cost; source-side deduplication also reduces bandwidth requirements |
| Hybrid cloud backup option | Cached on-premises backups eliminate long restore times of a pure cloud backup solution |
| Getting data in and out of the cloud via a physical device | Options of initial "seeding" of backups and delivery of restore data via physical disk to minimize initial backup and restore times |
| Incremental forever | Ensures efficient ongoing backups |
| Sub-file-level backup of changed files | Minimizes the amounts of data to be backed up, especially with large files |

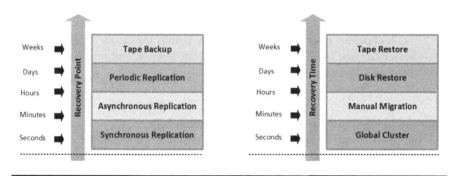

**Figure 6.19    Technology solution dependency of RTO and RPO.**

The size of investments depends on required RTO and RPO since shorter RTO and RPO times assume more advanced and expensive technology solutions.

## DR Site in Cloud and Disaster Recovery as a Service (DraaS)

A lot of small and medium businesses were not able to afford a DR solution at all, and they eventually had a procedure for shipping backup media off-site. Since virtualization and public cloud technology have become ubiquitous, new

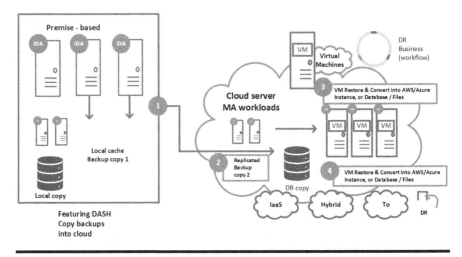

**Figure 6.20　DR site in the cloud.**

services emerged, offering disaster recovery in the public cloud. Hanna defines disaster-recovery-as-a-service as

> a productized service offering in which the provider manages server image and production data replication to the cloud, disaster recovery run book creation, automated server recovery within the cloud, automated server failback from the cloud, and network element and functionality configuration, as needed.
>
> (Hanna, 2018)

Figure 6.20 represents a typical DR to cloud architecture

The real strength of the public cloud is that a customer can get resources on demand and pay for resource utilization only. So, an organization can have whole DR infrastructure ready with minimal costs if it is not running.

## Building a Modern DR Platform

Even if an organization chooses a public cloud for DR site location, the starting point for architecting a solution is BIA and required RPO and RTO. An organization can choose between two primary options.

In the first option, with more relaxed RPO and RTO, an organization can prepare all required services in the cloud environment, copy the backup from the primary site to the cloud, and, if needed, restore a backup in the cloud environment and start services.

Almost every major backup vendor (Commvault, Veritas, IBM, Dell/EMC, and a significant number of new players in this market) offers this functionality as well as major cloud providers.

The second option, which could be valid for the business-critical services with more aggressive RTO and RPO, is to make a cloud replica of the production environment with data replication, using continuous data protection (CDP) software, database logs (e.g., Oracle Data Guard), or snapshots. This option could be costly since replicated VM-s are always-on, even when they are not in use.

Both options can be used regardless of whether the primary data center is located on-premise or in the cloud.

Regardless of which option an organization chooses, there are a few points to consider:

- Does the organization have an adequate business continuity plan containing clear procedures and guidelines on how to make a switch and use the DR environment?
- Is there enough Internet bandwidth to support smooth replication?
- How often should replication be run to meet RPO?
- Can end users and customers connect to the DR environment?

The hardest problem to solve in this situation is how to restore VM-s back to the primary site, mainly because that process has enormous bandwidth requirements.

For an organization that does not have enough resources to prepare and manage the DR plan, there is the possibility of using third-party providers that offer managed disaster recovery services (Disaster Recovery as a Service [DRaaS]). An organization needs to be sure that it has enough internal resources to support DR planning, testing, and maintenance processes, and, most importantly that it will be able to execute the plan if needed. Using DRaaS can remove (or at least lower) those risks and free internal resources. Nevertheless, for every business, it is essential to have control of the DR process, to understand it, test it, and be involved in all phases.

We can see that necessary BCP/DRP steps are not changed if an organization uses the cloud as a DR platform. It still needs to conduct BIA, risk analysis, develop the plan, test it, and maintain it. It even uses the same data protection techniques, backup, and snapshot, as it would use for an on-premise DR center. However, the cloud option provides greater flexibility, and enables the DR center with a minimal upfront investment, with reasonable RTO and RPO.

For a larger organization with demanding RTO and RPO, the cloud DR option could be quite expensive. The cloud DR option is intended for a virtualized workload or even physical servers, which can be virtualized, but legacy systems are not supported.

## Conclusion

The sixth chapter was about business continuity implementation in the real world, designing optimal BC solutions using BBN and BCM, and challenges and opportunities arising from the data center shift toward the cloud. There are different standards that can be the basis for BCM/DRM planning and implementation, and the most significant are NIST 800–34, COBIT, ISO/IEC 27031, and ISO 22301/22313. The essential step in the BCM process is BIA, an inventory of crucial business functions and related applications and other resources needed to run those processes. The main goal of the BIA is to correlate system components with business activities and, based on that analysis, determine the effects of potential disruption. Getting the business side's attention to this task is especially tricky because most organizations suppose that BIA is the task of the IT department. Even in that case, the BCM project manager (very often this role is given to head of IT by default) must take all necessary steps to finish BIA. One of the methods is to make the first BIA draft himself and then go to the business unit managers and ask them for their feedback and sign-off.

There are different methods and techniques for ensuring business continuity. But the best strategy is to work on prevention and on reducing the probability of an incident happening. The primary way for the rising IS availability level is the elimination of single points of failure in the system.

Bayesian belief networks (BBN) models can be used to analyze the potential impact of investment in IT systems and IT governance on the availability of information systems. One of the most critical measures, which can be implemented for improving IS availability, is establishing a monitoring mechanism to monitor the primary and DR center and the status of their components, as well as replication between them.

Besides monitoring, tests are an essential part of BC/DR management. An organization must run tests on a regular basis to verify the preparedness level, to implement a BC/DR plan. Test results must be used for continuous improvement purposes, meaning that before a new test, an organization should correct problems discovered on the last examination. DR/BCP must reflect every change implemented in the organization's IS, and keep pace with development in the IT field.

HCI is a new paradigm in IT architecture and it is becoming a part of most data centers. It uses virtualized and software-defined compute, storage, and networking components. One of the main reasons to implement HCI architecture, according to IDC research from 2017, is that implementing disaster recovery is more comfortable here than in classic data center architecture.

From the BC aspect, an even more significant change in the IT landscape is the increased use of cloud technologies. But depending on the cloud model used (IaaS, PaaS, SaaS, FaaS), there are different risks an organization needs to mitigate. BIA and business continuity plans are still unavoidable, but risk types may be different.

Container technology has one extremely fast adoption rate, regardless of whether the organization hosts applications in an on-premise data center or the cloud. An organization must be aware of all aspects of a containers platform and modified BCP to protect containerized applications and data.

Backup in the traditional sense is used less and less in the modern data center. Usage of tape as a backup medium is rapidly declining, and snapshot and CDP technologies are used more and more.

The public cloud is more often used as a backup target regardless of whether it is a backup of a personal computer or an enterprise application. The most efficient method for cloud backup is a hybrid option, which helps overcome bandwidth and latency issues. It assumes that backups are first stored to an on-premises disk or gateway, and that after backup is completed, it is replicated to the cloud. An additional benefit of this approach is that the last few backups, kept on-premise, can be used in the restore process, instead of copying data from the cloud, which can be a very slow process.

More and more organizations are basing their DRP on using a public cloud as a DR site. Instead of shipping backup media to a secondary site, they replicate data to the site on the cloud (it could be a hot or warm site). If an organization does not have enough resources internally, it can outsource the whole DRM process and use DRaaS. Even if an organization uses the cloud as a DR platform, it still needs to conduct BIA, risk analysis, develop the plan, test it, and maintain it. However, the cloud option provides greater flexibility, and enables a DR center with minimal upfront investment, with a reasonable RTO and RPO.

## Discussion Questions

1. What are the leading standards in the BC/DR field?
2. What is BIA, and who are the main participants in the BIA process?
3. What are the main steps in the BIA process?
4. Explain the process of assessing a downtime impact briefly.
5. What are the components of a holistic BC solution?
6. Explain what BBN is and how it can be used for designing an optimal BC solution.
7. List the key steps of the BCP management and testing process.
8. What is an HCI and what are the main benefits?
9. Explain the terms IaaS, PaaS, SaaS, and FaaS.
10. What are the main concerns when an organization decides to run a backup to the cloud?

## Notes

1. All definitions were given in Chapter 3. In this chapter we repeat some of them to make it easier for a reader to follow the chapter.

2. www.continuitycentral.com/news06645.html
3. Modified from Jason Buffington (2019)
4. ISO 22301 uses synonym Maximum acceptable outage (MAO)
5. ISO 22301 uses synonym Minimum business continuity objective
6. IT service can have vital and less important components. For example, the vital function of an ATM is the payment of money, while the printing of the certificate of redemption is not a vital function.
7. Similar functionality exists on VMware virtualization
8. Process Engineering The application is described in the ITIL Service design page 167.
9. "Outsourcing of Information and Transaction Processing", Board of Governors of the Federal Reserve System, www.federalreserve.gov/boarddocs/srletters/2000/SR0004.HTM, pogledano 3.5.2005.

# References

Bakkaloglu, M., Wylie, J.J., Wang, C., Ganger, G.R. (2002). *On Correlated Failures in Survivable Storage Systems* (CMU-CS-02-129), Parallel Data Laboratory. Paper 107

Bauer, E. (2010). *Design for Reliability: Information and Computer-Based Systems*, John Wiley & Sons, IEEE Press.

BCI. (2019). Glossary | BCI. Retrieved July 31, 2019, from www.thebci.org/knowledge/business-continuity-glossary.html

BSI_Standards_Limited. (2012). *BS ISO 22301:2012 Societal Security – Business Continuity Management Systems – Requirements*, BSI Standards Limited.

Byrum, A., Jones, B., Beaudry, P., Schulz, Y., Paredes, N., Clayton, T. (2016). *Create a Right-Sized Disaster Recovery Plan.*, Info-Tech Research Group.

Cai, Z. (2008). *Risk-Based Proactive Availability Management – Attaining High Performance and Resilience with Dynamic Self-Management in Enterprise Distributed Systems*. Georgia Institute of Technology.

Calzolari, F. (2006). *High Availability Using Virtualization*. Universita di Pisa.

Castagna, R. (2013). Business backup trends: Storage Purchasing Intentions fall 2012 survey results. Retrieved from *Storage* magazine website: http://searchitchannel.techtarget.com/photostory/2240176644/Business-backup-trends-Storage-Purchasing-Intentions-fall-2012-survey-results/1/Spending-plans-for-data-backup-solutions#contentCompress

Castagna, R.. (2012). *Storage Essential Guide Cloud Backup and Cloud Disaster Recovery*. Tech Target.

Cemerlic, A., Yang, L., Kizza, J. (2008). Network intrusion detection based on Bayesian networks. *Proceedings of the 20th International Conference on 20th International Conference on Software Engineering and Knowledge Engineering*, SEKE 2008, 1–4. Retrieved from www.utc.edu/Faculty/Li-Yang/MyPaper/SEKE08-Cemerlic-Yang.pdf

Chou, D. (2018). *Cloud Service Models (IaaS, PaaS, SaaS) Diagram*. Retrieved August 25, 2019, from https://dachou.github.io/2018/09/28/cloud-service-models.html

Conradi, H., Fuggetta, A. (2002). Improving software process improvement. *Software, IEEE* (August). Retrieved from http://ieeexplore.ieee.org/xpls/abs_all.jsp?arnumber=1020295

Crump, G. (2015). Data backup and disaster recovery made simple. Retrieved August 26, 2019, from https://searchdatabackup.techtarget.com/tip/Data-backup-and-disaster-recovery-made-simple

Dejaeger, K., Verbraken, T. (2012). Towards comprehensible software fault prediction models using Bayesian network classifiers (forthcoming). *Transactions on Software, 1*(1), 1–22.

ESG. (2017). ESG master survey results: Real-world SLAs and availability requirements. Retrieved August 18, 2019, from www.esg-global.com/research/esg-master-survey-results-real-world-slas-and-and-availability-requirements

Feng, N., Wang, H.J., Li, M. (2014). A security risk analysis model for information systems: Causal relationships of risk factors and vulnerability propagation analysis. *Information Sciences, 256*, 57–73. https://doi.org/10.1016/j.ins.2013.02.036

Fenton, N., Hearty, P., Neil, M., & Radlinski, L. (2010). Software Project and Quality Modelling Using Bayesian Networks. In F. Meziane & S. Vadera (eds.), Artificial intelligence applications for improved software (pp. 1–25). IGI Global. https://doi.org/10.4018/978-1-60566-758-4.ch001

Fineman, M. (2010). *Improved Risk Analysis for Large Projects : Bayesian Networks Approach.* Queen Mary, University of London.

Franke, U., Johnson, P., König, J., Marcks von Würtemberg, L. (2012). Availability of enterprise IT systems: an expert-based Bayesian framework. *Software Quality Journal, 20*(2), 369–394. https://doi.org/10.1007/s11219-011-9141-z

Gantz, J., Reinsel, D. (2011). *Extracting Value from Chaos State of the Universe : An Executive Summary,* IDC.

Gartner. (2011). *Hype Cycle for Business Continuity Management and IT Disaster Recovery Management,* Gartner.

Gartner. (2019). Magic quadrant for hyperconverged infrastructure. Retrieved August 25, 2019, from www.gartner.com/doc/reprints?id=1-5VKQPDW&ct=181130&st=sb&isGated=true&timestamp=1566725789512

Garvey, M.D., Carnovale, S., Yeniyurt, S. (2015). An analytical framework for supply network risk propagation: A Bayesian network approach. *European Journal of Operational Research, 243*(2), 618–627. https://doi.org/10.1016/j.ejor.2014.10.034

Gnanasundaram, S., Shrivastava, A. (eds.). (2012). *Information Storage and Management* (2nd ed.). John Wiley & Sons.

Gran, B.A. (2002). Use of Bayesian Belief Networks when combining disparate sources of information in the safety assessment of software-based systems. *International Journal of Systems Science, 33*(6), 529–542. https://doi.org/10.1080/00207720210133589

Gupta, J.N.D., Sharma, S.K. (eds.) (2008). *Handbook of Research on Information Security and Assurance.* https://doi.org/10.4018/978-1-59904-855-0

Hanna, T. (2018). What's changed: 2018 gartner magic quadrant for disaster recovery as a service. Retrieved September 6, 2019, from https://solutionsreview.com/backup-disaster-recovery/whats-changed-2018-gartner-magic-quadrant-for-disaster-recovery-as-a-service/

Henrion, M. (1989). Some practical issues in constructing belief networks, in: L.N. Kanal, T.S. Levitt, & J.F. Lemmer (eds.), *Uncertainty in Artificial Intelligence 3.* Elsevier Science Publishers, 161–173.

Hinz, D.J., Malinowski, J. (2006). Assessing the risks of IT infrastructure – A personal network perspective. *HICSS '06. Proceedings of the 39th Annual Hawaii International*

*Conference on System Sciences*, *00*(C), 1–8. Retrieved from http://ieeexplore.ieee.org/xpls/abs_all.jsp?arnumber=1579641

Hu, Y., Zhang, X., Ngai, E.W.T., Cai, R., Liu, M. (2013). Software project risk analysis using Bayesian networks with causality constraints. *Decision Support Systems*, *56*(1), 439–449. https://doi.org/10.1016/j.dss.2012.11.001

Ibrahimovic, S., Bajgoric, N. (2016). Modeling information system availability by using Bayesian belief network approach. *Interdisciplinary Description of Complex Systems*, *14*(2), 125–138. https://doi.org/10.7906/indecs.14.2.2

Ibrahimović, S., Bajgorić, N. (2018). The Role of Information System Monitoring in Improving System Availability. In N. Bajgoric (ed.), Always-On Enterprise Information Systems for Modern Organizations (pp. 184–207). IGI Global. https://doi.org/10.4018/978-1-5225-3704-5

Ibrahimović, S., Turulja, L., Bajgorić, N. (2017). *Maximizing Information System Availability through Bayesian Belief Network Approaches*, IGI Global.

ISACA. (2019). Glossary. Retrieved July 31, 2019, from www.isaca.org/Pages/Glossary.aspx?tid=1334&char=D

ISO. (2012). *ISO/DIS 22313 : Societal security – Business continuity management systems – Guidance*. International Organization for Standardization.

ISO/IEC. (2008). *ISO/IEC 24762 Information technology – Security techniques – Guidelines for information and communications technology disaster recovery services* (Vol. 2008).

ISO/IEC. (2011). *ISO/IEC 27031:2011(en), Information technology – Security techniques – Guidelines for information and communication technology readiness for business continuity*. Retrieved from www.iso.org/obp/ui/#iso:std:iso-iec:27031:ed-1:v1:en

Lande, S., Zuo, Y., Pimple, M. (2010). A survivability decision model for critical information systems based on bayesian network. *5th Annual Symposium on Information Assurance*. Retrieved from www.albany.edu/wwwres/conf/iasymposium/proceedings/2010/ASIA10Proceedings.pdf#page=32

Lauría, E.J.M., Duchessi, P.J. (2006). A Bayesian Belief Network for IT implementation decision support. *Decision Support Systems*, *42*(3), 1573–1588. https://doi.org/10.1016/j.dss.2006.01.003

Lauría, E.J.M., Duchessi, P.J. (2007). A methodology for developing Bayesian networks: An application to information technology (IT) implementation. *European Journal of Operational Research*, *179*(1), 234–252. https://doi.org/10.1016/j.ejor.2006.01.016

Li, H., Sun, J. (2011). Principal component case-based reasoning ensemble for business failure prediction. *Information & Management*, *48*(6), 220–227. https://doi.org/10.1016/j.im.2011.05.001

Liu, D., Deters, R., Zhang, W.J. (2010). Architectural design for resilience. *Enterprise Information Systems*, *4*(2), 137–152. https://doi.org/10.1080/17517570903067751

Marcus, E., Stern, H. (2003). *Blueprints for high availability* (2nd ed.). Retrieved from http://frank.depriester.free.fr/muse/docs/HA/Wiley – Blueprints For High Availability (2nd ed) (2003).pdf

Microsoft. (2013a). *Poster Companion Reference : Hyper-V Storage*.

Microsoft. (2013b). *Poster Companion Reference : Hyper-V Virtual Machine Mobility*.

Neil, M., Häger, D., Andersen, L. (2009). Modelling operational risk in financial institutions using hybrid dynamic Bayesian networks. *Journal of Operational Risk*, *4*(1), 3–33. https://doi.org/10.21314/jop.2009.057

Neil, M., Marquez, D., Fenton, N. (2008). Using Bayesian networks to model the operational risk to information technology infrastructure in financial institutions. *Journal of Financial Transformation, 22,* 131–138. Retrieved from http://econpapers.repec.org/RePEc:ris:jofitr:0929

NIST. (2014). Security and privacy controls for federal information systems and organizations security and privacy controls for federal information systems and organizations. *Sp-800-53Ar4,* 400+. https://doi.org/10.6028/NIST.SP.800-53Ar4

Pearl, J. (1986). Fusion, propagation, and structuring in belief networks. *Artificial Intelligence, 29*(1986), 241–288. Retrieved from www.sciencedirect.com/science/article/pii/000437028690072X

Pott, T. (2018). The pros & cons of hyperconvergence. Retrieved August 25, 2019, from www.hyperconverged.org/2018/06/27/hyperconvergence-pros-and-cons-2/

Raderius, J., Narman, P., Ekstedt, M. (2009). Assessing system availability using an enterprise architecture analysis approach. *Service-Oriented Computing–ICSOC....* Retrieved from www.springerlink.com/index/U485G47R746164MP.pdf

Radliński, Ł., Fenton, N., Neil, M. (2007). Improved decision-making for software managers using Bayesian networks. *Software Engineering and Applications (SEA 2007),* 1–13. Retrieved from http://scholar.google.com/scholar?hl=en&btnG=Search&q=intitle:Improved+Decision-Making+for+Software+Managers+Using+Bayesian+Networks#0

Reinsel, D., Gantz, J., Rydning, J. (2018). *The Digitization of the World From Edge to Core.* Retrieved from www.seagate.com/files/www-content/our-story/trends/files/idc-seagate-dataage-whitepaper.pdf

Report, I. (2015). High-value business applications on x86: The need for true fault -tolerant systems. Retrieved December 14, 2015, from www8.hp.com/h20195/v2/GetPDF.aspx/4AA5-8631ENW.pdf

Rubens, P. (2017). What Are Containers and Why Do You Need Them? | CIO. Retrieved August 25, 2019, from www.cio.com/article/2924995/what-are-containers-and-why-do-you-need-them.html

Schroeder, B., Gibson, G.A. (2007). Disk failures in the real world : What does an MTTF of 1, 000, 000 hours mean to you ? *5th USENIX Conference on File and Storage Technologies,* 1–16.

Sharma, S., & Routroy, S. (2016). Modeling information risk in supply chain using Bayesian networks. *Journal of Enterprise Information Management, 29*(2), 238–254. https://doi.org/10.1108/JEIM-03-2014-0031

Sikdar, P. (2017). *Practitioner's Guide to Business Impact Analysis.* CRC Press/Taylor & Francis.

Simonsson, M., Robert, L., Johnson, P. (2008). A Bayesian network for IT governance performance prediction. *ICEC 'Proceedings of the 10th International Conference on Electronic Commerce.* Retrieved from http://dl.acm.org/citation.cfm?id=1409542

Singh, J. (2009). Modeling application availability. *Proceedings of the 2009 Spring Simulation Multiconference,* 1–4. Retrieved from http://dl.acm.org/citation.cfm?id=1639932

Sommestad, T., Ekstedt, M. (2009). Cyber security risks assessment with bayesian defense graphs and architectural models. *System Sciences,* 1–10. Retrieved from http://ieeexplore.ieee.org/xpls/abs_all.jsp?arnumber=4755419

Swanson, M., Lynes, D., Swanson, M., Gallup, D. (2010). *NIST Special Publication 800–34 – Contingency Planning Guide for Federal Information Systems.* National Institute of Standards and Technology.

Taylor, S., Cannon, D., Wheldon, D. (2007). *ITIL Service Operation*. Office of Government Commerce.

Taylor, S., Case, G., Spalding, G. (2007). *ITIL Continual Service Improvement*. https://doi.org/10.1007/978-1-4614-3897-7_7

Taylor, S., Lacy, S., MacFarlane, I. (2007). *ITIL Service Transition*. The Stationery Office, TSO.

Taylor, S., Vernon, L., Rudd, C. (2007). *ITIL Service Design*. https://doi.org/10.1002/0471744719.ch1

Virtualization24x7. (2015). Virtualization the Future: What Is RPO, RTO, WRT, MTD? Retrieved August 19, 2019, from http://virtualization24x7.blogspot.com/2015/11/what-is-rpo-rto-wrt-mtd.html

Weber, P., Suhner, M. (2001). System architecture design based on a Bayesian networks method. *10th International Symposium on Applied Stochastic Models and Data Analysis*. Retrieved from http://hal.archives-ouvertes.fr/docs/00/12/84/57/PDF/Weber_2001_ASMDA_version_hal.PDF

Wei, W., Wang, H., Yang, B., Liu, L. (2011). A Bayesian network based knowledge engineering framework for IT service management. *IEEE Transactions on Services Computing, 99*, 1–14. Retrieved from http://ieeexplore.ieee.org/xpls/abs_all.jsp?arnumber=5928314

Yu, Y., Zheng, G., Qian, Z. (2009). Software reliability model analysis including internal structure based on bayesian network. *2009 Fourth International Conference on Cooperation and Promotion of Information Resources in Science and Technology*, (0592), 247–251. https://doi.org/10.1109/COINFO.2009.82

Zhang, R., Cope, E., Heusler, L. (2009). A Bayesian network approach to modeling IT service availability using system logs. *SOSP Workshop on the Analysis of System Logs*, (Vm). Retrieved from http://cipsm.rogrid.pub.ro/SSI/1. Modele si arhitecturi de sisteme de incredere/Availability modeling/bayesian_1.pdf

## Chapter 7

# IT Auditing – System Administration – Business Continuity – IT Capability

## Background

Audit practice has considerable experience because various terms are used, such as: inspection, control, revision, checking, auditing, and supervision. Each of these terms implies comparing the actual situation with the situation that should be, establishment and analysis of the deviations and risks, and/or proposal or recommendation of measures to contribute to the achievement of the entity or to provide correct information.

Different authors classify types of audits in different ways. For example, it is possible to find a classification of audit types concerning the following three criteria:

1. place of audit body (internal audit, external audit, supervision by the regulator, etc.)
2. audit subject (financial audit, compliance audit, information system audit, etc.)
3. scope and time when the audit is performed (preliminary audit, final audit, continuous audit, follow-up audit, etc.)

An internal audit is performed by the employees of internal audit units within the organization, and the primary objective of an internal audit is to provide recommendations to improve the internal control system and generally to improve the business processes and overall operations of the organization. If the organization has an internal audit function in place that regularly audits the information system security, the probability of adopting adequate security measures and preventing attacks or lowering the negative consequences is increased. The internal audit focuses on all processes and activities within the company and aims to provide quality feedback on the performance, efficiency, and economy of the business operations, so that management can focus on processes and activities that should be improved, to achieve business goals.

An audit performed by an independent organization or individual with no interest in the company itself is called an external audit. An external audit expresses an opinion about the management and security of the information system, or rates the information system processes' maturity, depending on audit methodology. Supervision is performed by the competent authority for regulating a particular industry (e.g., the banking system, etc.), and examines the compliance of the company operations with certain laws and sublegal acts. Organizations usually hire an external auditor once a year, depending on the obligation imposed by regulation, while an internal audit carries out its activities continuously throughout the year. Internal and external audits are interconnected and complement each other.

A financial audit or audit of financial statements is the examination of documents, reports, and other information to obtain sufficient, adequate, and reliable evidence to determine whether the financial statements present a true and fair view of its financial position, results of operations, and cash flows. The purpose of a compliance audit is to determine the extent to which the audit client complies with rules, policies, laws, contractual obligations, or state regulations. The primary purpose of IT auditing is to assess whether or not an information system is meeting stated organizational objectives and to ensure that the system is not creating an unacceptable level of risk for the business.

A preliminary audit is usually conducted before the end of the financial year to identify on-time certain irregularities and weaknesses in the accounting system. After a preliminary audit, a management letter is sent to the client. The letter lists those elements that need to be corrected before the final financial statement is prepared. During the final audit, the measures taken by the client are reviewed and evaluated. The continuous audit is a method that enables internal auditors to gain assurance about the functionality of internal controls by conducting continuous examinations of their work and issuing a review report at a time when the report is relevant to the company's management. A follow-up audit is an audit in which auditors determine the appropriateness, effectiveness, and timeliness of management actions concerning the implementation of previously issued recommendations.

# IT Auditing

The backbone of modern information systems consists of computers that process business data and provide information when management decisions are being made. Today, when the ratio of price and potential benefits of computers has reached a high scale, attention should be focused on making the most of the potential of data-processing equipment. This, in turn, requires careful, thorough, and systematic control and audit. The purpose of an information system audit is to verify and determine whether the existing controls within an organization's information system operate following existing policies, operating procedures, and regulations.

Organizations can make progress if they recognize that an audit of an information system can bring added value. The audit of the information system can be considered as a tool toward determining the value, function, and utility of information resources to fully exploit their strategic potential. There are many important factors regarding why control and audit are considered to be of crucial importance in trying to achieve expectations concerning the efficiency and effectiveness of information systems, for example:

a) cost of data loss;
b) costs of making inappropriate or wrong decisions;
c) misuse of IT equipment;
d) value of equipment, programs, and staff;
e) cost of computer-related errors;
f) preserving privacy; and
g) controlled improvement of the use of IT equipment, and so on.

By an audit of an information system, it can be determined whether the information and the information system satisfy the following three criteria:

a) availability: business information systems are available for business
b) security: whether data stored in these systems are available only to authorized users
c) integrity: whether this data is accurate, timely, and reliable

An audit of the information system assesses the adequacy of environmental, physical security, logical security, and operational controls designed to protect hardware, software, and data against unauthorized access and accidental or intentional destruction or alteration, and to ensure that information systems are functioning efficiently and effectively to help the organization achieve its strategic objectives. Moreover, an audit of the information system has another important goal: determining whether the organization meets the relevant regulations, rules, or conditions.

An audit of the information system presents the process of collecting and evaluating evidence to determine whether a computer system (information system) safeguards assets, maintains data integrity, achieves organizational goals effectively, and consumes resources efficiently.

The property of the information system of a company consists of machines and equipment (hardware), applications and data files (software), digitized knowledge, system documentation, auxiliary devices, materials, and so on. Just like any other form of property, the assets of the information system must be protected by the internal control system.

Data integrity is a feature of data that guarantees that data has not been altered since it was created. From an audit point of view, data integrity is an extremely important concept. This means that data must have certain properties such as completeness, precision, accuracy, and clarity. If the integrity of data is compromised or uninhibited, the organization loses its reputation. An effective information system guides an organization toward achieving its business goals, and an effective information system uses the minimum of resources to achieve the required goals.

The specific nature of the information system audit requires that IT auditors possess the skills and knowledge necessary to properly audit the information system. Also, if they perform audit engagements, IT auditors should apply standards that relate specifically to the audit of information systems. There are many standards that auditors can use in their work, such as: COBIT, ITIL, ISO 27001, PCI DSS, and so forth.

## Control as a Component of Management of Information System

Control is an important component of information system management. Managing the system means taking appropriate measures to ensure that the system functions in the desired way. The control determines which measures should be taken to achieve predefined management objectives. Controls can be implemented to prevent, detect, and correct unwanted events and processes in the information system.

Regarding this term, three important aspects of the controls should be noted. First, control is the system. Thus, control includes a set of interconnected components that, acting uniquely and harmoniously, help achieve the set goals of the information system. For example, a user password that can be used to access users with specific resources can be considered a form of control. However, the password becomes a control mechanism only in the context of a system that allows secure selection of passwords, verification of its authenticity, secure storage, and more.

Second, control focuses on unwanted events or processes in the information system. An unwanted event can occur, and the process is activated, due to unauthorized, inaccurate, incomplete, redundant, ineffective, or inefficient entry into the system. For example, entering inaccurate data into the system can be considered an unwanted event, which results in the wrong data-processing results in the system.

Third, controls are applied to prevent, detect, or correct unwanted events and/ or processes. The general purpose of the control is to reduce the expected losses that would occur if an unwanted event arises or an unwanted process occurs in the system. Control works in the following two ways:

a) preventive control reduces the likelihood of unwanted events and/or processes

b) detective and corrective controls reduce the amount of loss that would result from unwanted events and/or processes.

Preventive controls are controls whose primary task is to detect problems or adverse events before they occur, actually to anticipate them. Detective controls are those that detect an error, omission, or that compromise any part of the information system. Corrective controls aim to minimize the impact of the information system threat, whereby they identify the cause of the problem and automatically execute special instructions to correct the errors found.

Internal control consists of five interrelated components: the control environment, risk assessment, control activities, information and communication, and monitoring. One of the key tasks of the auditor is to determine whether appropriate controls are implemented in the company's information system. Should there be more control over certain unwanted events, the auditor should determine whether these controls are aligned or consistent. When reviewing the controls, the auditor may find it more efficient to first review the general controls affecting an application control before reviewing a specific application control, since the effectiveness of the application control is dependent on the adequacy of the general control.

Intensive use of computers in everyday business and digital transformation results in more information technology (IT) auditing and internal control standards and guidelines to assist auditors in their roles and responsibilities.

## Audit Risks

In this work, the auditor can face various challenges. For example, it may be necessary to determine material losses that have already occurred, or could occur, due to inefficient or ineffective operation of the information system. Therefore, the auditor must always take into account the fact that he could fail to determine the actual or potential losses caused by the inadequate operation of the system. Such risk is called an *audit risk*. In other words, audit risk is the risk that information could contain a material error that could be undetected during the audit engagement. The term "materiality" is one of the key concepts during the audit.

There is no specific formula in which materiality is calculated. This should be the assessment of IT auditors on the ground. For example, a particular system error can be very significant at the operational level, but at the management level, the same error may not be considered significant. The concept of materiality is closely related to the term "audit risk" and is one of the key elements to be considered when planning the audit.

On the other hand, when evaluating internal controls, an IT auditor can detect a minor error, but, combined with other errors and irregularities discovered, it can become a material error at the system level. Also, an IT auditor can detect several minor errors that are not material, each one individually, but when they are aggregated, they can point to a significant weakness in the system. These are the reasons why materiality is a significant concept during the audit. IT auditors should have a good understanding of audit risk and materiality during audit planning.

The auditor should always try to reduce the audit risk to an acceptable level (*desired audit risk*). The following model has been developed:

$$DAR = IR \times CR \times DR,$$

where

> DAR = Desired Audit Risk
> IR = Inherent Risk
> CR = Control Risk
> DR = Detection Risk

*Inherent risk* reflects the probability that there will be material loss in some segments of the audit before internal controls or mitigating factors are implemented. *Control risk* is the probability that internal controls in one segment of the audit will not prevent, detect, or correct material risks. Control risk is a consequence of an inappropriate internal control system within an organization. *Detection risk* reflects the likelihood that the audit procedures applied in a particular segment will not reveal material losses. Detection risk is the responsibility of the auditor since he or she chooses audit procedures.

The introduction and assessment of the internal control system and the assessment of audit risks are extremely important for the overall audit flow. Namely, a well-organized internal control system reduces audit risks, and in this case, the auditor can be satisfied with less evidentiary procedures. Inherent and control risk exists independently of the audit, while detection risk is directly related to the audit process. Audit efforts should be directed toward those areas of activity where the best results can be expected. Auditors must be flexible, adapt to new situations, and continuously make decisions about what to do next during the complete audit engagement.

## Performing an IS Audit

Individual audit engagement has the character of the project, which means it has a beginning and an end, as well as certain phases. Although the audit steps have a

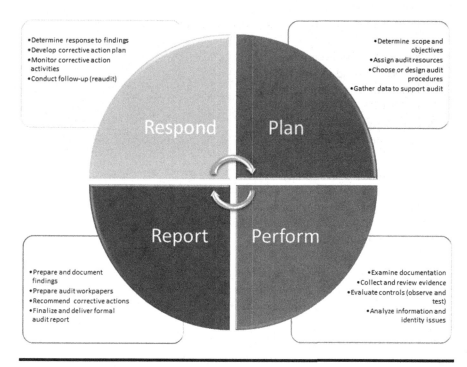

**Figure 7.1    IT audit process. (Gantz, 2013).**

sequential structure, due to rationalization, certain steps can be performed simultaneously depending on the nature of the activity. Auditing is a cyclical process consisting of risk assessment, analysis and evaluation of controls, reporting of facts and audit findings, and then reusing all of the information provided to assess risk and conduct new audit engagement. The IT audit process consists of the following steps: audit planning, audit performance, audit reporting, and responding to audit findings and recommendations (Figure 7.1.).

Each organization should define the audit methodology to conduct the audit in a standardized, consistent manner. Also, the audit methodology makes the job easier for the auditor. The audit methodology defines audit procedures, audit plans, and audit programs. The audit procedure determines how the audit is conducted from planning to reporting. The audit program consists of audit scope, audit objectives, and audit programs. An individual audit plan is required for each audit, as each audit has its specificities. During each audit, the auditor collects work documentation and audit evidence that varies depending on the specifics of the subject matter, audit scope, and objectives. The auditor must preserve the integrity and safeguard the audit evidence that he or she uses when making findings and writing the audit report.

Key phases of an IT audit as a process can be defined through the following steps:

1. **Preparation and planning**
   a. Defining audit scope
   b. Formulating audit objectives
   c. Identifying audit criteria
2. **Performing audit procedures**
   a. Documentation analysis
   b. Collection of audit evidence
3. **Preparat ion of an audit report**
   a. Analysis and evaluation of audit evidence
   b. Forming audit conclusions and opinions
   c. Reporting to management (stakeholders)
4. **Post-audit activities**

Audit management should provide sufficient resources for the audit team so that the audit objectives can be achieved. Therefore, the audit team should consist of an adequate staff with the necessary experience and skills to carry out the audit activity, and to conduct the audit in compliance with the basic postulates of the auditor (independence and objectivity). The auditing company should provide sufficient time for the audit team, so that the audit is not performed under the pressure of achieving inadequately formulated deadlines. Also, the audit team needs other resources such as hardware and software components necessary to perform assigned audit activities.

## *Preparation and Planning*

Regardless of the different ways of systematizing the audit phases that are encountered in the literature, planning the audit is an indispensable phase. At that stage, the objectives of the audit are set, general information is collected, the distribution of activities among the auditors is performed, and possible audit risks are identified. When the objectives of the audit are set, there should be considered reasons why this audit is being initiated, the specifics of the company and its information system, and the time and circumstances in which the audit will be conducted.

In March 2016, ISACA published a white paper titled Information Systems Auditing: Tools and Techniques Creating Audit Programs and explained five key steps when developing audit plans and programs.

1. Determine audit subject – What are you auditing?
2. Define audit objective – Why are you auditing it?
3. Set audit scope – What are the limits to your audit?
4. Perform pre-audit planning – What are the specific risk factors?

5. Determine audit programs and steps for data gathering – How will you test the controls for these risks?

The audit engagement should be adequately planned and monitored for the auditor to gather sufficient audit evidence and to draw adequate conclusions. During the planning process, potential audit topics and subjects are analyzed, as well as the expected impact and value of the audit.

The IT audit is most often conducted using a risk-based audit methodology, which means that risks are first identified and prioritized, then control mechanisms are evaluated, and in the end, controls are tested. If necessary, management may implement additional control mechanisms as a result of the audit's findings. Risk-based auditing combines business knowledge, risk assessment, and strategic audit before deploying audit resources.

The most commonly used methodology is based on a scoring system. Through the scoring system, the IT auditor assesses the risks as high, medium, and low risk, and then, by further calculation and depending on the type of risk, provides a numerical risk rating. Based on this assessment, the audit areas are prioritized. The risk factors to be assessed are usually financial risk, risk of data loss, the technical complexity of the process, adequacy of the internal control system, and so on. The auditor should evaluate all types of risk and then pay particular attention to high-risk areas during the audit.

When drafting the annual audit plan, the internal auditor should determine what to audit, when, and how frequently. When selecting the area to be audited, the auditor should also consider previous audit findings, historical facts about the company, the environment in which the company operates, external factors, and so forth. Risk-based audit planning makes it easier for the auditor to allocate audit resources. Also, with this type of planning, the audit risk is significantly reduced. By conducting a risk assessment, the auditor is already familiar with the company's business processes, goals, incidents, and operations, and obtains other company information that may be relevant during the audit.

For each audit, it is necessary to establish the objectives of the audit in the form of a statement defining the purpose of the audit. An audit typically covers several different audit objectives to be achieved during an audit engagement. However, defining audit objectives when auditing an information system has its specific characteristics. For example, wide-ranging audit objectives should narrow down and define specific audit objectives. For example, an audit objective may be to determine whether a company adequately manages malware protection. Accordingly, the auditor should determine whether the internal control system operates in such a way that internal controls reduce the risk of malicious code infection to an acceptable level. Since the definition of audit objectives is one of the key steps in planning an information system audit, the very performance of the audit depends on adequately set audit objectives and the understanding of the relationship between audit objectives and IS control objectives.

With a clearly defined scope and set of objectives, the audit company (or internal audit unit) should identify and assign the necessary auditors and other resources, review existing controls and information that will be used during the audit, and determine criteria, appropriate procedures, standards, and protocols to be followed. In the preparation phase of the audit work, the ranking of information system components should be performed, taking into account the two factors mentioned above – their importance (criticality) for the information system and their exposure to risks.

Auditors need to understand the business processes of the client's business domain. Each company's information system can consist of many applications and systems, which can include several geographical locations, and support various activities and functions within the organization.

## Performing Audit Procedures

At the very beginning of the audit work, the auditors will have to collect all available relevant documentation that will help them in the first steps of the work to orient themselves to the problem they are tackling, which will also serve them as the reference basis for the collection of the necessary documents, reimbursements, analyses, and for making certain judgments or estimates.

Auditors primarily need to collect and review key documentation relating to the company's operations in the subject matter of the audit. However, auditors should also review other documentation that may be obtained from external sources from the environment in which the company operates. Auditors may also use reports from other institutions. It is not possible to specify precisely what documentation the auditor should review. The auditor should collect and review everything that can assist him or her during the audit engagement.

External documentation could be laws, sublegal acts, contracts, agreements, decisions of competent bodies, reports, and so on. Internal documentation is the company's strategies, policies, procedures, rules, reports, and many others that relate to different aspects of business processes and information systems. All documentation should be reviewed and analyzed by the auditors to gain better insight into the operations and condition of the system to be audited. In such a way, the auditors will get a comprehensive view of the processes that are in the environment of that system, which could have an impact on performing the audit engagement and forming an audit opinion.

All documentation that the auditor collects during the audit engagement is called *working documentation*. Working documentation contains the auditor's notes on the planning and performance of the audit, the nature and extent of the audit procedures performed, the results of such procedures, and the conclusions drawn from the audit evidence. The working documentation includes materials (work files) that the auditor prepares personally or collects from others in connection with performing the audit. The working documentation must be complete and detailed, which means that the entire audit procedure can be reconstructed based on such working documentation. This documentation may be recorded on paper and stored on electronic or other media. The auditor's working documentation

a) assists in planning and conducting the audit;
b) assists in monitoring and reviewing the audit; and
c) records audit evidence from work performed that serves as a basis for the auditor's opinion.

The working documentation is the property of the auditor and not the client. After completing the audit and submitting the audit report, the client is no longer entitled to request access to the working documentation. He could have done this during the audit, or before the audit report was issued. The working documentation is confidential and can only be used for audit purposes following the right to protect confidentiality.

The objective of the audit engagement is to collect sufficient relevant audit evidence that will later serve for the formation of an audit opinion and assessment of the company's information system state. Audit evidence is also used to write and present an audit report. Gathering audit evidence is a task whose execution requires interdisciplinary knowledge, expertise, and specific skills.

Audit evidence is any information that the auditor collects during the audit engagement process, or to determine whether a particular IT segment (subject to audit) is in line with the predefined criteria, or whether it meets certain objectives. Audit criteria could be standards, norms, laws, sublegal laws, regulations, or the organization's internal acts like a set of policies, procedures, or requirements. Audit results are only as good as the criteria used for the evaluation.

The quality involved in collecting and documenting data is vital. Auditors must be creative, flexible, and careful when looking for appropriate evidence. It is important to keep an objective distance from the information presented, but auditors must also be open to other opinions and arguments.

Evidence can be categorized as physical evidence, documentary evidence, as evidence obtained through testimony, or as analytical evidence. In recent years, digital evidence has been increasingly present. To create adequate conclusions and form an audit opinion, the auditor must collect sufficient, competent, relevant, appropriate, and reliable audit evidence. Evidence is sufficient if sufficient to support the audit findings. Evidence sufficiency depends on the conditions in which the client operates, as well as on the auditor's assessment and his willingness to take responsibility for a potentially inaccurate audit report. The evidence that is used to support an audit finding is relevant if it has a logical, reasonable relationship with those findings. Evidence is competent if it is consistent with the facts. Appropriateness refers to whether the evidence is related to a particular objective being verified. Reliability refers to determining the quality and type of evidence.

The principle of documenting is one of the oldest audit principles, according to which the auditor must collect sufficient appropriate evidence, through appropriate audit procedures, to make correct conclusions that will enable him to formulate an audit opinion. Audit evidence is all the information that the auditor collects and uses in examining the compliance of the information system with predetermined criteria for evaluation. They must have appropriate qualitative and quantitative characteristics.

Tests of controls refer to the procedures directed toward either the effectiveness of the design or the operation of a control. In designing tests of automated controls, the auditor may need to obtain supporting evidence that the operation of controls directly related to the assertions and other indirect controls on which these controls depend, is effective. A large part of the audit work consists of gathering and evaluating evidence.

The collection of evidence should enable the auditor to do the following:

a) understand the organization's activities and applications in the audited system,
b) assess the risk level to which the system and the accompanying applications are exposed,
c) understand the control objectives in the system,
d) evaluate the control levels and quality over the risks to which the system and accompanying applications are exposed, and
e) undertake the reliability tests of the controls they are intended to rely on.

In IT audits, key evidence collection activities typically include those shown in Figure 7.2: reviewing documentation provided by the organization or gathered from interviews with personnel, observing operational procedures or activities, testing controls, and checking technical configuration settings for IT components.

Audit tests are divided into control tests and evidence tests. After conducting the control tests, the implementation of evidence tests will follow.

Control tests refer to testing the functioning and efficiency of an internal control system within a company. The internal control system is of great importance for meeting the strategies and goals of the company and for the economical and efficient use of resources, because an effective internal control system reduces the possibility of errors and fraud to a minimum. The internal control system must be designed in such a way to effectively cover all significant risks to which the company is exposed.

Establishing a stable and efficient internal control system is the task of the company management, while the auditor independently performs tests of these controls to determine a realistic and objective situation, identify possible key deficiencies of control mechanisms, and make recommendations for eliminating the observed deficiencies. Audit tests performed by the auditor are performed on representative samples.

The auditor tests the effectiveness of information system controls that are relevant to the audit objectives. During this audit phase, IT auditors are provided with

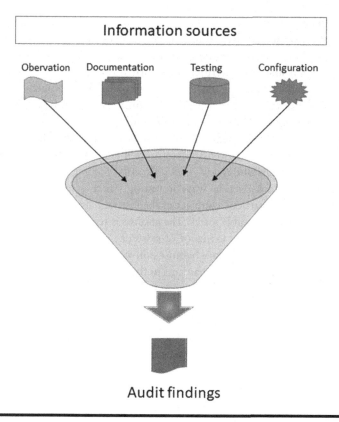

**Figure 7.2   Audit findings. Gantz, 2013.**

detailed information on control policies, procedures, and objectives, and perform tests of control activities. The purpose of these tests is to determine whether the controls are functioning effectively. General controls, as well as application controls, must be effective to help ensure the confidentiality, integrity, availability, and reliability of significant data.

The methods most often used by auditors in testing internal controls are: interview, inspection, observation, validation, conducting a survey, technical testing of the system, and so on. The aforementioned methods should be combined to obtain final confirmation of the efficiency or inefficiency of the internal control system from many sources.

The objective of the auditor is, through the *interview*, to gather as much quality information as possible to serve as audit evidence from individuals who know the most about certain issues related to the information system activity, those who directly deal with these issues in their everyday work. At the preparatory stage, auditors need to accurately identify the objectives of the interview and make a list of information that they want to collect. When conducting interviews, auditors should separate the facts from their own opinion of the respondents. Auditors also need to seek to correctly understand and interpret the information gathered by the respondent and to determine their meaning in the context of global audit objectives. Interviews as a method of testing an internal control system must always be used in conjunction with another method since the information gathered in such an oral manner cannot serve as formal audit evidence, but only as a good orientation basis for more detailed analysis. Interviews also help determine if employees understand their role and accept their responsibilities.

*Inspection* is a more reliable way of testing, since it also examines written documents related to a particular subject of the test, but also requires physical verification of documents or tangible assets. The auditor is required to confirm and verify both the written and physical evidence of existence. *Observation* as a testing technique is considered reliable evidence because it involves the process of monitoring the effectiveness of certain control mechanisms in the course of their functioning, "live". The particular internal control system is tested on a single sample basis. *Validation* is a technique by which the auditor validates the information. For example, the auditor can ask different employees the same question and compare the answers. Also, the auditor can ask the same question in different ways at different times in different situations. The auditor can compare the answers to the checklist questions with the condition he or she observed while reviewing a particular system or process at the client's location.

*Conducting the survey* is used to assess the suitability and quality of control in the systems. Answers to questions from the questionnaire indicate the existence, absence, or inapplicability of some control procedures. The auditors then analyze the sample of collected responses, trying to make an appropriate judgment about the controls in the audited information system. Auditors can fill out the questionnaire themselves during the process of interviewing staff or monitoring information system activities. Questionnaires can help in structuring the interview process. Auditors should be well educated in the use and implementation of the survey; otherwise, the answers they receive might be inaccurate, incomplete, or unreliable.

*Technical testing of the system* is performed using certain software tools for recording (scanning) the system. Such tools can collect large amounts of data, but they can also act selectively, collecting only those data that the auditors are interested in. Programs collect and record a lot of information, but they are designed and written to minimize the regular operation of computer equipment and the entire information system. They are not aggressive or invasive, but function as some kind of passive observers and recorders in the system. With these tools, it is also possible to perform different types of tests to determine the actual or assumed behavior of the system in different situations.

The auditor may also collect evidence based on the sample. A sample-based audit involves testing less than 100% of items of statistical mass. In addition to statistical, there are also nonstatistical methods of samples. Both methods can give satisfactory results, that is, appropriate audit evidence. Regardless of the sampling method, inherent and control risks are always present. If the sample is not well defined, there is high detection risk. However, other factors may increase the risk of detection. If the auditor is willing to tolerate a larger mistake, a smaller sample is sufficient and vice versa. When selecting a sample, the random number plate, system selection, random selection, and selection of the part (blocks) is most often applied. The errors found in the sample should be used to predict the error in the whole mass from which the sample was taken.

## Preparation of an Audit Report

After collecting all or at least the satisfactory amount of audit evidence required, the auditor should evaluate the evidence to determine the extent to which the assets of the audited information system are protected and the data integrity is maintained, and also how the system contributes to increasing the efficiency of the company's business processes. Besides other information, as a minimum, the audit report should include the audit finding, conclusions, and recommendations.

Audit findings are specific evidence collected by the auditor to meet the audit objective, provide answers to audit questions, verify hypotheses, and so on. Audit findings consist of the following elements: criteria (what should be), condition (what is), and effects (what are the consequences) plus the cause (why deviations from norms or criteria exist when problems are identified). Thus, all four elements are not always mandatory during the audit: for example, the element criteria do not always need to be addressed if a problem-oriented approach is applied.

After gathering sufficient relevant evidence, the auditor should evaluate it. The auditor should verify that the deviations he or she has observed are representative of the auditing control environment. The sample selected by the auditor must be large enough to represent the behavior of the entire population for which the irregularity was observed. The auditor should confirm the identified weaknesses and irregularities with the audit client.

The preparation of an audit report should not be a task for the auditor to approach routinely. IT auditors should demonstrate and prove creativity, inventiveness, expertise, and competence. The auditor should know the purpose of the report and adjust the report to the needs of the stakeholders. The structure, style, and level of detail in a report depend on that information.

The content of the report should be logical. The report should include an audit scope and objectives, as well as a description of the audit subject. Initially, a summary report should be prepared, highlighting all key findings and irregularities, based on which recommendations were issued. The main content of the report relates to the findings that were made during the audit. At the end of the report, a list of all recommendations should be provided, together with priorities and deadlines for their implementation. The report should also include an assessment of the state of the information system or the maturity of the processes that were audited.

In conclusion, it should be noted whether the subject of the audit meets the audit objectives. All conclusions within the audit report must be factual and documented.

The value of the audit report largely depends on how the audit results are communicated. The added value a company receives from an audit report may not be apparent immediately but only after a shorter or longer period. Audit recommendations may require changes to the process or implementation of controls, which may take a long time. The IS auditor should present the key findings of the audit in the final meeting and explain the key risks, values, and benefits that can be achieved if the audit recommendations are implemented.

Presentation of the audit report and submission of its integral version to all relevant addresses formally ends the audit implementation phase. However, in reality, the life cycle of the audit work does not end there, since it is necessary to undertake activities to implement the recommendations. If the auditee can demonstrate to the auditor that they care about the audit process, that they understand how it is conducted, and then come up with a list of findings, observations, and corrective actions by themselves, the relationship would be strengthened and it would make better use of the auditor's knowledge and experience.

Control Objectives for Information and Related Technologies (COBIT) is a framework created by the Information Systems Audit and Control Association (ISACA) for information technology (IT) management and IT governance. The framework defines a set of generic processes for the management of IT, with each process defined together with process inputs and outputs, key process-activities, process objectives, performance measures, and an elementary maturity model.

In COBIT 5, process maturity has been replaced by the concept of process capability. This is based on the ISO/IEC 15504 standard "Information technology – Process assessment". ISO/IEC 15504 and the process capability model in COBIT 5 define six capability levels, which is presented in Table 7.1 below:

## *Post-Audit Activities*

After the audit of the information system and the presentation of the audit report, the auditor's work has not been completed. Namely, the management of the company should leave a certain period to all persons and organizational units for careful reading and analysis of the audit report, and after the expiration of that deadline, organize a meeting at which a plan of all activities arising from the findings and recommendations of the auditor will be established, agreed upon, and coordinated.

All the organizational units of the company that were included in the audit and all authorized individuals of the work for which the audit found that they should experience certain changes, improvements, modifications, or improvements should

**Table 7.1  COBIT 5 Capability Levels**

| Level | Description |
|---|---|
| Level 0: Incomplete process. | The process is not placed or it cannot reach its objectives. At this level, the process has no objective to achieve. For this reason, this level has no attribute. |
| Level 1: Performed process. | The process is in place and achieves its purpose. This level has only "Process Performance" as a process attribute. |
| Level 2: Managed process. | The process is implemented following a series of activities such as planning, monitoring, and adjusting. The outcomes are established, controlled, and maintained. This level has "Performance Management" and "Work Product Management" as process attributes. |
| Level 3: Established process. | The previous level is not implemented following a defined process that allows the achievement of the process outcomes. This level has "Process Definition" and "Process Deployment" as process attributes. |
| Level 4: Predictable process. | This level implements processes within a defined boundary that allows the achievement of the process outcomes. This level has "Process Management and "Process Control" as process attributes. |
| Level 5: Optimizing process. | This level implements processes in a way that makes it possible to achieve relevant, current, and projected business goals. This level has "Process Innovation" and "Process Optimization" as process attributes. |

*Source*: (Pasquini & Galiè, 2013)

be invited to the meeting. The meeting may also be attended by an auditor who has identified a certain deficiency and stated it in the audit report. His role will be advisory, to elaborate some of his opinions and claims in detail; present any necessary additional evidence to some of his findings; instruct employees who are expected to perform certain actions in each specific case and the situation; point out the possibilities of improving certain existing ones and the introduction of new controls; suggest priorities, order, dynamics, and deadlines for the implementation of planned activities related to the removal of observed shortcomings in information processes; advise in planning financial, material, human, and other resources for the implementation of corrective measures; and so on.

For the audited company to benefit from the audit itself, it is necessary to take action for recommendation implementation. The internal audit, together with the competent organizational units whose work the recommendations relate to, should take corrective actions, follow deadlines, and report on the status of the recommendations and the activities undertaken.

## IT Auditing and IT Capability

IT auditing is an integral part of IT governance. It is recognized as a critical IT process in the COBIT and ITIL governance frameworks. IT audits can be used for various purposes. For example, an IT audit can determine whether an organization's strategy is aligned with an IT strategy and whether the organization applies its own IT policies and procedures. Furthermore, an IT audit can determine whether the IT budget and plan have been prepared and executed following the organization's business rules. Moreover, an IT audit can verify that business transactions have been properly processed. In other words, an IT audit identifies risks and controls implemented on applications and business processes, and then tests whether those controls work appropriately.

The primary purpose of an information system audit is to assess whether the company information system meets business needs and is aligned with the business objectives. Also, the audit should determine whether the risks associated with the company information system are at an acceptable level. One of the key benefits of an audit to a company is that the audit systematically and analytically identifies and documents control mechanisms within the information system, and raises awareness if it is determined that controls are inadequate in certain areas.

In addition to the direct, explicit benefits, it is believed that IT audits provide additional, value-added benefits. Some of these benefits include:

1. Improved return on investment in information technology through improved IT governance.
2. Using audit documentation to improve operational efficiency through business (and IT) process reengineering or improved business process management.
3. Using audit observations to improve risk mitigation through enhanced enterprise risk management (ERM) awareness.
4. Improved business continuity planning and associated systems disaster recovery planning.
5. Improved systems development quality.
6. Increased organizational communication and trust development through facilitation among various stakeholders.

Since IT capability refers to the use of information technologies to meet the company's information needs, IT capability can help the company lower the likelihood of material weaknesses. IT capability not only affects internal controls along multiple dimensions but also simultaneously affects the audit process through direct and indirect mechanisms. IT capability affects the audit process via both a direct path by reducing perceived business risks arising from IT use, and an indirect path by enabling an effective internal control system.

Therefore, if the company's IT capability is very strong, the company's internal control system is also considered to be efficient. In this regard, IT audit can rely on controls implemented within the information system, and the risk assessment performed by the auditor will not indicate several high-risk areas. A well-organized internal control system reduces audit risks, and in this case, the auditor can be satisfied with less evidentiary procedures. In this regard, the IT auditor is convinced that the internal control system is at an acceptable level. A better organized internal control system means a lower number of tests and checks by an external audit and less probability of errors in the external audit findings. But sophisticated and complex IT environments require additional audit effort, and the audit companies have to engage more specialized and expensive technical resources.

## IT Auditing and Sysadmin

As system administration is discussed in previous chapters, this part of the chapter will briefly introduce the best practices and some key tasks that the IT auditor needs to perform to audit system administration with a focus on VMware virtualization administration, application containers, and cloud administration.

The controls can be divided into the following three categories: management, logical, and physical. Given that the information system is as secure as its most vulnerable part, a layered approach for the construction of a layered infrastructure, involving different combinations of management, logical, and physical controls, is necessary. Using these categories and controls significantly reduces the risk of violating the basic principles of the information system.

The IS auditor should prepare an individual audit plan along with an accompanying checklist. An audit plan typically consists of the audit subject, audit purpose, and audit scope; the methodology to be used; the timing of activities; and the tasks assignment among members of the audit team. Given that each company is specific both in the industry in which it operates, concerning the policy and management commitment, and regarding the environment in which it operates, the audit program should be adjusted to the specificities of that company. Also, companies use different information systems, applications, and infrastructure, and the audit program should be adjusted to the needs of the company.

During the audit engagement, an external auditor may interview the control functions within the company, such as the chief information security officer (CISO) or the internal auditor. The CISO may provide more internal information on whether any significant problems or incidents have occurred in the previous period regarding the system administration. An internal audit may state whether the system administration has been subject to an audit in the previous period, and what are the key recommendations related to the subject area. An auditor can also obtain a copy of penetration or vulnerability testing of the company and gain more information concerning security. All this information could be useful for the auditor to perform testing and make adequate conclusions.

When auditing VMware virtualization administration, the IT auditor should, at a minimum, pay attention to the following elements:

1. Obtain and review the company's policies and procedures related to virtualization.
2. Interview adequate personnel to gain more information about virtualization, policies, procedures, and other issues.
3. Determine if the company has implemented adequate segregation of duties.
4. Review the current organizational scheme concerning the VMware ESX/ ESXi™ operating environment.
5. Determine the version of the VMware hypervisor(s) installed.
6. Determine the host operating system and versions for VMWare Server.
7. Check which storage array is available to VMware.
8. Select the virtualized servers according to their significance and materiality and review them.
9. Check if the root password is changed/personalized; determine whether two employees know the root password; examine if the root password is securely stored.
10. Check whether ESX is configured in Lockdown Mode; Check whether the ESXi shell is protected.
11. Determine that audit logs exist for Remote Logging and are reviewed periodically.
12. Review patch procedures.
13. Check whether the company applies best practices concerning hardening.
14. Determine whether disk storage is properly isolated.
15. Review VM maintenance concerning creation, modification, and removal of VMS.
16. Determine if the company applies change management best practices; review whether VM changes are reviewed and approved before introduction into the production environment.
17. Check whether the company applies best practices concerning capacity planning.

When auditing application containers, the IT auditor should, at a minimum, pay attention to the following elements:

1. Obtain and review the company's policies and procedures related to application containerization.
2. Interview the adequate personnel to gain more information about application containerization, policies, procedures, and other issues.
3. Determine if the company has implemented adequate segregation of duties.
4. Check whether the users have appropriate access according to their business needs.

5. Confirm that users cannot log on directly to the host without authentication to an orchestration layer.
6. Determine the type of network and check whether is suitable for the company operations.
7. Confirm that individual containers cannot access each other and the host over the network.
8. Determine whether registries are conducted over a secure channel.
9. Determine whether confidentiality and security of images are implemented and maintained.
10. Review patch procedures.

When auditing cloud computing, the IS auditor should, at a minimum, pay attention to the following elements:

1. Obtain and review a copy of the contract and service level agreement (SLA) with the service provider.
2. Check whether SLA is adequate and that the monitoring system for SLA is established, including penalties.
3. Determine if the reporting relationship between the service provider and the company is clearly defined.
4. Check whether technology controls are clearly defined (information usage, access controls, security controls, location management, privacy controls, encryption, etc.).
5. Determine whether incident management, business continuity and disaster recovery, and backup facilities are clearly defined.
6. Check whether contract termination or renegotiation, as well as audit rights, are clearly defined.
7. Review the incident monitoring reports and SLA reports for a representative period.
8. Determine that audit logs exist and are reviewed periodically.
9. Determine that encryption keys are securely protected against unauthorized access, separation of duties exists between the key managers and the hosting organization, and the keys are recoverable.

# IT Auditing of Business Continuity and Disaster Recovery

This section will briefly introduce the best practices and some key tasks that the IT auditor needs to perform to audit business continuity and disaster recovery.

The purpose of this section of the chapter is to provide minimum assumptions and procedural instructions to IT auditors responsible for reviewing BCM and DRP. Business continuity planning should enable an organization to reduce the overall impact of a crash or other adverse and unanticipated events (the consequences of which may cause interruption of business processes) to an acceptable level by using adequate recovery measures in the shortest possible time. Ensuring recovery is achieved by taking measures to prevent adverse events, limit their impact, and recover in the event of business process interruptions.

When auditing BCM and DRP, the IS auditor should, at a minimum, perform the following activities:

1. Understand and review business continuity strategy
2. Evaluate Business Impact Analysis
3. Review Business Continuity Plans
4. Evaluate business continuity manuals and procedures
5. Review adequacy of BCP teams
6. Review the test of BCP
7. Evaluate secondary data center

The IS auditor should prepare an individual BCP audit plan along with an accompanying checklist. An audit plan typically consists of the audit subject, audit purpose and audit scope, the methodology to be used, the timing of activities, and the tasks assignment among members of the audit team. Given that each company is specific both in the industry in which it operates, concerning the policy and management commitment, and regarding the environment in which it operates, the audit program should be adjusted to the specificities of that company. Also, companies use different information systems, applications, and infrastructure, and the audit program should be adjusted to the needs of the company. The following is a general list of the tasks that an auditor should perform when auditing a BCP.

## *Review the Business Continuity Plan*

When reviewing a BCP, the IT auditor should, at a minimum, take the following basic actions:

1. Obtain a copy of the following documents: business continuity strategy and policy, business continuity plan, business impact analysis, disaster recovery plan, corresponding manuals, and procedures.
2. Review whether these documents are up-to-date and approved by the competent authorities, whether they meet the set goals and the business needs of the company, and whether they are consistent with each other.
3. Review whether the RTO and RPO parameters are defined within the Business Impact Analysis, and check whether all critical business processes and activities are defined.
4. Determine whether the priorities for the recovery of information system resources are defined, as well as a list of all resources needed to reestablish critical business processes.

5. Check whether all critical systems and applications have been identified, together with the priorities of their establishment (note that outsourced activities are included).

6. Obtain a member list for each recovery/continuity/response team, and check that duties and responsibilities are clearly defined.

7. Obtain a list of suppliers to call in case of an emergency and review it.

8. Interview sample-based staff to determine if persons know their responsibilities and duties, and check that the telephone contact list is up-to-date.

9. Evaluate whether all written emergency procedures are complete, appropriate, accurate, current, and easy to understand.

## Examine Plan Testing

When examining Plan Testing, the IT auditor should, at a minimum, check take the following basic actions:

1. Obtain copies of test plans and review them.

2. Review backup procedures for all areas covered by BCP and determine compliance.

3. Determine the type of scenario to be tested, and check the adequacy of the scenario (whether various real-world tests are periodically performed, whether company affiliates are included in testing, whether adequate test samples are selected, etc.).

4. Assess whether test participants follow BCP manuals and procedures.

5. Obtain a copy of the test report, then determine the time and location of the test and participants, and determine if the test results are satisfactory.

6. Determine whether the company performs testing periodically and whether the testing is conducted after significant changes within the company and its information system.

7. Obtain copies of previous test reports and verify that errors identified in the previous testing have been corrected.

8. Check if the BCP and all supporting documentation including manuals and procedures are located at the secondary data center.

## Evaluate Secondary Data Center

When evaluating the secondary data center, IT auditor should, at a minimum, take the following basic actions:

1. Determine whether the secondary data center is at a sufficient distance from the primary data center. If the secondary data site is the responsibility of another company, obtain a copy of the contract and review if the contract elements are suitable.

2. Determine whether the secondary data center contains all the necessary servers, media, and documentation, as well as applications and other software, hardware, system software, infrastructure, telecommunication lines, necessary supplies, and so on.

3. Determine the security of secondary data centers to ensure that it has the proper physical and environmental access controls (UPS, smoke detectors, limited access only to authorized users, temperature and humidity controls, raised flooring, etc.).

## Conclusions

The internal quality of the information system is ensured by the system of internal controls, and the quality level of the information system is determined by an internal or external audit. Internal controls are implemented in such a way that appropriate control mechanisms are put into effect within the information system, which reduces the weaknesses of the system and/or reduces the likelihood of threats. The implementation of controls alone is not sufficient, but it is necessary to periodically evaluate the effectiveness of these controls. By checking (auditing) the effectiveness of implemented controls, it is possible to assess the level of IT risk and to determine the quality level of control procedures. In other words, an audit is a process of reviewing and verifying performance and evaluating the quality of the system under review as a whole or a part of it.

An audit of the information system is a complex process of collecting and evaluating evidence to determine whether a computer system (information system) safeguards assets, maintains data integrity, achieves organizational goals effectively, and consumes resources efficiently. The main benefit of an IT audit is to evaluate whether the information system is working properly, for example, whether it processes inputs into outputs work correctly, whether only authorized individuals can access specific data and applications, whether data is stored securely, and so forth. According to different studies, an IT audit adds value to the company in a way that certain processes are improved like business continuity planning, system development quality, return on investment in IT through improved IT governance, and so on.

The audit has evolved over the years. In previous years, the traditional "old school" approach of auditing was used. Following this, the risk-based auditing approach has been increasingly used in which auditors make their audit plans based on a risk assessment. Nowadays, a continuous audit approach is widespread in the world. Continuous auditing can do 100% of population testing. The advantages of continuous auditing include the availability of timely information, prompt correction of errors, improved audit effectiveness and efficiency, and improved employee alertness.

Today's digital revolution is present at every corner in the business world, incorporated into every function, including IT auditing. It is unknown in which direction IT audit will continue to evolve when "faster, better, cheaper" is required in every single business. To survive in the market and remain competitive, organizations must transform their business digitally, with the term "digital or die" best reflecting changes in the business scene. On the other hand, cyberattacks – disruptions to the normal functioning of the information system and loss of sensitive information caused by malicious events – are becoming widespread.

Considering the fact that many organizations are digitally transforming, which entails certain new risks, IT auditors face many challenges today and are expected to rethink their fundamental processes, question long-established practices, and adapt their function to the digital era in the future.

## Discussion Questions

1. What is the difference between an IT audit and a financial audit?
2. List the key criteria by which the audit types are classified.
3. What are the main differences between an internal and an external audit?
4. What are the main purpose and goals of the IT audit?
5. Explain briefly the types of controls in the information system.
6. List the key phases of the IT audit process and briefly explain the process of IT auditing.
7. List the five key steps in the audit planning phase when developing audit plans and programs.
8. What key methods does the auditor use to gather/collect audit evidence?
9. List the key elements of the audit report.
10. Which elements should IT auditors consider during the engagement of IT auditing of BCP and DRP?

## References

Agarwala, S. (2016). How to be the most wanted IS auditor. *ISACA Journal, 1*, 32–24.

Ana-Maria, S., Bizoi, M., Filip, F.G. (2010). Audit for information systems security. *Informatica Economică, 14*, 43–48.

Buchanan, S., Gibb, F. (1998). The information audit: An integrated strategic approach. *International Journal of Information Management, 18*(1), 29–47.

Champlain, J.J. (2003). *Auditing Information Systems* (2nd ed.). John Wiley & Sons.

*CISA Review Manual.* (2015). (26th ed.). ISACA.

Gantz, S.D. (2013). *The Basics of IT Audit : Purposes, Processes, and Practical Information.* Elsevier Science.

Gelbstein, E. (2016). Trust, but Verify. *ISACA Journal*, *1*, 12–13.

Gelbstein, E. (2017). Risk-based audit planning for beginners. *ISACA Journal*, *2*, 1–4.

Gheorghe, M. (2010). Audit methodology for IT governance. *Informatica Economica*, *14*(1), 32–42.

Hoffman, B.W., Sellers, R.D., Skomra, J. (2018). The impact of client information technology capability on audit pricing. *International Journal of Accounting Information Systems*, *29*(November 2016), 59–75.

ISACA. (2016). *Information Systems Auditing: Tools and Techniques: Creating Audit Programs*. White Paper.

ISACA. (2019a). Audit Programs based on COBIT 5 and COBIT 2019: Application Container Audit Program. Retrieved from www.isaca.org/knowledge-center/research/pages/audit-assurance-programs.aspx

ISACA. (2019b). Audit Programs Based on COBIT 5 and COBIT 2019: Cloud Computing Audit Program. Retrieved from www.isaca.org/knowledge-center/research/pages/audit-assurance-programs.aspx

ISACA. (2019c). Audit Programs based on COBIT 5 and COBIT 2019: VMware Serve -Virtualization Audit Assurance Program. Retrieved from www.isaca.org/knowledge-center/research/pages/audit-assurance-programs.aspx

Kim, S.L., Teo, T.S.H., Bhattacherjee, A., Nam, K. (2015). IS auditor characteristics, audit process variables, and IS audit satisfaction: An empirical study in South Korea. *Information Systems Frontiers*, *19*(3), 577–591.

Kumalić, J. (2008). How to implement performance audit. In *IX International Symposium – Competetiveness and European road of Bosnia and Herzegovina*. Revicon d.o.o. Sarajevo, 417–443.

Majdalawieh, M. (2009). Paradigm shift in information systems auditing. *Managerial Auditing Journal*, *24*(May), 352–367.

Merhout, J., Havelka, D. (2008). Information technology auditing: A value-added IT governance partnership between IT management and audit. *Communications of the Association for Information Systems*, *23*, 463–482.

Moeller, R.R. (2010). *IT Audit, Control, and Security*. John Wiley & Sons.

Panian, Ž. (2004). *Control and Audit of Information Systems*. Sinergija-nakladništvo d.o.o.

Panian, Ž., Spremić, M. (2007). *Corporate Governance and Audit of Information Systems*. Zgombić & Partneri – nakladništvo i informatika d.o.o.

Pasquini, A., & Galiè, E. (2013). COBIT 5 and the Process Capability Model. Improvements Provided for IT Governance Process. Proceedings of FIKUSZ, 13, 67-76.

Petraşcu, D. (2010). Internal audit: Defining, objectives, functions, and stages. *Studies in Business and Economics*, *5*(3), 238–246.

Rosário, T., Pereira, R., & da Silva, M. M. (2012). Formalization of IT Audit Management Process. In *IEEE 16th International Enterprise Distributed Object Computing Conference Workshops*, 1–10.

Sayana, S.A. (2002). The IS audit process. *Information Systems Control Journal*, *1*, 20–22.

Senft, S., Gallegos, F. (2009). *Information Technology Control and Audit* (3rd ed.). CRC Press Taylor & Francis Group.

Spremic, M. (2007). Methods of conducting information systems audit. *Proceedings of the Faculty of Economics in Zagreb*, *5*, 295–312.

Stanišić, M. (2014). Audit of Information Systems Controls. *Information Systems in Accounting and Audit*, (2005), 588–594.

Stoor, G. (2016). Challenges addressed by fundamentals. *ISACA Journal*, 6, 1–3.

Turulja, L., Bajgorić, N. (2016). Innovation and information technology capability as antecedents of a firm's success. *Interdisciplinary Description of Complex Systems*, *14*(2), 148–156.

Tušek, B., Žager, L. (2006). *Audit*. Croatian Association of Accountants and Financial Professionals.

Yang, D.C., Guan, L. (2004). The evolution of IT auditing and internal control standards in financial statement audit: The case of the United States. *Managerial Auditing Journal*, *19*(4), 544–555.

# Chapter 8

# IT Capability and Organizational Business Performance

*"The advance of technology is based on making it fit in so that you don't really even notice it, so it's part of everyday life".*

**Bill Gates**

## Introduction

Information technology (IT) is a unique business resource that enables better organizational business performance year by year. How IT adds value to the business is a topic that has been discussed for more than half a century now. Managing IT in a systematic way to optimize the contribution to the value is a very significant strategic issue for organizations. Therefore, it is also necessary to know the methods of measuring IT value. In other words, it is clear that IT can potentially provide a sustainable competitive advantage for organizations, but it is necessary to manage resources to enable this properly. Hence, this chapter aims to discuss the concept of **organizational IT capability**, how to evaluate and measure IT capability, and how it relates to an organization's business performance. In this regard, bibliometric citation and co-occurrence analysis were used. The bibliometric analysis applies a set of quantitative methodologies based on statistical analytical techniques, taking into account the analysis of citations made in scientific articles and thus assessing the impact of articles published with their reference and dissemination (Ferreira, Fernandes, & Ratten, 2016).

The main objective of this chapter is to answer the following questions:

1. What is organizational IT capability?
2. How can organizational IT capability be measured?
3. What is the relationship between BCM and organizational IT capability?

## Methodology

Our analysis consisted of two parts. First, a qualitative analysis of papers obtained from the Web of Science (WoS) citation database was conducted following the steps of the systematic literature review. Subsequently, an overview of available professional sources, standards, as well as best practices was conducted. We followed PRISMA (Preferred Reporting Items for Systematic Reviews and Meta-Analyses) guidelines for conducting systematic reviews of research. The PRISMA diagram of the search is presented in Figure 8.1.

For bibliometric analysis, the citation database of Web of Science and VOSviewer software were used. Specifically, this chapter incorporated the Web of Science™ Core Collection database, searching by the string *"("information technology capabilit*" OR*

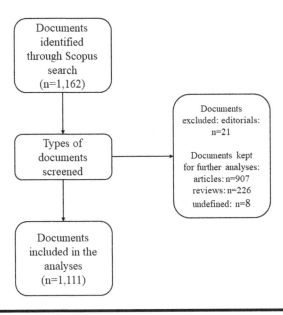

**Figure 8.1   PRISMA process of literature identification.**

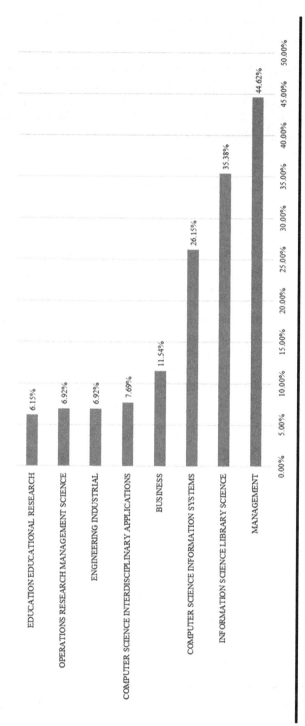

**Figure 8.2  Scientific fields of papers.**

*"IT capabilit*") OR ("information technology competenc*" OR "IT competenc*")"* in the title[1] (Timespan: All years. Indexes: SCI-EXPANDED, SSCI, A&HCI, ESCI.). This search process returned a total of 138 documents with the date of publication ranging from 1994 to the present. We excluded editorials, letters, meeting abstracts, and news items. One hundred thirty papers were left for analysis with a total of 5,799 citations in WoS. Moreover, Figure 8.2 shows the leading scientific fields in which documents have been published, noting that some articles may belong to more than one area at a time. As can be seen from Figure 8.2, most existing works deal with BCM primarily from a management perspective (Xing, Zeng, & Zio, 2019).

Citation analysis is used to obtain indicators of scientific performance concerning citation results (De Bellis, 2009). The ten most cited papers were identified and are presented in Table 8.1. In addition, Figure 8.3 presents references with ten or more citations, grouped into ten clusters. Additional content analysis might help identify the cluster logic and rationale, but that is not the subject of this chapter.

The map of key words was created based on a co-occurrence matrix (Sinkovics, 2016). The minimum threshold is set at five occurrences. The most popular key words are presented on the co-occurrence map shown in Figure 8.4. Research topics and trends can be identified from the clusters of key words. Interestingly, while papers have been identified from the field of IT capabilities, the most prominent key word is firm performance, followed by competitive advantage and the resource-based view. Only after that do the key words of systems, IT capability, and information technology appear. This analysis suggests that IT capability is mainly treated from a business and management perspective.

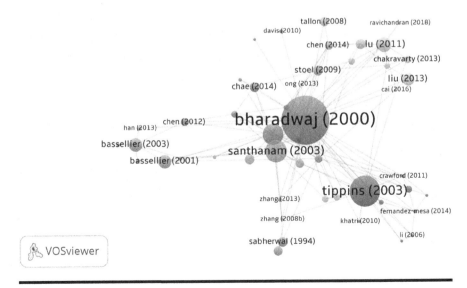

**Figure 8.3   Citation analysis – most influential papers (VOSviewer output).**

The analysis revealed five clusters. The first, a red cluster, based on the key words, can be linked to investments in IT, R&D, and innovation. Second, the green cluster can be related to the IT infrastructure, its adoption, and management. The key words of the third, blue cluster, relate to the resource-based perspective and the different resources of the organization. The fourth (yellow) and fifth (purple) clusters are smaller and difficult to relate to a single container.

## IT Capability and Assessment Approaches

IT capability is the strategic use of IT competencies and resources to achieve the goals of an organization. In other words, IT capability suggests the combination of IT-based assets, services, and processes or procedures that support business operations in a way that adds value (Bharadwaj, Sambamurthy, & Zmud, 1999). However, in order to be able to critically examine the concept of organizational IT capability as well as the ways it is evaluated, the findings of the most influential papers in the field identified by the literature review are presented below.

The basic conclusion that can be drawn from the analysis performed is that two approaches are used to assess the organizational IT capability. The first, a scientific approach, is focused more on business value and IT management. The other, relates to the technical side of the capability and evaluates using specific standards, best practices, and benchmarking. Hence, after reviewing the literature, **two approaches to assess organizational IT capability** can be outlined: 1) an approach present in the scientific literature; and 2) an approach present in standards and best practices. Both approaches, as well as IT capability conceptualization, are briefly presented below.

### *An Approach Present in Scientific Research*

First, based on the methodology explained above, the most influential papers in the field have been identified (see Table 8.2), and, based on a qualitative content analysis of those papers, a method of measuring/evaluating IT capability is offered. This certainly does not mean that there are no other measurement methods.

The most influential study in the field is Bharadwaj (2000), with more than double the citations from a study that is in second place. He defined IT capability as the organizational "ability to mobilize and deploy IT-based resources in combination or copresent with other resources and capabilities". Moreover, IT capability is measured with three dimensions: the tangible resources consisting of the physical IT infrastructure components; the human IT resources incorporating the technical and managerial IT skills; and the intangible IT-enabled resources such as knowledge assets, customer orientation, and synergy (Bharadwaj, 2000). Physical IT assets represent the core of an organization's entire IT infrastructure and consist of

**Table 8.1  Most Influential Papers in WoS on IT Capability/Competence**

| | Reference | Article Title | WoS Number of Citations | Average Citations per Year | Google Scholar Number of Citations |
|---|---|---|---|---|---|
| 1 | (Bharadwaj, 2000) | A resource-based perspective on information technology capability and firm performance: An empirical investigation | 1,532 | 76.60 | 5,008 |
| 2 | (Tippins & Sohi, 2003) | IT competency and firm performance: Is organizational learning a missing link? | 691 | 40.65 | 1,924 |
| 3 | (Santhanam & Hartono, 2003) | Issues in linking information technology capability to firm performance | 397 | 23.35 | 1,227 |
| 4 | (Bhatt & Grover, 2005) | Types of information technology capabilities and their role in competitive advantage: An empirical study | 357 | 23.80 | 1,159 |
| 5 | (Lu & Ramamurthy, 2011) | Understanding the Link Between Information Technology Capability and Organizational Agility: an Empirical Examination | 201 | 22.33 | 622 |
| 6 | (Bassellier, Benbasat, & Reich, 2003) | The influence of business managers' IT competence on championing IT | 164 | 9.65 | 504 |
| 7 | (Bassellier, Reich, & Benbasat, 2001) | Information technology competence of business managers: A definition and research model | 162 | 8.53 | 546 |
| 8 | (Liu, Huang, Wei, & Huang, 2015) | The impact of IT capabilities on firm performance: The mediating roles of absorptive capacity and supply chain agility | 142 | 20.29 | 399 |
| 9 | (Stoel & Muhanna, 2009) | IT capabilities and firm performance: A contingency analysis of the role of industry and IT capability type | 102 | 9.27 | 309 |
| 10 | (Chae, Koh, & Prybutok, 2014) | Information Technology Capability and Firm Performance: Contradictory Findings and Their Possible Causes | 101 | 16.83 | 275 |

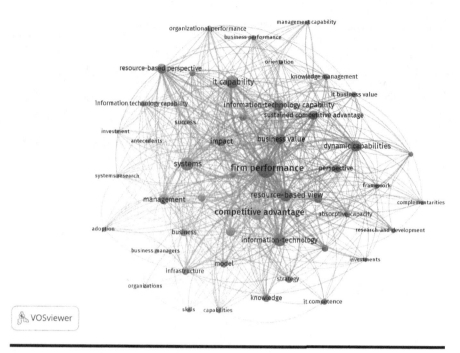

**Figure 8.4** Key words co-occurrence analysis (VOSviewer output).

computer and communication technologies, and technical platforms and databases. Human resources consist of two types of skills: technical (IT skills such as programming, systems analysis, and design, and competencies in emerging technologies) and management IT skills (capabilities such as effective IS management, project management, and leadership). The intangible IT-based capabilities analyzed in this paper are customer orientation, knowledge assets, and synergies. Synergy refers to the resources and opportunities sharing across organizational departments (Bharadwaj, 2000).

Tippins and Sohi (2003) aimed to develop a conceptualization of IT competency. They defined this competence as "the extent to which a firm is knowledgeable about and effectively utilizes IT to manage information within the firm". They viewed this construct as multidimensional, consisting of IT knowledge, IT operations, and IT objects. Thus, IT knowledge is defined as "the extent to which a firm possesses a body of technical knowledge about objects such as computer based systems" (Tippins & Sohi, 2003). IT operations are considered as "the extent to which a firm utilizes IT to manage market and customer information". Finally, IT objects refer to "computer-based hardware, software, and support personnel" (Tippins & Sohi, 2003). Measuring indicators are quite broad and do not treat specific technology in the organization. For example, IT objects refer to having an MIS department and a designated manager of that department, creating applications

**Table 8.2  Content Analysis of the Most Influential Papers**

| | Reference | IT Capability Definition | IT Capability Measurement |
|---|---|---|---|
| 1 | (A.S. Bharadwaj, 2000) | He defined the IT capability as organizational "ability to mobilize and deploy IT-based resources in combination or copresent with other resources and capabilities". | • The tangible resource – IT infrastructure<br>• Human IT resources – technical and managerial IT skills<br>• The intangible IT-enabled resources |
| 2 | (Tippins & Sohi, 2003) | They defined the IT competency as "the extent to which a firm is knowledgeable about and effectively utilizes IT to manage information within the firm". | • IT knowledge<br>• IT operations<br>• IT objects |
| 3 | (Santhanam & Hartono, 2003) | They did not provide a clear definition of IT capability but rather a tentative definition of capability – "a unique set of capabilities mobilized by a firm that cannot has". | They measured IT capability using the Standard Industrial Classification (SIC) scheme and identified firms with superior IT capability. |
| 4 | (Bhatt & Grover, 2005) | They defined capabilities as "the ability of firms to build unique competencies and capabilities that can leverage their resources". | IT capabilities are characterized by value, competitive, and dynamic capabilities as three distinct types of capabilities.<br>• IT infrastructure<br>• Competitive IT capabilities – IT business experience, relationship infrastructure<br>• IT business experience –<br>• Relationship Infrastructure |
| 5 | (Lu & Ramamurthy, 2011) | They defined IT capability as a "firm's ability to acquire, deploy, combine, and reconfigure IT resources in support and enhancement of business strategies and work processes". | • IT infrastructure capability<br>• IT business spanning capability<br>• IT proactive stance |

*(Continued)*

**Table 8.2 (Continued)    Content Analysis of the Most Influential Papers**

|   | Reference | IT Capability Definition | IT Capability Measurement |
|---|---|---|---|
| 6 | (Bassellier et al., 2003) | This paper deals with the information technology competence of business managers (not organizations), which is not the primary objective of this chapter. | |
| 7 | (Bassellier et al., 2001) | This paper deals with the information technology competence of business managers (not organizations), which is not the primary objective of this chapter. | |
| 8 | (Liu et al., 2015) | They defined IT capability as a "firm's ability to assemble, integrate, and deploy IT resources to meet business needs". | • IT operational capability<br>• IT transformational capability |
| 9 | (Stoel & Muhanna, 2009) | They defined the capability as "a special type of resource, encompassing a firm's capacity to coordinate and deploy other resources to effect a desired end". | They used the rankings provided by *Information Week* in their annual special issue, IW 500, in this study to identify firms with superior IT capabilities. Internally focused IT capability Externally focused IT capability |
| 10 | (Chae et al., 2014) | They adopted conceptualization from IT capability from (A.S. Bharadwaj, 2000) and (Santhanam & Hartono, 2003) | The IT leader group of firms considered to have superior IT capabilities and selected from *Information Week 500*, IW 500. |

when needed, allocating funds for IT, and owning a computer network. It is clear that the way of measuring these dimensions may have represented trends in 2003, but that they need to be revised in line with the development of IT.

Santhanam and Hartono (2003) tested the robustness of the IT capability concept and its relationship to company performance. IT capability was treated as a unique set of capabilities mobilized by a firm, and that cannot be easily duplicated. They measured IT capability following the standard industrial classification (SIC) scheme employing benchmarking for comparison. Furthermore, Bhatt and Grover (2005) analyzed the impact of IT infrastructure, IT business experience, and relationship infrastructure on a firm's competitiveness, concluding that the quality of the IT infrastructure does not influence the competitive advantage, while the quality of IT business expertise and the related infrastructure do.

Similar to previous research, Lu and Ramamurthy (2011) conceptualized IT capability as a multidimensional construct reflected in its three dimensions: IT infrastructure capability, IT business spanning capability, and IT proactive stance. IT infrastructure capability is an ability that captures the extent to which a firm is good at managing data management services and architectures, network communications services, and application portfolios and services. IT business spanning capability refers to the ability of a firm's management to anticipate and leverage IT resources to support and enhance its business goals. In other words, this capability implies the ability by which a firm develops a clear IT strategic vision, integrates business and IT strategic planning, and enables management's ability to understand the value of IT investment (Lu & Ramamurthy, 2011). IT proactive stance is a process related to the continuous search for ways to explore or leverage IT resources to create and leverage business opportunities (Lu & Ramamurthy, 2011). It is interesting to note that the way IT infrastructure capability is measured, is improved in relation to Tippins dan Sohi (2003), and is measured with specific:

■ Data management services & architectures technologies (databases, data warehousing, data availability, storage, accessibility, sharing, etc.)
■ Network communication services (connectivity, reliability, availability, LAN, WAN, etc.)
■ Application portfolio and services (ERP, ASP, reusable software modules/components, emerging technologies, etc.)
■ IT facilities' operations/services (servers, large-scale processors, performance monitors, etc.) (Lu & Ramamurthy, 2011)

Also, Liu et al. (2015) considered IT capability as a multidimensional construct consisting of IT operational and IT transformational capability. IT operational capability refers to the deployment of IT applications to provide reliable and consistent IT support to running businesses, and IT transformation capability points out the use of new IT applications to transform businesses to create new business opportunities (Liu et al., 2015). Both of these types of capabilities do not address specific information technologies and processes but general system scalability and compatibility, and innovation.

Stoel and Muhanna (2009) analyzed the relationship between IT capability and organizational business performance under the environmental influence. Their results suggest that the relationship between IT capabilities and organizational performance is more complex than has been theorized. They concluded that the external environment appears to be a significant contingency. Finally, Chae et al. (2014), Bharadwaj (2000), and Santhanam and Hartono (2003) concluded that there is no significant relationship between IT capability and firm performance.

In conclusion, there are more conceptualizations of organizational IT capability in the literature. However, these definitions are very similar and are essentially based on a resource-based view, that is, the ability of an organization to assemble, integrate, and deploy IT resources to meet business needs and to create value. In other words, resources that are unique, inimitable, and valuable represent the capabilities of the organization. However, although the definitions of organizational IT capability are very similar, the dimensions analyzed in the papers are quite different. Some research evaluates an organization's IT capability by using a survey, with measurement indicators that are very broadly defined and more focused on managing it or those that are more technically oriented. Table 8.3 represents one of the measurement scales used in research studies. This scale is prominent because it covers a significant part of IT architecture that has been overlooked by other scales.

As we can see in the second item, even the availability of the network is evaluated (which is not the case with most other measurement scales). However, following the recommendations of this book, BCM and IT revision should be an integral part of the evaluation of a company's IT capabilities. Another scale that provides a good basis for assessing IT capability is the scale from the study by Chen et al. (2014). However, indicators related to technical issues should be improved. This topic is covered in Chapter 9.

## An Approach Present in IT Standards/Best Practices

The *IGI-Global Dictionary* defines IT capability as the ability of an organization to recognize business needs in terms of IT, to deploy IT to enhance business processes cost effectively, and to provide long-term support and maintenance for IT systems. Thus, an organization's ability, by virtue of its IT assets and expertise, to create business value should be considered a capability (CIO wiki).

IT capability, according to CIO wiki, comprises four main components: IT strategy, IT processes, IT organization, and IT infrastructure (see Figure 8.5).

IT organization refers to skills, structure, and expertise, while infrastructures suggests hardware, software, applications, networks, databases, and tools. While it is important to determine how IT capability is measured, it should be noted that the needs of each organization are not the same. IT is a service provider for organizations, and the organization itself and its employees are its customers. IT must enable the business and ensure that its customers are satisfied with the basic services, and that all IT operations are efficient and cost effective (CIO wiki).

IT capability can be illustrated in the capability catalog used to establish a common language and framework about the services to be consumed and delivered to the business (see Figure 8.6). The catalog points to five parts (with constituent elements) of management capabilities, including infrastructure management, data management, application management, customer relationship management, and finally, IT planning, service delivery, and governance. In addition, the ability catalog can be used as a basis for defining what core and non-core capabilities are. Core competencies are those for which internal expertise must be developed, as they are often crucial to the business and to gain a competitive edge. On the other hand, non-core capabilities are less crucial to competitiveness and are often

**Table 8.3  The Measurement Scale for IT Capability**

| *Dimension* | *Items/Indicators* |
|---|---|
| IT Infrastructure Capability | *Relative to other firms in your industry, please evaluate your organization's IT infrastructure capability in the following areas on a 1 to 7 scale (1 = poorer than most, 7 = superior to most).* |
| | Data management services & architectures (e.g., databases, data warehousing, data availability, storage, accessibility, sharing, etc.) |
| | Network communication services (e.g., connectivity, **reliability, availability**, LAN, WAN, etc.) |
| | Application portfolio & services (e.g., ERP, ASP, reusable software modules/components, emerging technologies, etc.) |
| | IT facilities' operations/services (e.g., servers, large-scale processors, performance monitors, etc.) |
| IT Business Spanning Capability | *Relative to other firms in your industry, please evaluate your organization's IT management capability in responding to the following on a 1 to 7 scale (1 = poorer than most, 7 = superior to most).* |
| | Developing a clear vision regarding how IT contributes to business value |
| | Integrating strategic business planning and IT planning |
| | Enabling functional area and general management's ability to understand the value of IT investments |
| | Establishing an effective and flexible IT planning process and developing a robust IT plan |
| IT Proactive Stance | *Relative to other firms in your industry, please evaluate your capability in acquiring, assimilating, transforming, and exploiting IT knowledge in the following areas on a 1 to 7 scale (1 = strongly disagree, 7 = strongly agree).* |
| | We constantly keep current with new information technology innovations |
| | We are capable of and continue to experiment with new IT as necessary |
| | We have a climate that is supportive of trying out new ways of using IT |
| | We constantly seek new ways to enhance the effectiveness of IT use |

(*Source*: Lu & Ramamurthy, 2011)

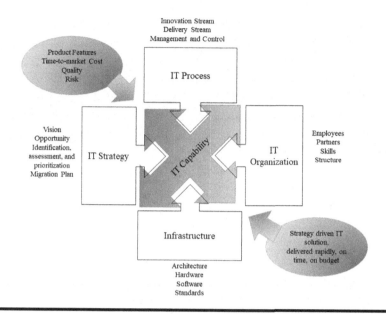

**Figure 8.5    Components of IT capability.** CIO wiki (available at https://cio-wiki.org/wiki/IT_Capability, accessed: February 2020).

| Customer interface | Business relationship management | Business and desktop application portfolio strategy | Business intelligence and analytics | End-user support | End-user computing and devices (for example, laptops, peripherals) | |
|---|---|---|---|---|---|---|
| **Application and management** | Application design and architecture | Application development | Testing and QA | **IT planning, service delivery, and governance** | | |
| | Application support | Release, configuration and change management | Enterprise application integration and middleware | Security and risk management | IT service management | Financial management |
| **Data management** | Data governance and master data management | Storage and backup services | Database services | Innovation management | Enterprise architecture | Program and project management (PMO) |
| **Infrastructure management** | Date center and network operations | Server administration and management | Data network | Vendor and contract management | Capacity management | Training |
| | IT asset management | | Telecommunications infrastructure | | | |

**Figure 8.6    The IT capability catalog.** CIO wiki (available at https://cio-wiki.org/wiki/IT_Capability, accessed: February 2020).

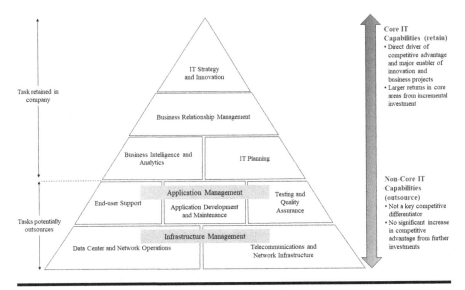

**Figure 8.7    Core IT capabilities.** CIO wiki (available at https://cio-wiki.org/wiki/IT_Capability, accessed: February 2020).

outsourced. The core capabilities are presented in Figure 8.7. The figure shows that IT strategy, planning, and business intelligence and analytics are considered core capabilities, while infrastructure and application management are non-core capabilities.

## COBIT Maturity Model

Control Objectives for Information and Related Technology (COBIT) can be used for the assessment of organizational IT capability as well. COBIT is an IT governance control framework that helps organizations meet business challenges in the areas of regulatory compliance, risk management, and in aligning IT strategy with organizational objectives. COBIT's management guidelines contain a framework for the control and measurability of IT by providing tools to assess and measure the enterprise's IT capability for the 37 identified COBIT processes. In this regard, APO02 (Recognizing and Sterically Addressing Current IT Capability Issues) is related to this (Cobit 5, 2012). However, COBIT's IT maturity model can also be used to evaluate IT capabilities, as it includes all aspects of IT capability from awareness, policies, tools, skills, responsibility, goal setting, and measurement. The COBIT 4.1-maturity model for process improvement purposes is used for assessing a process maturity, defining a target maturity level, and identifying the gaps (ISACA, 2012a). The concept of the maturity level of IT arises because of the need to create a simple benchmark by which it would be possible to distinguish between different

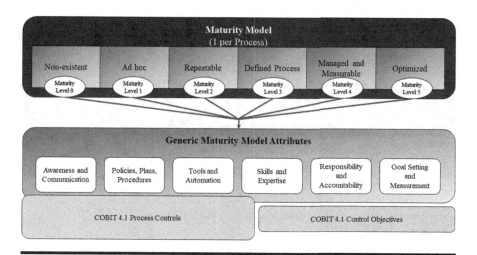

**Figure 8.8  Summary of the COBIT 4.1 maturity model. ISACA (2012a).**

states of organizational IT capability. Summary of the COBIT 4.1 maturity model is presented in Figure 8.8.

Using the COBIT 4.1 maturity model for process improvement purposes requires the use of the following COBIT 4.1 components. First, it is necessary to assess whether the control objectives for the process have been met. Then, the maturity model included in the management guidelines for each procedure can be used to obtain a process maturity profile. Additionally, the generic maturity model in COBIT 4.1 provides six different attributes that are applicable to each process, and that help obtain a more detailed view at the maturity level of the process. Process controls are general objectives of control that also need to be reviewed when a process assessment is performed. Moreover, the COBIT 5 process maturity model can be used to assess IT processes. Figure 8.9 summarizes the model.

The implementation of COBIT begins with an assessment of the overall maturity of the IT processes in the organization. It is the initial stage that gives an overview of the current state of maturity of the information system or processes. Organizational management is responsible for choosing procedures based on the information that is provided and further analyzed and enhanced. The ability to apply it selectively only to the systems of management interest is a highly desirable function of COBIT.

The maturity model can lead to improvements in stability when monitoring information processes and systems. The model defines the metrics and goals that are achieved by measuring the performance of information processes. The COBIT specifications for each process specify the criteria to be considered when evaluating. Its specification defines a table that establishes the status of the maturity attribute for each of the five grades.

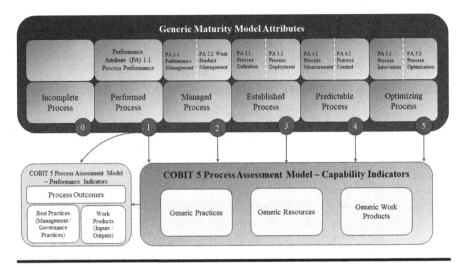

**Figure 8.9** **Summary of COBIT 5 process maturity model.** *ISACA (2012a).*

In general, there are three steps in assessing process capability, including 1) identifying performance objectives, 2) planning and monitoring process performance, and 3) adjusting process performance to meet plans. There are six levels of capability that a process can achieve:

- 0 – Incomplete process – The method is not being implemented, or its intention is not being achieved. There is little or no proof that the process is systematically accomplished at this point.
- 1 – Performed process – The implemented process achieves its goal.
- 2 – Managed process – The performed process is now managed, and its products are properly established, controlled and maintained.
- 3 – Established process – The managed process is now implemented using a defined process that is able to achieve its results in the process.
- 4 – Predictable process – The established process operates within defined limits to achieve its process results.
- 5 – Optimizing process – The predictable process is continually improving to meet relevant current and projected business goals

Figure 8.10 shows a comparison of COBITs 4.1. and 5 maturity models. They overlap to some extent, so organizations that have used the COBIT 4.1 model can reuse existing assessment data and reclassify it to COBIT 5 assessment.

The main drawback of the COBIT maturity model is that an increase in the level of maturity of the process also means the pursuit of even greater control and documentation. Such practices are often inapplicable in business environments that are highly dynamic because too much time is spent documenting existing processes rather than proactively acting.

| COBIT 4.1 Maturity Attribute | COBIT 5 Process Capability Attribute | | | | | | | | |
|---|---|---|---|---|---|---|---|---|---|
| | Process Performance | Performance Management | Work Product Management | Process Definition | Process Deployment | Process Measurement | Process Control | Process Innovation | Process Optimization |
| Awareness and communication | | | | ■ | | | | | |
| Policies, plans, and procedures | | | | | | | ■ | | |
| Tools and automation | | | | ■ | | | | | |
| Skills and Expertise | | | | | ■ | | | | |
| Responsibility and accountability | | | | ■ | | | | | |
| Goal setting and measurement | | ■ | | | | ■ | | | |

**Figure 8.10  Comparison Table of Maturity Attributes (COBIT 4.1) and Process Attributes (COBIT 5). COBIT 5 (2017).**

## IT Capability Maturity Framework – IT-CMF

One of the models that should be mentioned and highlighted here is the IT Capability Maturity Framework – IT-CMF – that has been discussed in Chapter 3. The model is a comprehensive framework of proven management practices, assessment approaches, and improvement strategies covering 37 management disciplines or Critical Capabilities (CCs). For each capability, IT-CMF incorporates a comprehensive suite of maturity profiles, assessment methods, and improvement road maps. Maturity assessment is based on a set of questionnaires or interviews conducted by an expert team.

IT-CMF (presented in Figure 3.16) focuses on IT processes but also on the capabilities and value delivered to the business. In other words, this model is comprehensive and covers all critical IT capabilities, and is easy to implement. By using IT-CMF, it is possible to identify practical ideas for how IT can improve its capabilities.

The IT-CMF model evaluates and improves organizational IT capabilities. It is planned to derive greater business value from IT. The IT-CMF is structured around four macro capabilities, each of which embraces a number of critical capabilities. The IT-CMF is structured around four key strategic areas, or macro capabilities: managing IT like a business, managing the IT budget, managing IT capability, and managing IT for business value. Managing IT like a business, settles the direction for the overall IT capability. In managing the IT budget, the strategic direction is translated into an IT budget to power activities and programs. Managing IT capability is the production engine, where two primary activities are performed: maintaining existing IT services and developing new IT solutions. Managing IT for business value ensures that these activities and programs deliver value (CIO wiki). The IT-CMF

| High | | | |
|---|---|---|---|
| | 5 | Optimizing | • Value-centric IT management<br>• State-of-the-art practices and outcomes |
| | 4 | Advanced | • Benefits from IT investments quantified and communicated<br>• Practices and outcomes well above industry average |
| | 3 | Intermediate | • IT/business interaction formalized for all critical capabilities<br>• Transparent investment decisions |
| | 2 | Basic | • Delivering basic IT services<br>• Some IT/business interactions formalized |
| Low | 1 | Initial | • No formal processes<br>• Ad-hoc management of IT |

**Figure 8.11   Maturity levels of IT-CMF. IVI (2013).**

classifies 36 basic capabilities within these four macro capabilities (see Figure 3.16). The maturity levels of this model are presented in Figure 8.11.

- Initial – At the first level of maturity, there is a lack of formal practices and processes effectiveness. The effectiveness of practices is based on the ad-hoc and informal success of individuals.
- Basic – A formal governance structure is established at the second level of maturity, with a basic understanding of the IT function, but without considering the entire business.
- Intermediate – The third level of maturity implies that IT structures and management approaches are coordinated both within the company and with the stakeholders, on the basis of which formal metrics and reporting systems are set.
- Advanced – The fourth level of maturity is characterized by consistent and coordinated approaches that contribute to continuous advancements that are above the industry average.
- Optimizing – The fifth level of maturity involves defining policies, procedures, and standards to maximize efficiency, which is closely linked to internal and external stakeholders. At this level, the organization is recognized as an industry leader.

Detailed assessments following the IT-CMF usually require four to six weeks. The final analysis provides organizations with insight into the current level of maturity of the target areas, as well as a road map to improve IT capabilities and turn them into more business value. Figure 8.12 shows a hypothetical example of the assessment (available at www.bcg.com/publications/2010/transformation-tech-function-managing-it-business-value.aspx. accesses: February 2020). The figure shows that 9 processes are at the basic level (level 2), while 7 processes are at an advanced level. Compared to the industry average (yellow line), the example organization is better in 5 areas (with lines above the yellow line – e.g., process CFP) and worse in 12 areas (with lines below the yellow line – e.g., process ITG).

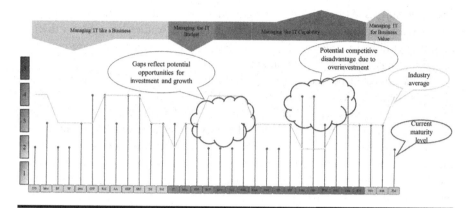

**Figure 8.12  A high-level IT-CMF assessment (hypothetical example).**
*Dreischmeier, Iyer and Matzke (2014).*

The method of measuring IT capabilities is very significant, and a combination of scientific and technical approaches may be appropriate. In this regard, Kmieciak, Michna, and Meczynska (2012) stated that IT, perceived only in terms of hardware and software, cannot provide a competitive advantage because it is too easily duplicated. More on combining the two approaches is presented in Chapter 9.

## *IT Capability and BCM*

A comprehensive literature review conducted confirms the discussion outlined in Chapter 3. BCM should be an integral part of organizational IT capability. It is important that organizations also assess their BCM while evaluating their IT capability. Some models of IT maturity tackle BCM, too. Most IT maturity models also address BCM. When it comes to more technical research, they treat the technical side of IT capability and BCM as an integral part of it. Studies that are more concerned with management and the social sciences, however, employ a narrower definition of IT capability, and BCM is rarely considered part of it. BCM is the capability of the organization to continue the delivery of products or services at acceptable predefined levels following a disruptive incident (Hassel & Cedergren, 2019), and it should be an integral part of overall organizational IT capability.

## IT Capability and Organizational Performance

Understanding the relationship between IT investments and organizational business performance has become a major and enduring interest of researchers and professionals. Although much progress has been made, significant gaps remain in our understanding. For example, while numerous studies have shown that IT spending is linked to increased business performance, other studies are reporting mixed findings (Stoel & Muhanna, 2009).

The relationship between IT investments and organizational business performance has been analyzed in research since the 1970s, but no definitive conclusion has emerged on this relationship (Bhatt & Grover, 2005; Chae et al., 2014). Specifically, the relational assumption that IT should contribute to productivity has proven to be incorrect (Dué, 1993). IT is considered a key factor driving economic growth in industrial societies. Investing in IT is considered as a potential for reducing costs, increasing productivity, and improving living standards. However, since the 1970s, productivity growth has slowed in most of the world's economies, while IT spending has grown. In other words, organizations invest resources in procuring IT-related products because these investments are assumed to provide economic returns to firms. However, research that has attempted to confirm this premise has produced mixed results, creating a productivity paradox (Santhanam & Hartono, 2003). The analysis of this relationship in the identified most influential papers is presented in Table 8.4.

As already mentioned, the indirect impact of organizational IT capability on business performance is often analyzed through some other capability. In this regard, Kala Kamdjoug, Nguegang Tewamba, and Fosso Wamba (2019) confirm the mediating effects of the information security management system on the relationship between IT capability and business performance.

## IT Productivity Paradox

American economist Robert Solow said in 1987, "You can see the computer age everywhere but in the productivity statistics". This was the beginning of the productivity paradox, the premise that advances in computing power have not made workers more productive. The productivity paradox suggests that productivity growth in the United States slowed down in the 1970s and 1980s, even though IT grew rapidly at the same time. Such statistics are contrary to the logic that job automation should increase overall factor productivity.

The productiveness growth of the United States economy as a whole has slowed and has been recorded in many other countries as well, and often within individual industries that have made a major investment in IT amid substantial improvements in computing power and IT spending. Thus, the productivity paradox has its roots in microeconomic research results, which has failed in confirming the assumption that high-technology investment benefits productivity (Cohen, DeLong, & Zysman, 2000). This phenomenon has also become known as the "IT productivity paradox", "new technology productivity paradox" or simply the "*technology paradox*" (Braque & Medina, 2002; Hajli, Sims, & Ibragimov, 2015). Analyzing the productivity paradox of IT investment, Brynjolfsson and Hitt (1996) point out that IT investments create intangible benefits that have a positive impact on

**Table 8.4   Content Anlysis of the Most Influential Papers**

|   | *Reference* | *IT capability and Organizational Performance* |
|---|---|---|
| 1 | (A.S. Bharadwaj, 2000) | This study empirically examined the relationship between superior IT capability and superior organizational business performance and found the relationship to be significant and positive. |
| 2 | (Tippins & Sohi, 2003) | They did not analyze the direct impact of IT capability on organizational performance. Specifically, the proposed model consisted of a relationship between organizational learning and business performance, and the moderating impact of IT capability on that relationship, as well as the relationship between IT capability and organizational learning. |
| 3 | (Santhanam & Hartono, 2003) | They have shown that companies with superior IT capability have superior current and sustained performance compared to industry average performance. |
| 4 | (Bhatt & Grover, 2005) | They empirically tested the relationship between IT capabilities and competitive advantage of the firm. The results showed that the quality of the IT infrastructure did not have a significant effect on competitive advantage, while the quality of IT business expertise and the relationship infrastructure did. |
| 5 | (Lu & Ramamurthy, 2011) | They analyzed the impact of IT capability on organizational agility. |
| 6 | (Bassellier et al., 2003) | This relationship was not analyzed in the study. |
| 7 | (Bassellier et al., 2001) | This relationship was not analyzed in the study. |
| 8 | (Liu et al., 2015) | This paper dealt with the analysis of how IT capability influences the integration of supply and demand over the Internet, which further influences the improvement of organizational performance. |
| 9 | (Stoel & Muhanna, 2009) | Their results suggested that the relationship between IT capabilities and organizational performance is more complex than has been theorized. |
| 10 | (Chae et al., 2014) | Their results showed no significant link between IT capability and firm performance. |

organizational business performance. For this reason, many scholars have proposed an analysis of other organizational capabilities in the relationship between IT capabilities and business performance (Chen, Wang, Nevo, Benitez-Amado, & Kou, 2015). Specifically, the capabilities through which the IT capability influences the organizational business performance, such as, for example, organizational agility (Chakravarty, Grewal, & Sambamurthy, 2013; Lu & Ramamurthy, 2011), knowledge management (Pérez-López & Alegre, 2012), quality management practices (Pérez-Aróstegui, Bustinza-Sánchez, & Barrales-Molina, 2014), and so on.

Over the past decades, many researchers have periodically revised the IT productivity paradox. While some confirm its existence, some deny its existence (Hajli et al., 2015). In this regard, Hajli et al. (2015) conducted research to analyze the IT paradox of productivity in the twenty-first century. Their results show that spending on IT is still high. Their research found a high correlation between growth per capita and growth in ICT investment. Furthermore, the results indicate the existence of the phenomenon of the IT productivity paradox in 1995–2005. The study concludes that the existence of the IT productivity paradox still cannot be confirmed or denied (Hajli et al., 2015).

We have already reported inconsistency in measuring IT capabilities. In this regard, Brynjolfsson (1993) pointed out that one of the reasons for the productivity paradox can be a way of measuring IT, claiming that "the shortfall of IT productivity is as much due to deficiencies in our measurement and methodological tool kit as to mismanagement by developers and users of IT" (Kmieciak et al., 2012).

Many scholars argue that the relationship between IT capability and organizational business performance has been debated without clear results. However, Brynjolfsson and Hitt (1998) argue that throughout most studies, there has been a consistent finding that IT has a positive and significant impact on firm production, contrary to claims of a "productivity paradox". Also, Hajli et al. (2015) point out that ICT is constantly delivering positive results, implying that there has been no IT productivity paradox.

Furthermore, in research, there is an inconsistency in perceiving IT. The paradox is primarily associated with IT investments. In other words, research has confirmed that IT investments have no direct impact on the productivity or business performance of the organization. IT investments are not the same as the IT capability of an organization. We have already explained the concept of IT capabilities. In this regard, it is clear that some organizations may have high IT investments but may not have the capacity to reap the benefits of IT. Perhaps the inconsistency of the earlier results should be sought precisely in the difference between the treatment of IT and the ways of measuring IT capabilities. Relying on a resource-based view, IS scholars have argued that the difference in performance from IT rests on differences in IT capabilities as opposed to differences in IT spending per se (Stoel & Muhanna, 2009). IT, perceived only in terms of hardware and software, cannot provide a competitive advantage because it is too easily duplicated (Kmieciak et al., 2012). Also, researchers have pointed out that IT investments are made with long-term goals in mind, and there is a time lag in obtaining benefits (Santhanam & Hartono, 2003). Maybe this time lag is just about building organizational IT capabilities.

## Conclusion

Information technology has become one of the most important resources of contemporary organizations. However, it is often a challenge for management to properly define and determine IT in the organization, as well as to assess the adequacy of its use. One common way of conceptualizing IT is through organizational IT capabilities (Tippins & Sohi, 2003). IT capability refers to the way a company uses information technology to manage information resources successfully. The concept of IT capability encompasses the possession of information technologies as well as their appropriate use to meet the information needs of the organization (Mithas, Ramasubbu, & Sambamurthy, 2011).

While some research has shown that there is a significant positive relationship between organizational IT capability and business performance, other authors have empirically found that there is no direct relationship between the two. In order to explain the inconsistency of the findings, one reason offered is that the causal link between organizational IT capability and business performance is "too long", and that it requires consideration of the mediation role of any of the organizational capability concepts, that is, the capabilities of a company that mediates the relationship between IT capabilities and business performance. Organizational IT capability is considered a significant tool that complements the other organizational capabilities. In other words, IT capability, combined with other organizational capabilities, can generate a positive synergistic effect and increase competitiveness.

All this raises the question of how to assess the IT capability of an organization. In this regard, this chapter aimed to identify ways in which an organization can evaluate its IT capability. The results of the literature search led to the identification of two ubiquitous approaches. Namely, in the scientific literature, the concept of organizational IT capability is treated very narrowly and undermines the management aspect. On the other hand, there is a more comprehensive approach to international standards and practice. Finally, the issue of linking BCM to organizational IT capability is addressed, and the results of our analysis indicate that organizations seeking higher IT capability must address their BCM capability as well, especially when international standards and best practices are considered.

## Real-World Example

This example illustrates how the IT-CMF was used to assess improvements in capability and provide guidance on prioritizing recommendations for change in Intel. Figure 8.13 shows the improvement achieved in each critical capability and highlights key measures used to drive improvements. It is important to note that the IT-CMF was just one of the tools used to help focus IT improvements initiatives, and, in this capacity, it provided the CIO with business intelligence on the maturity of IT capabilities (Curley & Kenneally, 2011). Figure 8.14 shows that seven areas were listed as high-right priority areas, of which only five were prioritized because the rate of progress in IT management has been deemed adequate, and no further changes beyond the previously planned ones were needed.

The case is adopted from Curley & Kenneally (2011).

## Discussion Questions

1. What is organizational IT capability?
2. Discuss two approaches to measuring IT capability.
3. Which approach is more appropriate for measuring IT capability? Why?
4. How does COBIT address BCM?
5. Explain COBIT's IT maturity model.
6. Explain IT-CMF.
7. Discuss maturity levels of IT-CMF.

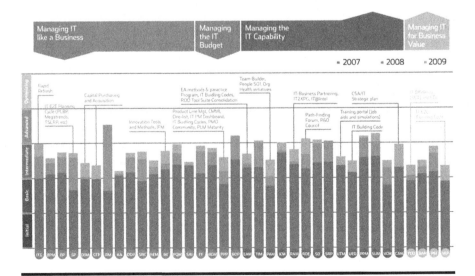

**Figure 8.13   Intel IT Maturity improvement. Curley and Kenneally (2011).**

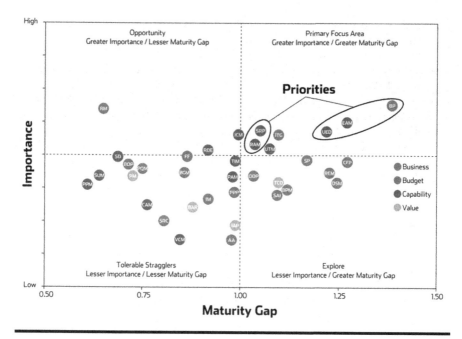

**Figure 8.14 Critical Capability Prioritization. Curley and Kenneally (2011).**

8. Discuss the relationship between organizational IT capability and organizational business performance.
9. Explain the IT productivity paradox.
10. Discuss the IT paradox in today's business.

# References

Bassellier, G., Benbasat, I., Reich, B.H. (2003). The Influence of business managers' IT competence on championing IT. *Information Systems Research*, *14*(4), 317–336. https://doi.org/10.1287/isre.14.4.317.24899

Bassellier, G., Reich, B.H., Benbasat, I. (2001). Information technology competence of business managers: A definition and research model. *Journal of Management Information Systems*, *17*(4), 159–182. https://doi.org/10.1080/07421222.2001.11045660

Bharadwaj, A., Sambamurthy, V., Zmud, R.W. (1999). IT capabilities: theoretical perspectives and empirical operationalization. *Management Science*, (January), 378–385. https://doi.org/10.1145/352925.352962

Bharadwaj, A.S. (2000). A resource-based perspective on information technology capability and firm performance: an empirical investigation. *MIS Quarterly*, *24*(1), 169–196. https://doi.org/10.2307/3250983

Bhatt, G.D., Grover, V. (2005). Types of information technology capabilities and their role in competitive advantage: An Empirical Study. *Journal of Management Information Systems*, *22*(2), 253–277. https://doi.org/10.1080/07421222.2005.11045844

Braque, S., Medina, J.A. (2002). The technology paradox: Characteristics, causes and implications for IT management. *International Journal of Information Technology, 8*(1), 1689–1699. https://doi.org/10.1017/CBO9781107415324.004

Brynjolfsson, E. (1993). The productivity paradox of information technology. *Communications of the ACM, 36*(12). Retrieved from http://dl.acm.org/citation.cfm?id=163309

Brynjolfsson, E., Hitt, L. (1996). Paradox lost? Firm-level 3vidence on the returns to information systems spending. *Management Science, 42*(4), 541–558.

Brynjolfsson, E., Hitt, L.M. (1998). Beyond the productivity paradox: Computers are the catalyst for bigger changes. *Communications of the ACM, 41*(8), 49–55. https://doi.org/10.1145/280324.280332

Chae, H., Koh, C., Prybutok, V. (2014). Information technology capability and firm performance: Contradictory findings and their possible causes. *MIS Quarterly, 38*(1), 305–326.

Chakravarty, A., Grewal, R., Sambamurthy, V. (2013). Information technology competencies, organizational agility, and firm performance: Enabling and facilitating roles. *Information Systems Research, 24*(4), 976–997. https://doi.org/10.1287/isre.2013.0500

Chen, Y., Wang, Y., Nevo, S., Benitez-Amado, J., Kou, G. (2015). IT capabilities and product innovation performance: The roles of corporate entrepreneurship and competitive intensity. *Information & Management, 52*(6), 643–657. https://doi.org/10.1016/j.im.2015.05.003

Chen, Y., Wang, Y., Nevo, S., Jin, J., Wang, L., Chow, W.S. (2014). IT capability and organizational performance: The roles of business process agility and environmental factors. *European Journal of Information Systems, 23*(3), 326–342. https://doi.org/10.1057/ejis.2013.4

*COBIT 5: A Business Framework for the Governance and Management of Enterprise IT.* (2017).

Cohen, S.S., DeLong, J.B., Zysman, J. (2000). Tools for thought: What is new and important about the "e-conomy"? University of California, Berkeley. Available at: https://escholarship.org/uc/item/0c97w1gn.

Curley, M., Kenneally, J. (2011). *Using the IT-CMF to Improve IT Capability and Value Creation: An Intel IT Case Study.* Innovation Value Institute.

De Bellis, N. (2009). *Bibliometrics and Citation Analysis: From the Science Citation Index to Cybermetrics.* Scarecrow Press.

Dreischmeier, R., Iyer, S., Matzke, C. (2014) *The IVI's IT Capability Maturing Framework: Taking IT in Financial Institutions to the Next Level.* Boston Consulting Group. Available at: www.bcg.com/documents/file116131.pdf.

Dué, R.T. (1993). The productivity paradox. *Information Systems Management, 10*(1), 68–71. https://doi.org/10.1080/10580539308906917

Ferreira, J.J.M., Fernandes, C.I., Ratten, V. (2016). A co-citation bibliometric analysis of strategic management research. *Scientometrics, 109*(1), 1–32. https://doi.org/10.1007/s11192-016-2008-0

Hajli, M., Sims, J.M., Ibragimov, V. (2015). Information technology (IT) productivity paradox in the 21st century. *International Journal of Productivity and Performance Management, 64*(4), 457–478. https://doi.org/10.1108/IJPPM-12-2012-0129

Hassel, H., Cedergren, A. (2019). Exploring the conceptual foundation of continuity management in the context of societal safety. *Risk Analysis, 39*(7), 1503–1519. https://doi.org/10.1111/risa.13263

ISACA. (2012a). A business framework for the governance and management of enterprise IT. ISACA, Rolling Meadows, IL, USA.

ISACA. (2012b). *COBIT 5 Implementation.* ISACA. Retrieved from www.isaca.org/COBIT/Pages/COBIT-5-spanish.aspx

IVI – Innovation Value Institute. (2013). *IT Capability Maturity Framework.* Innovation Value Institute.

Kala Kamdjoug, J.R., Nguegang Tewamba, H.J., Fosso Wamba, S. (2019). IT capabilities, firm performance and the mediating role of ISRM: A case study from a developing country. *Business Process Management Journal, 25*(3), 476–494. https://doi.org/10.1108/BPMJ-11-2017-0297

Kmieciak, R., Michna, A., Meczynska, A. (2012). Innovativeness, empowerment and IT capability: evidence from SMEs. *Industrial Management & Data Systems, 112*(5), 707–728. https://doi.org/10.1108/02635571211232280

Liu, H., Huang, Q., Wei, S., Huang, L. (2015). The impacts of IT capability on internet-enabled supply and demand process integration, and firm performance in manufacturing and services. *International Journal oLogistics Management, 26*(1), 172–194. https://doi.org/10.1108/IJLM-11-2013-0132

Lu, Y., Ramamurthy, K.R. (2011). Understanding the link between information technology capability and organizational agility: An empirical examination. *MIS Quarterly, 35*(4), 931–954. https://doi.org/10.1007/978-3-642-49298-3

Mithas, S., Ramasubbu, N., Sambamurthy, V. (2011). How information management capability influences firm performance. *MIS Quarterly, 35*(1), 237–256.

Pérez-Aróstegui, M.N., Bustinza-Sánchez, F., Barrales-Molina, V. (2014). Exploring the relationship between information technology competence and quality management. *Business Research Quarterly, 18*(1), 4–17. https://doi.org/10.1016/j.brq.2013.11.003

Pérez-López, S., Alegre, J. (2012). Information technology competency, knowledge processes and firm performance. *Industrial Management & Data Systems, 112*(4), 644–662. https://doi.org/10.1108/02635571211225521

Santhanam, R., Hartono, E. (2003). Issues in linking information technology capability to firm performance. *MIS Quarterly, 27*(1), 125–153.

Sinkovics, N. (2016). Enhancing the foundations for theorising through bibliometric mapping. *International Marketing Review, 33*(3), 327–350. https://doi.org/10.1108/IMR-10-2014-0341

Stoel, M.D., Muhanna, W.A. (2009). IT capabilities and firm performance: A contingency analysis of the role of industry and IT capability type. *Information & Management, 46*(3), 181–189. https://doi.org/10.1016/j.im.2008.10.002

Tippins, M.J., Sohi, R.S. (2003). IT competency and firm performance: Is organizational learning a missing link? *Strategic Management Journal, 24*(8), 745–761. https://doi.org/10.1002/smj.337

Xing, J., Zeng, Z., Zio, E. (2019). Dynamic business continuity assessment using condition monitoring data. *International Journal of Disaster Risk Reduction, 41*, 1-12. https://doi.org/10.1016/j.ijdrr.2019.101334

# Chapter 9

# Development of IT Capability

## Background

The concept of organizational IT capability, how to evaluate and measure IT capability, and how it relates to an organization's business performance are presented in Chapter 8. The IT Capability Maturity Framework (IT CMF) was introduced in Chapter 3. It has already been clarified that scholarly approaches to measuring IT capabilities are evident in the literature, but that there are models present in practice as well. The former focus more on business values and the latter focus on technical aspects too. However, this chapter will be based on a model belonging to the second group. Hence, this chapter involves an explanation of the components of the IT CMF.

The IT CMF focuses on four integrated strategies and 37 associated critical processes against which the IT organization's level of maturity can be assessed according to five levels. A detailed description will be given.

## Information Technology Capability Maturity Framework

Nowadays, the key five digital forces: globalization, millenialization, prosumerization, business virtualization, and plaformization, are changing business operations and society as a whole. Given that powerful computing devices and inexpensive digital communication are present in the world today, there are many opportunities for more agile and innovative firms to gain market dominance. The IT-CMF enables business and IT leaders to collectively assess their current maturity, to define target maturity goals, and to agree on what is important – so that they can set priorities for action.

The IT-CMF can also be seen as a manual that helps companies manage all IT segments to leverage IT investments with the aim of meeting their business goals and addressing specific challenges. The IT-CMF, as comprehensive and credible guidance, not only provides a framework for maturity assessment but also provides a tool for improving specific IT capabilities. Creating and improving IT capability is a process that must be well defined, managed, and monitored. In the age of the digital economy, companies must continually innovate business and IT processes to keep pace over their competitors. So, by implementing the IT-CMF, organizations can create added value from IT; in other words, they can assess the current situation and create realistic concrete plans for improvement. The potential of information technology (IT) in today's digital age is enormous, and it is necessary to ensure that business leaders recognize the key IT benefits and realize them in their organization.

Maturity-based approaches to managing IT are very popular nowadays. The IT-CMF defines five maturity levels concerning the efficiency and effectiveness of specific capabilities. This framework helps organizations evaluate each segment systematically and analytically and guides what actions to take to improve each process. The maturity of the process is driven by the growth of each IT capability from the existing level to the next level with transformations over time. Maturity levels together with approaches, scope, and outcomes are given in Table 9.1.

To begin, the process of business innovation and differentiation and positioning of IT in line with market dynamics involves first understanding existing IT capabilities. After that, there should be determined which IT capabilities are most strategically important. Before making the final decision to move from a reactive to a proactive stance, IT capabilities should be prioritized as well as a strategic plan for implementation and development. According to the IT-CMF framework, the activities of an organization's IT function are divided into the key for macro capabilities (MCs) that underpin value-oriented IT. Four macro capabilities that continually improve the value delivered from IT capability are the following:

1. Managing IT like a business
2. Managing the IT budget
3. Managing the IT capability
4. Managing IT for business value

All four of these macro capabilities should be aligned with the overall business strategy of the company. The relationship between these four macro processes is shown in Figure 9.1. These four macro capabilities operate in a continuous feedback loop to optimize how IT is managed.

*Managing IT like a business* means that the company undertakes a business-like approach to organize, manage, and control IT function. This approach optimizes

**Table 9.1  General Maturity Level Heuristics**

| Level | Approaches<br>*Quality of<br>Routines/Practices<br>or Activities* | Scope<br>*The Breadth of<br>Coverage/Focus* | Outcomes<br>*Predictability<br>between Actions<br>and Consequences* |
|---|---|---|---|
| 1 – Initial | Approaches are inadequate and unstable. | Scope is fragmented and incoherent. | Repeatable outcomes are rare. |
| 2 – Basic | Approaches are defined, but inconsistencies remain. | Scope is limited to a partial area of a business function or domain area; deficiencies remain. | Repeatable outcomes are achieved occasionally. |
| 3 – Intermediate | Approaches are standardized, inconsistencies are addressed. | Scope expands to cover a business function (typically IT) or domain area. | Repeatable outcomes are often achieved. |
| 4 – Advanced | Approaches can systematically flex for innovative adaptations. | Scope covers the end-to-end organization/ neighboring domain areas. | Repeatable outcomes are very often achieved. |
| 5 – Optimizing | Approaches demonstrate world-class attributes. | Scope extends beyond the borders of the organization/ neighboring domains. | Repeatable outcomes are virtually always achieved. |

*Source*: (Curley et al., 2017)

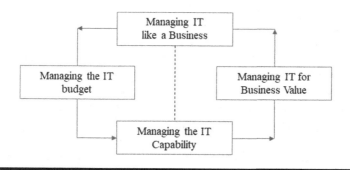

**Figure 9.1  Closing the loop on value. Curley & Kenneally, 2007.**

the contribution of technology to the company as a whole in a way that IT is run efficiently and effectively to meet the company's goals.

*Managing the IT budget* means that the company creates a sustainable economic model and strategically invests in IT. Concerning that, the company can free up resources for innovation and growth while managing the budget. The budget spending also needs to be monitored.

*Managing IT capability* is crucial to delivering sustainable competitive advantage from IT. This involves a systematic approach to managing IT's assets. It is also very important to maintain and improve a system that creates business value from IT, as well as the core competencies that the IT organization requires to deliver IT business value.

*Managing IT for business value* means that the company designs and measures processes to help ensure that value is designed in and released through the usage of IT-enabled investments. According to that requirement, the company should optimize the business value of IT.

Each of the macro capabilities supports key goals and strategies. Besides strategies, four macro capabilities involve a library of 37 critical capabilities (CC), which are broken down into 315 building blocks.

Complete IT-CMF framework is shown in Figure 9.2.

In the following text, each critical capability is described, together with briefly summarized explanations based on available literature research.

## *Managing IT Like a Business*

Managing IT like a business consists of 16 critical capabilities, which are presented in Table 9.2.

The following is a brief explanation of individual CC of "Managing IT like a Business" macro capability:

1. *Accounting and Allocation capability* helps the company better manage IT costs as well as adequately invest in IT. Financial management through the IT function is necessary to meet the business needs of the company and to make rational use of IT resources. In this regard, it is necessary to strike a balance between IT costs and IT investments.
2. *Business Planning capability* refers to the creation of an appropriate IT strategy. The IT strategy is a long-term plan that spans three to five years and needs to be revised and updated. Operational plans are drawn up based on an IT strategy and cover one year. Operational plans define the key activities and projects of the IT function, the timetable for the activities, and the necessary financial and human resources.
3. *Business Process Management capability* helps the company better understand the flow of business activities so that business processes can be clearly defined. In this way, the company is well prepared for any changes or reengineering

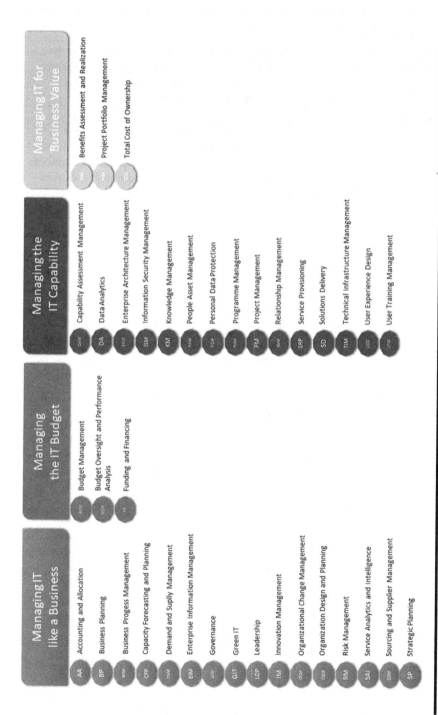

**Managing IT like a Business**

- AA Accounting and Allocation
- BP Business Planning
- BPM Business Progess Management
- CFP Capacity Forecasting and Planning
- DSM Demand and Suplly Management
- EIM Enterprise Information Management
- GOV Governance
- GIT Green IT
- LDP Leadership
- IM Innovation Management
- OCM Organizational Change Management
- ODP Organization Design and Planning
- RM Risk Management
- SAI Service Analytics and Intelligence
- SSM Sourcing and Supplier Management
- SP Strategic Planning

**Managing the IT Budget**

- BUM Budget Management
- BOA Budget Oversight and Performance Analysis
- FF Funding and Financing

**Managing the IT Capability**

- CAM Capability Assessment Management
- DA Data Analytics
- EAM Enterprise Architecture Management
- ISM Information Security Management
- KM Knowledge Management
- PAM People Asset Management
- PDP Personal Data Protection
- PGM Programme Management
- PM Project Management
- RM Relationship Management
- SRP Service Provisioning
- SD Solutions Delivery
- TIM Technical Infrastructure Management
- UCD User Experience Design
- UTM User Training Management

**Managing IT for Business Value**

- BAR Benefits Assessment and Realization
- PPM Project Portfolio Management
- TCO Total Cost of Ownership

**Figure 9.2   37 Critical capabilities. Innovation Value Institution, 2019.**

**Table 9.2  Description of Critical Capabilities – Managing IT Like a Business**

| Critical Capability | Description |
|---|---|
| Accounting and Allocation | The Accounting and Allocation (AA) capability is the ability to define and manage the policies, processes, and tools used for calculating the costs of IT and distributing them across the organization. |
| Business Planning | The Business Planning (BP) capability is the ability to produce an approved document that provides implementable detail for the IT strategy, setting out the IT function's tactical objectives, the operational services to be provided, and the financial and other resources and constraints that apply in the coming planning period. |
| Business Process Management | The Business Process Management (BPM) capability is the ability to identify, design, document, monitor, optimize, and assist in the execution of both existing and new organizational processes. |
| Capacity Forecasting and Planning | The Capacity Forecasting and Planning (CFP) capability is the ability to model and forecast demand for IT services, infrastructure, facilities, and people. |
| Demand and Supply Management | The Demand and Supply Management (DSM) capability is the ability to manage the IT services portfolio in such a way that there is a balance between the demand for, and the supply of, IT services. |
| Enterprise Information Management | The Enterprise Information Management (EIM) capability is the ability to establish effective systems for gathering, analyzing, disseminating, exploiting, and disposing of data and information. The data can be held in any medium – all forms of digital storage, film, paper, or any other recording mechanism used by the organization. |
| Governance | The Governance (GOV) capability is the ability to evaluate, direct, and monitor the current and future use of an organization's IT resources in support of strategic objectives. |
| Green Information Technology | The Green Information Technology (GIT) capability is the ability to minimize the environmental impact of IT and to make the best use of technology to minimize environmental impact across the organization. |
| Innovation Management | The Innovation Management (IM) capability is the ability to identify, fund, and measure technology-driven business innovation. |

*(Continued)*

**Table 9.2 (Continued)   Description of critical capabilities – Managing**

| Critical Capability | Description |
|---|---|
| Leadership | The IT Leadership (LDP) capability is the ability to guide the organization in making the optimal use of technology and related assets to drive business value. |
| Organization Change Management | The Organizational Change Management (OCM) capability is the ability to plan for and manage IT-related change and to support organizations as they go through it. OCM covers gaining and maintaining a commitment to change, implementing and evaluating the impact of change, and embedding sustainable change processes in the organization. |
| Organization Design and Planning | The Organization Design and Planning (ODP) capability is the ability to manage the IT function's internal structure and its interfaces with other business units, suppliers, and business partners. |
| Risk Management | The Risk Management (RM) capability is the ability to identify, assess, prioritize, treat, and monitor the exposure to and the potential impact of IT-related risks that can directly affect the business. |
| Service Analytics and Intelligence | The Service Analytics and Intelligence (SAI) capability is the ability to define and quantify the relationships between IT infrastructure, IT services, and IT-enabled business processes. |
| Sourcing and Supplier Management | The Sourcing and Supplier Management (SSM) capability is the ability to evaluate, select, integrate, and manage IT suppliers in line with defined sourcing and supplier management strategies. |
| Strategic Planning | The Strategic Planning (SP) capability is the ability to formulate a long-term vision and translate it into an actionable strategic plan for the IT function. |

*Source*: (Innovation Value Institute, 2019)

of the process. If the goals of a particular business process are understandable and precise, performing the supporting activities is more reliable and efficient.

4. *Capacity Forecasting and Planning capability* enable the company to better understand IT services and plan a timely expansion of capacity as needed. Thus, it is necessary to anticipate the replacement of certain resources so that IT resources can be added cost effectively.

5. *Demand and Supply Management capability* is focused on the balance between business demands and the IT services provided by the IT function. In this regard, the IT function should effectively respond to the business

requirements regarding the development and upgrade of the system, as well as other IT services required for the daily operations of the company.

6. *Enterprise Information Management capability* helps the company operate with quality data. Information is the most valuable resource of the digital economy. There are various platforms today that enable data analysis and processing to support timely and appropriate business decision-making.

7. *Governance capability* helps the company establish employee accountability mechanisms both in performing business tasks and in making decisions. Also, it is necessary to establish a system of supervision over activities and operations to perform them following rules, procedures, and legislation.

8. *Green Information Technology capability* refers to the fact that IT operations should be managed in an environmentally sensitive manner. In this regard, it is recommended that IT resources are disposed of and destroyed appropriately so that they do not harm the environment. Also, business processes can be redesigned to use sensitive IT solutions, such as working paperless.

9. *Innovation Management capability* helps the company use technology-driven innovation to solve business challenges. One of the essential conditions for adapting a company to a turbulent environment is to constantly invest in innovation because it is a very good way to gain a market advantage over other competitors.

10. *Leadership capability* refers to the company's ability to motivate employees to perform their tasks responsibly, and together contribute to the achievement of goals. If the company develops leadership capability to the optimum level, the organization will have better IT vision, stakeholder interaction, and business interaction with partners, which adds to the company's value.

11. *Organization Change Management capability* refers to the ability of the company to adequately manage change management of IT solutions and IT services, including elements of an effective change management process from request for change, impact analysis, approve/deny change, implement change, and review/report on change. Also, the company should evaluate the impact of change and enable a sustainable change process.

12. *Risk Management capability* aims to help the company identify, assess, evaluate, and manage IT risks, and take actions to mitigate identified risks that are not acceptable to the company. The company should manage IT-related risks such as those related to IT security, IT sabotage, data protection, and so on.

13. *Service Analytics and Intelligence* capability refer to the ability of the company to monitor, model, and analyze different processes to establish a clear understanding of the relationship between business processes and underlying IT infrastructure and processes, all with the aim of optimizing the delivery of IT services for business value.

**Table 9.3   Description of Critical Capabilities - Managing the IT Budget**

| Critical Capability | Description |
|---|---|
| Budget Management | The Budget Management (BGM) capability is the ability to oversee and adjust the IT budget to ensure that it is spent effectively. |
| Budget Oversight and Performance Analysis | The Budget Oversight and Performance Analysis (BOP) capability is the ability to compare actual IT expenditure against budgeted IT expenditure over extended periods. Where appropriate, it offers management the opportunity to reprofile or reprioritize budget forecasts and allocations. |
| Funding and Financing | The Funding and Financing (FF) capability is the ability to determine the funding level required for IT and to allocate it appropriately. |

*Source*: (Innovation Value Institute, 2019)

14. *Sourcing and Supplier Management capability* is the ability of the company to manage the obligations and responsibilities of both parties (company and supplier), relationship objectives, and contractual deliverables, and to monitor contracted clauses regarding SLA, incident management, continuity management, auditing capabilities, and so on.

15. *Strategic Planning capability* means that the company needs to ensure that IT strategic planning is aligned with strategic business plans. The company should identify challenges and opportunities where IT function can improve business performance and affect the business side.

## *Managing the IT Budget*

Managing the IT budget consists of three critical capabilities, which are presented in Table 9.3.

The following is a brief explanation of individual CC of "Managing the IT budget" macro capability:

1. *Budget Management capability* is the ability of the company to understand their IT cost structure and drivers as they look to expand the scope of optimization from IT cost to IT cost and value.

2. *Budget Oversight and Performance Analysis capability* refers to the ability of a company to monitor, control, reprioritize, and rebalance the planned IT budget.

3. *Funding and Financing capability* aims to help the company provide sources of funding for an organization. Also, IT resources need to be properly allocated and managed.

**Table 9.4   Description of Critical Capabilities – Managing IT for Business Value**

| Critical Capability | Description |
|---|---|
| Benefits Assessment and Realization | The Benefits Assessment and Realization (BAR) capability is the ability to establish the outcomes focus for the selection and management of IT-enabled business change initiatives to ensure that their potential value is delivered. BAR addresses the cultural and behavioral change needed to create and to sustain value from those initiatives. In this way, BAR ensures that business benefits are planned, dynamically adjusted, and achieved. |
| Project Portfolio Management | The Project Portfolio Management (PPM) capability is the ability to select, approve, and balance project portfolio components (projects, programs, or sub-portfolios) to deliver the organization's strategic objectives and its operational needs. |
| Total Cost of Ownership | The Total Cost of Ownership (TCO) capability is the ability to identify, compare, and control all direct and indirect costs associated with IT assets and IT-enabled business services. |

*Source*: (Innovation Value Institute, 2019)

## *Managing IT for Business Value*

Managing IT for business value consist of three critical capabilities, which are presented in Table 9.4.

The following is a brief explanation of individual CC of "Managing IT for business value" macro capability:

1. *Benefits Assessment and Realization capability* means that the company needs to raise awareness that the IT function creates sustainable business value from IT-enabled change. The technology does not add value by itself, but it enables the employees to maximize the value of IT-enabled change.
2. *Project Portfolio Management capability* focuses on monitoring and reporting on IT projects and programs. The company should monitor the project activities, progress deviation, accompanying risks, and other factors concerning projects and programs to ensure that the projects are successful.
3. *Total Cost of Ownership capability* refers to the ability of the company to track, compare, and control all direct and indirect costs (including people, processes, and methodologies) associated with IT assets (infrastructure and systems) and services to maximize value.

## Managing the IT Capability

Managing the IT Capability consist of 15 critical capabilities, which are presented in Table 9.5.

The following is a brief explanation of individual CC of "Managing the IT Capability" macro capability:

1. *Capability Assessment Management* helps the company identify its IT strengths and weaknesses, and also identify areas where it can make improvements and further progress.
2. *Data Analytics capability* relates to the ability of the company to understand current activities, facilitate problem-solving, and enable prediction to plan future activities.
3. *Enterprise Architecture Management capability* helps the company understand its current composition, utility, costs, and sources of value generation. The company should envision and develop projects to meet strategic objectives, reduce complexity by implementing technical standards and operating rules, enhance productivity across the organization by unifying and integrating data linkages, and so on.
4. *Information Security Management capability* helps the company define and implement adequate information security policies and procedures to protect confidentiality, integrity, and availability of data.
5. *Knowledge Management capability* helps the company leverage relevant information, knowledge, and ideas to support better and faster decision-making. The company should gather know-how and also promote knowledge-sharing behavior.
6. *People Asset Management capability* is focused on managing the information technology unit to employ a sufficient number of IT employees who possess the necessary skills and experience.
7. *Personal Data Protection capability* refers to the company's ability to protect personal data. Also, the data need to be available for the company when needed, and the company needs to maintain data integrity.
8. *Program Management capability* refers to the company's ability to stimulate robust and competent programs, develop an appropriate organizational structure, and provide adequate resources and support mechanisms to enable timely delivery of projects and programs.
9. *Project Management capability* refers to the ability to apply project management methodologies, which consist of the following phases: initiate program, plan, execute, monitor, control, and close projects. The project should include costs, human resources, schedules, and so on.
10. *Relationship Management capability* is the ability of an IT function to maintain good business relationships with other organizational units, then to define common interests, and to minimize internal conflicts. Openness, respect, and sharing of business information is the basis for optimizing this capability.

**Table 9.5  Description of Critical Capabilities – Managing the IT Capability**

| Critical Capability | Description |
|---|---|
| Capability Assessment Management | The Capability Assessment Management (CAM) capability is the ability of the organization to conduct current state evaluations and plan improvements for its portfolio of IT capabilities. Current state evaluations involve gathering and documenting data about the specific IT capabilities in the organization. The results then inform the planning and execution of improvement actions to deal with any deficiencies. |
| Data Analytics | The Data Analytics (DA) capability is the ability to specify analytical objectives, to identify data sets likely to enable those objectives, to apply analytical methods and techniques appropriate to those objectives, and to interpret, communicate, and exploit the analytical results to deliver value for the organization. |
| Enterprise Architecture Management | The Enterprise Architecture Management (EAM) capability is the ability to envision, plan, design, lead, manage, and control organizations, systems, and/or processes in current, transitionary, and future states, and the relationships between them. Architecture conceptualizations may be layered to represent specific types of relationships – for example, those between applications, business services, internal IT services, security, networking, data storage, and so on. |
| Information Security Management | The Information Security Management (ISM) capability is the ability to manage approaches, policies, and controls that safeguard the integrity, confidentiality, accountability, usability, and availability of information. |
| Knowledge Management | The Knowledge Management (KM) capability is the ability to identify, capture, classify, analyze, share, and exploit knowledge to improve organizational performance. |
| People Asset Management | The People Asset Management (PAM) capability is the ability to meet the organization's requirements for an effective IT workforce. |
| Personal Data Protection | The Personal Data Protection (PDP) capability is the ability to develop and deploy policies, systems, and controls for processing personal and sensitive personal data relating to living persons in all-digital, automated, and manual forms. It ensures that the organization safeguards the right to privacy of individuals whose information it holds and that the organization uses personal data strictly for specified purposes agreed upon with the data subjects. |

*(Continued)*

**Table 9.5 (Continued)   Description of Critical Capabilities – Managing the IT Capability**

| Critical Capability | Description |
|---|---|
| Program Management | The Program Management (PGM) capability is the ability to assemble and assign resources to identify, select, approve, oversee, and deliver value from program coordinated components (i.e., sub-programs and projects). |
| Project Management | The Project Management (PM) capability is the ability to assign resources to initiate, plan, execute, monitor, control, and close projects that deliver project objectives within agreed variances of cost, timeliness, quality, and scope of works. |
| Relationship Management | The Relationship Management (REM) capability is the ability to analyze, plan, maintain, and enhance relationships between the IT function and the rest of the business. |
| Service Provisioning | The Service Provisioning (SRP) capability is the ability to manage IT services to satisfy business requirements. This includes ongoing activities relating to operations, maintenance, and continuous service improvement, and also transitional activities relating to the introduction of services, their deployment, and their eventual decommissioning. |
| Solutions Delivery | The Solutions Delivery (SD) capability is the ability to design, develop, validate, and deploy IT solutions that effectively address the organization's business requirements and opportunities. |
| Technical Infrastructure Management | The Technical Infrastructure Management (TIM) capability is the ability to manage an organization's IT infrastructure across its complete life cycle of:<br>• Transitional activities, including building, deploying, and decommissioning.<br>• Operational activities, including day-to-day operations, maintenance, and continuous improvement. |
| User Experience Design | The User Experience Design (UED) capability is the ability to proactively consider the needs of users at all stages in the life cycle of IT services and solutions. |
| User Training Management | The User Training Management (UTM) capability is the ability to provide training that will improve user proficiency in the use of business applications and other IT-supported services. |

*Source*: (Innovation Value Institute, 2019)

11. *Service Provisioning capability* is the ability to manage the life cycle of IT services, meaning that the IT function should take action to maintain and continually improve IT services. Also, the IT function should ensure the availability of IT services and respond on time in the event of problems and incidents.

12. *Solutions Delivery capability* presents the ability of a company to purchase, develop, or upgrade IT solutions that will effectively and efficiently meet business needs and facilitate and expedite operations by employees.

13. *Technical Infrastructure Management capability* refers to the company's need to adequately manage IT components. In other words, the IT function should provide technical infrastructure stability, availability, and reliability.

14. *User Experience Design capability* refers to the usability and usefulness of IT services and solutions. IT solutions should be useful, which means that IT solutions should serve the purpose or business needs. Usability relates to the ease with which IT solutions can be used from an employee's perspective.

15. *User Training Management capability* means that the company needs to ensure that users and IT employees possess adequate knowledge, skills, and experience concerning their operations. The users need to be trained to be proficient and productive while using the company's business applications.

## Conclusion

The IT-CMF is a standardized and structured assessment tool that organizations can use to systematically identify gaps in IT capabilities that limit IT performance and assess their strengths and weaknesses. With the implementation of the IT-CMF, organizations can achieve incremental improvements in IT maturity through four macro-based capabilities, called a five-level maturity curve. Those four macro capabilities (Managing IT like a business, Managing the IT budget, Managing the IT capability, and Managing IT for business value) embrace several critical capabilities (CCs) that can contribute to agility, innovation, and the value of the organization. There are numerous examples of worldwide organizations using the IT-CMF to address their capability issues.

Since many organizations are constantly challenged to innovate and generate real value, the IT-CMF can enable them to devise more robust strategies, make better-informed decisions, and perform its activities in a more effective, efficient, and economical manner. With the help of the IT-CMF, organizations can evaluate the current state of each capability and define a road map to achieve improved capability maturity. To create more value from IT and to successfully respond to competitive forces, organizations need to reevaluate, assess, and evolve continually their existing IT practices, processes, and cultural norms across the entire organization.

# Discussion Questions

1. What does the acronym IT-CMF stand for?
2. What can the IT-CMF be used for?
3. How can organizations add value from IT by implementing the IT-CMF?
4. Explain briefly each macro capability.
5. Discuss the maturity levels concerning the efficiency and effectiveness of the capabilities.
6. What do four macro capabilities consist of?
7. List at least two critical capabilities per macro capability and describe them.
8. Briefly explain the following critical capabilities: Information Security Management capability, Personal Data Protection capability, and Risk Management capability.
9. Which activities can the organization undertake to improve and develop the following critical capabilities: Green Information Technology capability, Strategic planning capability, and Capacity Forecasting and Planning capability?
10. Why is User Training Management as a capability important for the organization?

# References

Carcary, M. (2011). Design science research: The case of the IT capability maturity framework (IT CMF). *Electronic Journal of Business Research Methods, 9*(2), 109–118.

Carcary, M. (2012). IT risk management : A capability maturity model perspective. *Electronic Journal Information Systems Evaluation, 16*(3), 3–13.

Carcary, M., Doherty, E., Thornley, C. (2015). Business Innovation and Differentiation: Maturing the IT Capability. *IT Professional, 17*(2), 46–53.

Curley, M., Kenneally, J. (2007). Methods and metrics to improve the yield of IT using the IT-CMF™ – An intel case study. *Proceedings – 2007 IEEE Conference on Exploring Quantifiable IT Yields, EQUITY 2007, 2001*, 27–38.

Curley, M., Kenneally, J., Carcary, M. (2017). *IT Capability Maturity FrameworkTM (IT-CMFTM)* (2nd ed.). Van Haren Publishing.

Gimpel, G., Westerman, G. (2012). Shaping the Future: Seven Enduring Principles for Fast-Changing Industries. *MIT Center for Digital Business, Working Papers*, 1–24.

Innovation Value Institution. (2019). IT Capability Maturity Framework™ (IT-CMF™). Retrieved from https://ivi.ie/critical-capabilities/

Ngosi, T., Helfert, M., Braganza, A. (2011). Increasing Knowledge Management Maturity in Organisations: A Capabilities – Driven Model, in: *Proceedings of the 3rd European Conference on Intellectual Capital* (p. 302).

Pintaric, N., & Bronzin, T. (2013). IT Capability Review, in: *Central European Conference on Information and Intelligent Systems Faculty of Organization and Informatics Varaždin Central European Conference on Information and Intelligent Systems* (p. 104). Faculty of Organization and Informatics Varaždin.

Upton, S. (2011). *Sustainable ICT – Action Planning for the New Economy*. IVI Executive Briefing Series.

# *Chapter 10*

# Real-World Stories

(Selected links to cases and white papers related to downtime, costs of downtime, business continuity, system administration, IT auditing, and IT capability)

## Outages. Downtime. System Failures. 2019'S IT Meltdowns

Retrieved September 6, 2019, from
https://data-economy.com/outages-downtime-system-failures-2019s-it-meltdowns/

---

## Deloitte Lacks Control

Retrieved August 9, 2019, from
https://data-economy.com/outages-downtime-system-failures-2019s-it-meltdowns/

---

## Microsoft Suffers Global Outage to Azure and Office 365 Services

Retrieved May 12, 2020, from
www.cloudpro.co.uk/it-infrastructure/7658/microsoft-suffers-global-outage-to-azure-and-office-365-services?_mout=1&utm_campaign=alphr_cloud_newsletter&utm_medium=email&utm_source=newsletter

## Security Practitioners Weigh In on the 18 Worst Data Breaches in Recent Memory

Retrieved August 6, 2019, from
www.csoonline.com/article/2130877/the-biggest-data-breaches-of-the-21st-century.html

## The Business Value of Leading-Edge High Performance

Retrieved September 12, 2019, from
https://s7d2.scene7.com/is/content/hpedam/a00029212enw

## The Astonishing Hidden and Personal Costs of IT Downtime (and How Predictive Analytics Might Help)

Retrieved September 12, 2019, from
www.zdnet.com/article/the-astonishing-hidden-and-personal-costs-of-it-downtime-and-how-predictive-analytics-might-help/

## What Every Small Business Owner Must Know about Protecting and Preserving Their Company's Critical Data and Computer Systems

Retrieved September 12, 2019, from
http://impacttg.com/wp-content/uploads/2019/04/IMPACT-FreeReport-ProtectNetwork-SMBs-FD.pdf

## IT Downtime Factors

Retrieved September 12, 2019, from
www.the20.com/blog/the-cost-of-it-downtime/

------------------------------------------------------------------------

## IT Outages: The Actual Cost and How to Prevent It Becoming a Reality

Retrieved September 12, 2019, from
www.information-age.com/prevent-outages-becoming-reality-123470751/

------------------------------------------------------------------------

## Average Cost Per Hour of Enterprise Server Downtime Worldwide in 2017 and 2018

Retrieved September 12, 2019, from
www.statista.com/statistics/753938/worldwide-enterprise-server-hourly-
downtime-cost/

------------------------------------------------------------------------

## 7 Greatest Causes of Data Loss

Retrieved September 12, 2019, from
www.databackuponlinestorage.com/7_Causes_of_Data_Loss

------------------------------------------------------------------------

## Dealing with Disgruntled IT Workers

Retrieved September 12, 2019, from
www.cio.com/article/2433507/dealing-with-disgruntled-it-workers.html

------------------------------------------------------------------------

## Network Issues Are Causing More Data-Center Outages

Retrieved March 27, 2019, from
www.networkworld.com/article/3373646/network-problems-responsible-for-more-data-center-outages.html?utm_source=Adestra&utm_medium=email&utm_content=Title%3A%20Network%20issues%20are%20causing%20more%20data-center%20outages&utm_campaign=Networkworld%20Data%20Center%20Alert&utm_term=Editorial%20-%20Data%20Center%20Alert&utm_date=20190327054907,

--------------------------------------------------------------------------

## 57 Simple Sys Admin Mistakes That Someday You'll Regret

Retrieved September 12, 2019, from
https://techtalk.gfi.com/57-simple-sys-admin-mistakes-that-someday-you-will-regret/

## The Decline and Fall of System Administration

Retrieved September 2, 2019, from
www.infoworld.com/article/2623478/the-decline-and-fall-of-system-administration.html

## Ransomware Hobbles the City of Atlanta

Retrieved February 20, 2020, from
https://invenioit.com/continuity/business-continuity-looks-like/

## Internet Disruption Report: March 2020

Retrieved May 12, 2020, from
https://internetdisruption.report/2020/04/22/internet-disruption-report-march-2020/#more-1522

## February 2020 Downtime Report

Retrieved May 12, 2020, from
https://uptime.com/blog/february-2020-downtime-report

## How Planning Reduces the Impact of Outages

Retrieved May 12, 2020, from
https://uptimeinstitute.com/resources/research-and-reports/how-planning-reduces-the-impact-of-outages

## Maintaining Operations and Business Continuity during COVID-19

Retrieved May 12, 2020, from
https://uptimeinstitute.com/covid-19-minimizing-critical-facility-risk

# Index

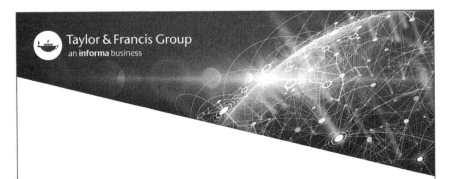

Printed in the United States
by Baker & Taylor Publisher Services